ECONOMIC ISSUES, PROBLEMS AND PERSPECTIVES

U.S. ECONOMIC RECOVERY AND STIMULUS MEASURES: ISSUES, OPTIONS, AND IMPACTS

Economic Issues, Problems and Perspectives

Additional books in this series can be found on Nova's website under the Series tab.

Additional E-books in this series can be found on Nova's website under the E-books tab.

America in the 21st Century: Political and Economic Issues

Additional books in this series can be found on Nova's website under the Series tab.

Additional E-books in this series can be found on Nova's website under the E-books tab.

ECONOMIC ISSUES, PROBLEMS AND PERSPECTIVES

U.S. ECONOMIC RECOVERY AND STIMULUS MEASURES: ISSUES, OPTIONS, AND IMPACTS

JESSICA D. SAPARITO
EDITOR

Nova Science Publishers, Inc.
New York

For permission to use material from this book please contact us:
Telephone 631-231-7269; Fax 631-231-8175
Web Site: http://www.novapublishers.com

LIBRARY OF CONGRESS CATALOGING-IN-PUBLICATION DATA

U.S. economic recovery and stimulus measures : issues, options, and impacts / editor, Jessica D. Saparito.
p. cm.
Includes index.
ISBN 978-1-61209-266-9 (hardcover)
1. United States--Economic policy--2009- 2. United States--Economic conditions--2009- 3. Unemployment--United States. 4. Tax incentives--Economic aspects--United States. 5. Recessions--United States. I. Saparito, Jessica D. II. Title: US economic recovery and stimulus measures. III. Title: United States economic recovery and stimulus measures.
HC106.84.U157 2010
339.50973--dc22
2010048368

Published by Nova Science Publishers, Inc. † New York

CONTENTS

PREFACE

The slowdown of economic activity was moderate through the first half of 2008, but at that point the weakening economy was overtaken by a major financial crisis that would exacerbate the economic weakness and accelerate the decline. Recent evidence suggests that the process of economic recovery has begun. On the other hand, significant economic weakness remains evident, particularly in the labor and housing markets. This new book examines the current issues, options and impacts of the U.S. economic recovery and stimulus measures.

Chapter 1- The recession that began in late 2007 was long and deep. It is likely to prove to be the worst economic contraction since the 1930s (but still much less severe than the Great Depression). The slowdown of economic activity was moderate through the first half of 2008, but at that point the weakening economy was overtaken by a major financial crisis that would exacerbate the economic weakness and accelerate the decline.

Chapter 2- According to the Business Cycle Dating Committee of the National Bureau of Economic Research (NBER), the U.S. economy has been in recession since December 2007. Congress passed and the President signed an economic stimulus package, the American Recovery and Reinvestment Act of 2009 (P.L. 111-5), in February 2009. The $787 billion package included $286 billion in tax cuts to help stimulate the economy. Among the tax reductions, many were tax incentives directed to business. The preliminary estimate of fourth quarter real gross domestic product (GDP) growth is 5.9%; the unemployment rate, a lagging indicator, averaged 9.6% in the third quarter and 10.0% in the fourth quarter of 2009. Federal Reserve Chairman Ben Bernanke expects the economy to continue growing at a modest pace, but predicts that bank lending will remain constrained and the job market will remain weak into at least 2010. To further assist unemployed workers, help business, and stimulate housing markets, Congress passed the Worker, Homeownership, and Business Assistance Act of 2009 (P.L. 111-92). The Obama Administration has advocated further business tax incentives to spur investment and employment, especially for small business. The House and Senate passed the Hiring Incentives to Restore Employment (HIRE) Act, which includes an employment tax credit. The President signed the act into law on March 18, 2010.

Chapter 3- Although the economy has begun growing again, it may be a while before the unemployment rate shows steady improvement. The unemployment rate is considered a lagging indicator, meaning that its ups and downs happen some time after the ups and downs of other indicators of economic activity. For example, more than a year elapsed before the unemployment rate trended downward following the end of the 1990-1991 and 2001 recessions. This led the two to be labeled jobless recoveries. By contrast, after four earlier recessions the unemployment rate began a sustained decline within four to five months.

Chapter 4- Congress in recent years passed a number of bills intended in part to jump-start a recovery in the labor market from the recession that began in December 2007. Policymakers are interested in how employment has responded to stimulus measures to determine how effective the legislation has been and to decide whether additional job creation legislation is warranted.

Chapter 5- After the long economic expansion that characterized much of the current decade, the nation entered its 11th postwar recession in December 2007. The size of job losses and the comparison to the Great Depression intensified congressional interest in passing legislation early in 2009 aimed at encouraging job creation and warding off further cuts in employment.

Chapter 6- The Federal Reserve (Fed) has been central in the policy response to the financial turmoil that began in August 2007. It has sharply increased reserves to the banking system through open market operations and lowered the federal funds rate and discount rate on several occasions. Since December 2008, it has allowed the federal funds rate to fall close to zero. As the crisis deepened, the Fed's focus shifted to providing liquidity directly to the financial system through new policy tools. Through new credit facilities, the Fed first expanded the scale of its lending to the banking system and then extended direct lending to non-bank financial firms. The latter marked the first time since the Great Depression that firms that are not banks or members of the Federal Reserve System have been allowed to borrow directly from the Fed. After the crisis worsened in September 2008, the Fed began providing credit directly to markets for commercial paper and asset-backed securities. All of these emergency facilities had expired by the end of June 2010, but central bank liquidity swap lines were reopened in May 2010 in response to the crisis in Greece. The Fed also provided emergency assistance to Bear Stearns, AIG, and Citigroup over the course of the crisis; the Fed still holds assets from and loans to AIG and assets from Bear Stearns.

Chapter 7- At the beginning of the 111th Congress, economic stimulus proposals have dominated the legislative agenda, with a broad recognition that business tax incentives are among the policy options to consider. Two prominent proposals, H.R. 1 and S. 1, both titled the American Recovery and Reinvestment Act of 2009, were the focus of this debate. Both proposals include business tax incentives which would increase the after-tax rate of return on domestic investment and were subsequently enacted in P.L. 111-5. In contrast, little attention has been given to international policy options. An exception to this is a plan to reduce the tax rate on repatriated dividends that has received some consideration. Under such a plan, the U.S. tax that U.S. firms pay when their overseas operations remit ("repatriate") their foreign earnings as dividends to their U.S. parent corporations would be reduced. This provision was considered, but not adopted, as a floor amendment to a Senate version of the American Recovery and Reinvestment Act of 2009.

Chapter 8- As part of the unprecedented accountability and transparency provisions included in the American Recovery and Reinvestment Act of 2009 (ARRA), the Council of Economic Advisers (CEA) is charged with providing to Congress quarterly reports on the effects of the Recovery Act on overall economic activity, and on employment in particular. In this fourth report, we provide an assessment of the effects of the Act through the secondquarter of 2010.

In: U.S. Economic Recovery and Stimulus Measures
Editor: Jessica D. Saparito
ISBN: 978-1-61209-266-9

Chapter 1

ECONOMIC RECOVERY: SUSTAINING U.S. ECONOMIC GROWTH IN A POST-CRISIS ECONOMY

Craig K. Elwell

SUMMARY

The recession that began in late 2007 was long and deep. It is likely to prove to be the worst economic contraction since the 1930s (but still much less severe than the Great Depression). The slowdown of economic activity was moderate through the first half of 2008, but at that point the weakening economy was overtaken by a major financial crisis that would exacerbate the economic weakness and accelerate the decline.

Recent evidence suggests that the process of economic recovery has begun. Real gross domestic product (GDP) has been on a positive track since mid-2009. The stock market has recovered from its lows, and employment has increased moderately. On the other hand, significant economic weakness remains evident, particularly in the labor and housing markets.

In the typical post-war business cycle, lower than normal growth during the recession is quickly followed by a recovery period with above normal growth. This above normal growth serves to speed up the reentry of the unemployed to the workforce. Once the economy reaches potential output (and full employment), growth returns to its normal growth path where the pace of aggregate spending advances in step with the pace of aggregate supply.

There is concern that this time the U.S. economy will either not return to its pre-recession growth path but perhaps remain permanently below it, or return to the pre-crisis path but at a slower than normal pace. Problems on the supply side and the demand side of the economy may lead to a weaker than normal recovery.

If the pace of private spending proves insufficient to assure a sustained recovery, would further stimulus by monetary and fiscal policy be warranted? One of the important lessons from the Great Depression is to guard against a too hasty withdrawal of fiscal and monetary stimulus in an economy recovering from a deep decline. The removal of fiscal and monetary stimulus in 1937 is thought to have stopped a recovery and caused a slump that did not end until WWII.

Opponents of further stimulus maintain that the accumulation of additional government debt would lower future economic growth, but supporters argue that additional stimulus is the appropriate near-term policy.

In regard to the long-term debt problem, it is true that for an economy operating close to potential output, government borrowing to finance budget deficits will in theory draw down the pool of national saving, crowding out private capital investment and slowing long-term growth. However, the U.S. economy is currently operating well short of capacity and the risk of such crowding out occurring and damaging future economic growth seems low.

Once the short-term problem of weak demand is solved and the economy has returned to a normal growth path, mainstream economists' consensus policy response for an economy with a looming debt crisis is fiscal consolidation—cutting deficits. Such a policy would have the benefits of low and stable interest rates, a less fragile financial system, improved investment prospects, and possibly faster long-term growth.

BACKGROUND

Severity of the 2008-2009 Recession

The recession that began in late 2007 was long and deep. It is likely to prove to be the worst economic contraction since the 1930s (but still much less severe than the Great Depression). The slowdown of economic activity was moderate through the first half of 2008, but at that point the weakening economy was overtaken by a major financial crisis that would exacerbate the economic weakness and accelerate the decline.[1]

When the fall of economic activity finally bottomed out in the second half of 2009, real gross domestic product (GDP) had contracted by nearly 4.0%, or by about $500 billion.[2] The decline in economic activity was much sharper than in the two most recent recessions, in 2001 and 1990 respectively. The most recent recession of similar severity was in 1973 in which real GDP fell about 3.2%. (However, the recent decline falls well short of the experience during the Great Depression when real GDP decreased by 30%).[3]

As output decreased the unemployment rate increased, rising from 4.6% in 2007 to a peak of 10.1% in October 2009, and remaining only slightly below that high into 2010. The U.S. unemployment rate has not been at this level since 1982, when in the aftermath of the 1981 recession it reached 10.8%, the highest rate of the post-war period. (During the Great Depression, the unemployment rate reached 25%). This recent rise in the unemployment rate translates to about 7 million persons put out of work. Another 8.5 million workers have been pushed involuntarily into part-time employment.[4]

The recession was intertwined with a major financial crisis that exacerbated the negative effects on the economy. Falling stock and house prices led to a large decline in household wealth (net worth), which plummeted by over $10 trillion or nearly 16% during 2008 and 2009. In addition, the financial panic led to an explosion of risk premiums (i.e., compensation to investors for accepting extra risk over relatively risk-free investments such as U.S. Treasury securities) that froze the flow of credit to the economy, crimping credit supported spending by consumers such as for automobiles, as well as business spending on new plant and equipment.[5]

The negative shocks the economy received in 2008 and 2009 were, arguably, more severe than what occurred in 1929. However, unlike in 1929, the severe negative impulses did not turn a recession into a depression, arguably because timely and sizable policy responses by the government helped to support aggregate spending and stabilize the financial system.[6] That stimulative economic policies would have this beneficial effect on a collapsing economy is consistent with standard macroeconomic theory, but without the counterfactual of the economy's path in the absence of these policies, it is difficult to establish with precision how effective these policies were.

Policy Responses to the Financial Crisis and Recession

Both monetary and fiscal policies as well as some extraordinary measures were applied to counter the economic decline. This policy response is thought to have forestalled a more severe economic contraction, helping to turn the economy into the incipient economic recovery by mid-2009. The policies already put in place are likely to continue stimulating economic activity in 2010.

In terms of monetary policy, the Federal Reserve (Fed) aggressively applied conventional monetary stimulus by lowering the federal funds rate to near zero and boldly expanding its "lender of last resort" role, creating new lending programs to better channel needed liquidity to the financial system and induce greater confidence among lenders. These actions were needed to get credit flowing to the wider economy. To bolster the liquidity of the financial system, during 2008 and 2009, the Fed took a variety of actions that more than doubled reserve bank credit by injecting nearly $1.5 trillion of new reserves into the financial system.[7]

In terms of fiscal policy, Congress and the Bush Administration enacted the Economic Stimulus Act of 2008 (P.L. 110-185).This act was a $120 billion package that provided tax rebates to households and accelerated depreciation rules for business. Congress and the Obama Administration passed the American Recovery and Reinvestment Act of 2009 (P.L. 111-5). This was a $787 billion package with $286 billion of tax cuts and $501 billion of spending increases that is projected to add fiscal stimulus equivalent to about 2% of GDP in 2009 and 2.5% of GDP in 2010.[8]

In terms of extraordinary measures, Congress and the Bush Administration passed the Emergency Economic Stabilization Act of 2008 (P.L. 110-343), creating the Troubled Asset Relief Program (TARP). TARP authorized the Treasury to use up to $700 billion to directly bolster the capital position of banks or to remove troubled assets from bank balance sheets.

Congress was an active participant in the emergence of these policy responses and has an ongoing interest in macroeconomic conditions. Current macroeconomic concerns include whether the economy is in a sustainable recovery, rapidly reducing unemployment, speeding a return to normal output and employment growth, and addressing government's long-term debt problem.

IS SUSTAINED ECONOMIC RECOVERY UNDERWAY?

Recent evidence suggests that the process of economic recovery has begun.

- Real GDP (i.e., GDP adjusted for inflation) increased at an annualized rate of 2.2% and 5.6% in the third and fourth quarters of 2009 and 2.7% in the first quarter of 2010. A major contributor to this upward momentum has been a shift by business from letting their inventories decrease to spending to increase inventories. This positive inventory effect was particularly pronounced in the third quarter of 2009, accounting for two-thirds the increase of real GDP. In the first quarter of 2010, inventories continued to boost real GDP and other components of aggregate spending also made a contribution, with consumer spending rising 3.0% and exports rising 11.3%.
- Manufacturing activity is increasing. By mid-2010, output had increased 6% over a year earlier and capacity utilization has risen from a low of 65% in mid-2009 to nearly 74% through mid-2010.
- Since mid-2009 employment has increased, but the gains have been modest.
- The stock market has rebounded and interest rate spreads on corporate bonds have narrowed. The Dow-Jones stock index had plunged to near 6500 in March 2009 but has risen substantially since then. Spreads on investment grade corporate bonds, a measure of the lenders perception of risk and credit worthiness of borrowers, have fallen from a high of 600 basis points in December 2008 to less than 100 basis points by mid-2010.[9]
- China and Asia's other emerging economies are having strong recoveries and the large advanced economies of Germany, France, and Japan have recently recorded positive output growth. Recovery in the rest of the world would likely transmit a positive impulse to the United States by boosting demand for U.S. exports.

On the other hand, significant economic weakness remains evident.

- Employment gains are only keeping pace with growth of the labor force, leaving the unemployment rate historically high at just below 10%.
- The housing market remains weak. Mortgage loan foreclosures continue to rise. House prices are still falling, continuing to have an adverse effect on the balance sheets of households and banks, and dampening the recovery of aggregate spending.[10]
- Despite low interest rates, the Fed reports that credit conditions remain tight, making getting loans difficult for consumers and businesses, and limiting many types of credit supported expenditures.

THE SHAPE OF ECONOMIC RECOVERY

In the typical post-war business cycle, lower than normal growth of aggregate demand during the recession is quickly followed by a recovery period with above normal growth of spending, perhaps spurred by some degree of monetary and fiscal stimulus. The degree of acceleration of growth in the first two to three years of recovery has varied across post-war business cycles, but has been at an annual pace in a range of 4% to 8%.[11] This above normal growth brings the economy back more quickly to the pre-recession growth path, and speeds up the reentry of the unemployed to the workforce.

Once the level of aggregate demand approaches close to the pre-recession level of potential output (or full employment), the economy returns to its pre-recession growth path where the growth of aggregate spending is slower because it is constrained by the growth of aggregate supply, which in recent years is estimated to have been at an annual pace of near 3.0%. (A subsequent section of the report looks more closely at aggregate supply.)[12]

There is concern, however, that this time the U.S. economy, without further policy actions, will either not return to its pre-recession growth path, perhaps remain permanently below it, or return to the pre-crisis path but at a slower than normal pace, or worse, dip into a second recession. Below normal growth would almost certainly translate into below normal recovery of employment, whereas a second round of recession could increase the already high unemployment rate. The next sections discuss problems on the supply side and the demand side of the economy that could lead to a weaker than normal recovery.

Demand Side Problems?

Whatever vigor is now occurring on the demand side of the economy is largely coming from fiscal stimulus and businesses inventory restocking, and these are likely to remain an important propulsive force through 2010. Fiscal stimulus and inventory rebuilding are, however, temporary sources of support of aggregate spending. Sooner or later fiscal stimulus will fall away. The Congressional Budget Office (CBO) projects that fiscal stimulus will peak in the first half of 2010 and make progressively smaller additions to demand in the second half of 2010 and thereafter.[13] Inventory building is a self limiting process that will not go on indefinitely; by 2011 stock-building will likely have only a small positive effect on aggregate demand.

A strong recovery of private sector demand, including consumer spending, investment spending, and exports is required to reduce unemployment and bring the economy quickly back to its pre-recession growth path. However, there are major uncertainties about the potential medium-term strength of each of these components that could dampen aggregate spending and constrain the economy's ability to generate a recovery period with above normal growth and quickly falling unemployment.

Consumption Spending

Personal consumption expenditures constitute the largest and most stable component of aggregate spending. During the first three post-war decades, personal consumption spending averaged a 62% share of GDP. However, that share rose significantly over the next three decades averaging about 65% in the 1980s, 67% during the 1990s, and about 70% between 2001 and 2007. The high level of household spending reached during the 2001-2007 expansion is unlikely to reemerge during the current recovery because it was supported by an unsustainable increase in household debt, decrease in personal savings, and ease of access to credit.

Household Debt

In the mid-1980s, after a long period of relative stability at a scale of around 45% to 50% of GDP, the debt level of households began to rise steadily, reaching over 100% of GDP by 2008. Such a substantial rise in the level of household debt was sustainable so long as rising home prices and a rising stock market continued to also rapidly increase the value of household net worth, and interest rates remained low, mitigating any rise in the burden of debt as a share of GDP.

The collapse of the housing and stock markets in 2008 and 2009 substantially decreased household net worth, which had, by the end of 2009, fallen $10 trillion below its level in 2007.[14] This large fall in net worth pushed the household debt burden to what may be an unsustainable level especially if interest rates rise. Repairing household balance sheets will probably require a large diversion of current income from consumption spending to debt reduction for several more years.[15]

The recent rise of the stock market from its low point in early 2009 has helped household wealth to recover. However, rising home equity, largely dependent on the path of house prices, has traditionally been the major contributor to household wealth. The rapid rise of home prices during the last economic expansion caused an equally rapid rise in home equity. Consumers borrowed against this equity to fund current spending. With the sharp fall of home prices, home equity was reduced substantially, erasing that source of funding. Home prices are still falling and the housing market is expected to remain weak for several more years. That weakness is likely to slow the rebuilding of household wealth, and be a drag on the rebound of consumer spending.[16]

In addition to diverting more personal income to saving, a continued weak labor market is likely to dampen income growth and, in turn, slow the recovery of consumer spending.

Credit Conditions

Easy credit availability in the pre-crisis economy enabled households to readily borrow against their rising home equity to fund added spending. Financial innovations allowed lenders to keep interest rates low and offer liberal terms and conditions to entice households to borrow. It seems likely that credit conditions will be tighter during the current expansion. Interest rates are still low but banks greatly tightened the terms and conditions of consumer loans during the crisis and recession and are likely to continue to do so in the near term. While not likely as important a cause of higher savings as high household debt, tighter credit conditions will make it less likely that households will exploit any increase in their home equity to fund current spending, further constraining consumer spending relative to what occurred during the 2001-2007 economic expansion.

Personal Saving

The U.S. personal saving rate had averaged about 10% of GDP consistently through the 1970s,1980s, and 1990s. But since then the personal saving rate has declined sharply, reaching a low of 1.0% by 2005.[17] It is likely that the evaporation of household saving was in large measure a consequence of the sizable increase in household net worth associated with increased house prices and stock prices occurring at that time. As wealth rose rapidly, it was less urgent to divert current income to saving.

The sharp reduction of household net worth during the recent recession dramatically changed the financial circumstances of households, reducing the use of debt financed spending. The need to repair household balance sheets is likely to induce households to pay down debt. The poor prospect for the appreciation of house prices will sharply limit the ability to use rising equity as a substitute for saving.

In addition, the above normal increase in economic uncertainty in the aftermath of the financial crisis and recession will likely mean that over the medium term, households could be more inclined to save. As the economic decline intensified, the personal saving rate increased, climbing to 2.6% in 2008 and 3.3% in 2009.[18] The financial imperatives behind greater personal saving are going to persist for some time and with the recovery of household income the ability to save will also improve, suggesting that the personal saving rate could continue to increase for several more years.

Slow Recovery of Consumer Spending?

If income rises, the personal saving rate stabilizes near 5%, that would translate into about a 3 percentage point increase over the rate that prevailed during the economy's 2001-2007 expansion, and in turn, a reduction in the consumption to GDP ratio, from about 70% to about 67%.

Therefore, for the U.S. economy to return to its normal pre-crisis growth rate, a 3% share of GDP will have to come from another component of aggregate demand.

Investment Spending

Investment spending is the third largest component of aggregate spending, averaging 17% to 18% of GDP in years of near normal output growth. (Government spending is second largest at about 20%.) The largest portion of total investment spending is business fixed investment, averaging 11% to 12% of GDP in periods of normal growth. The second component of total investment is residential investment, averaging 4% to 5% of GDP.

However, investment spending is very sensitive to economic conditions and more volatile than consumer spending. This sensitivity is at least in part because investment projects are often postponable to a time when economic conditions are more favorable. Its volatility makes investment spending an important determinant of the amplitude, down and up, of the typical business cycle.[19]

As aggregate spending fell and credit availability tightened in 2008, investment spending quickly weakened. As a share of GDP, investment spending fell from about 16% in 2007 to about 11% at the economy's trough in 2009. The sharp fall in real GDP from the second quarter of 2008 through the first quarter of 2009 was nearly fully accounted for by the sharp fall of investment spending over this same period. Investment spending was up modestly in the first quarter of 2010, elevating its share of GDP to 11.8%.

Typically, this same sensitivity also works in the opposite direction. Strongly rising investment spending, responding to improving market demand, reduced uncertainty, and expanding credit availability, often gives above normal contribution to the rebound of aggregate spending during the recovery phase of the business cycle.

Looking forward, however, some significant constraints on both residential and business investment raise uncertainty about whether investment spending will be a strong contributor to economic recovery, and therefore, whether it could be a component of aggregate spending capable of compensating for a weaker than normal recovery of spending by consumers.

The principal constraint on residential investment is likely to be the large inventory of vacant housing, left over from the 2002-2006 housing boom. It is estimated that the number of vacancies could be more than 2 million units above what would normally be expected at this stage of the business cycle. As discussed above, it is still not clear that the housing market has stabilized and new construction remains very weak. The rate of housing starts is likely to remain low for the next two years while the inventory overhang is worked down to a more normal level.

The prospect for nonresidential investment is likely to be better than for residential investment, but it is not clear that nonresidential investment will exceed its pre-crisis level. On the supply side, capacity utilization rates have climbed back from record lows of below 70% reached during the recession, but, at about 74% currently, are still only at the lows reached in the 1990 and the 2001 recessions and well short of the 80% to 85% that would typically correspond to operating near or at capacity.[20] On the demand side, business investment in new plants and equipment is most often a response to the expectation of increased demand for the products they produce. The main driver of that demand is consumer spending and as discussed above that spending has been tepid, with the not unlikely prospect that it may continue to be weak over the near term if households have made a lasting commitment to increased savings. Stronger foreign demand could also stimulate investment spending and in theory compensate for the weaker pull of domestic demand, but as discussed more fully below, foreign demand may also be weak. Also, problems in the financial sector have sharply reduced activity in commercial real estate, causing business investment in structures to continue to be flat.

Therefore, it seems unlikely that investment spending would provide the offset to any sizable fall in consumption's share of GDP over the near term.

Net Exports

The U.S. trade deficit shrank from about 6% of real GDP in 2006 to below 3% in 2009. Since the beginning of the recession in late 2007 through mid-2009, net exports have on balance made a significant positive contribution to real GDP in an otherwise declining economy. Economic weakness abroad caused U.S. exports to fall, but imports have fallen by more, providing a net positive push to current economic activity.[21]

The 3 percentage point swing in real net exports is, however, largely the consequence of the severe economic weakness in the United States over this period, and may not persist as the economy returns to a more normal condition. It is not clear that net exports can offset weak consumption over the medium to long term, boost spending, and help assure a sustained recovery at a near normal pace.

Boosting U.S. Net Exports through a Rebalancing of Global Spending

Increasing U.S. net exports to any degree requires that the trade deficit continue to decrease. For that to happen, trade surpluses in the rest of the world must simultaneously decrease. To achieve this adjustment of trade flows, a sizable rebalancing of domestic and external demand on the part of the deficit and surplus economies must occur. [22]

Because a trade deficit is a consequence of an economy spending more than it produces, rebalancing in this circumstance requires a decrease of domestic spending and increase of domestic saving. In contrast, because a trade surplus is a consequence of an economy spending less than it produces, rebalancing in this circumstance requires an increase of domestic spending and decrease in domestic saving.

This rebalancing of spending will cause the dollar to depreciate and foreign currencies to appreciate. A fall in the value of the dollar relative to the currencies of the surplus countries causes the price of foreign goods to rise for U.S. buyers and the price of U.S. goods to fall for foreign buyers. This change in the relative price of foreign versus domestic goods will cause the net exports of the deficit country to rise, giving the boost in spending needed to potentially offset reduced consumption spending. The change in relative prices would also cause the net exports of surplus countries to fall as more of current output is absorbed by increased domestic spending.

In the United States, as discussed above, some measure of rebalancing seems to be occurring, as evidenced by the increase in the personal saving rate. Although there are good reasons to expect this increase to be durable, there is the possibility that households would eventually revert to their pre-crisis low saving ways. However, even if household saving remains higher, it is likely that any significant increase in the overall U.S. national saving rate would also require an increase in government saving via smaller federal budget deficits.

Large U.S. budget deficits over the near term are providing a needed boost to weak aggregate spending during the early stages of an economic recovery. With the strengthening of private spending as the recovery matures, large government budget deficits would fade away, causing government saving to rise. What puts this fading away of budget deficits in doubt over the long-term is the prospect of having to fund the obligations attached to the rising demand of an aging U.S. population for healthcare, social security, and other entitlements. Without policy actions to address these long-term demands, it is not clear how the long-term budget deficits will fall.

Effective global rebalancing arguably also involves sizable adjustments by the largest surplus economies—Germany, Japan, and China. However, there are significant potential constraints on how substantially each of these three economies can "save less and spend more," perhaps limiting any sizable appreciation of their currencies relative to the dollar, and any associated boost in U.S. net exports.

The inability of Germany to move its exchange rate independently from the other Euro area economies reduces its flexibility of adjustment. In addition, the effects of recession have left limited room for further fiscal expansion and small ability to lower the household saving rate. While its level of debt is not high, recent German policy actions have stressed fiscal consolidation, tending to increase saving and dampen spending. Japan, which does have a very high level of public debt, has little to no room for fiscal expansion and a poor prospect of boosting household spending. Moreover, both Germany and Japan, faced with substantial near-term economic weakness in the aftermath of the global recession, may take steps to avoid the dampening of their net exports that a sizable appreciation of the exchange rate would cause.

China has the largest bilateral trade surplus with the United States and therefore has the potential to have a large impact on U.S. export sales and through that a significant positive impulse on the pace of the U.S. economic recovery. Also, economic growth has remained relatively strong in China through the recent global financial crisis and recession and aggregate demand is expected to be strong through the next two to three years. What is uncertain, however, is whether a greater share of this spending will be domestic demand, particularly consumption spending by Chinese households.

The very high rate of saving by Chinese households is thought to be a precautionary measure to compensate for a lack of social insurance. It likely also reflects limited access to consumer credit. The difficulty for the near-term task of sustaining economic recovery is that even if policy actions are taken to remove these constraints on consumer spending, households are likely to only gradually change their pattern of consumption and not provide a sharp near-term boost to domestic spending.

Also, a closer look at the sources of increase in China's domestic saving over the last decade reveals that the principal contributor to that growth was Chinese companies, not households. Therefore changing the saving practices of Chinese companies is likely to be an important aspect of any large increase in China's saving rate. It is argued by some that Chinese companies retain too large a share of their earnings. Better access to credit and changes in the governance rules of Chinese business would likely reduce the business saving rate. But, as with households, even if such policy initiatives are forthcoming, the change in the business saving rate is likely to emerge only gradually.[23]

Even with a successful rebalancing, it is unlikely that China alone can propel a boost in U.S. net exports sufficient to offset weak domestic demand and pace economic recovery. China's global trade surplus is estimated to be about 10% of GDP. However, China is only about one-third the size of the U.S. economy. Therefore, if China's trade were only with the United States, it would have to reduce its trade surplus by 3% of GDP to affect a 1 percentage point reduction of the U.S. trade deficit. But since, in fact, only about 16% of China's trade is with the United States, it would take a 15 percentage point change in China's trade balance (moving from a surplus equal to 10% of GDP to a deficit equal to 5% of GDP) to reduce the U.S. trade deficit by 1 percentage point. (This assumes that the fall of China's trade surplus is not offset by an increase of other trading partners surpluses.)

Other emerging Asian economies also run trade surpluses and adding these to the calculation makes the relative scale of rebalancing needed to achieve a given amount of improvement in the U.S trade deficit more feasible. However, all of emerging Asia is only about half the size of the U.S. economy. Therefore, if the U.S. share of the whole region's trade is similar to China's, emerging Asia would need to accomplish a sizable 7 percentage point change in its trade balance to generate a 1 percentage point change in the U.S. trade balance. As with China, for a reduction of the trade surpluses of other emerging Asian economies to happen quickly, their currencies will need to appreciate against the dollar.

All and all, there are reasons to doubt whether U.S. net exports can increase over the near term at a pace sufficient to fully compensate for the prospect of slower than normal growth of other components of U.S. domestic spending.

Supply Side Problems?

The supply side of the economy governs its capacity for producing goods and services. That capacity is a function of the economy's supplies of labor and capital and the level of technology used to turn labor and capital into the output of goods and services. In the short run, the potential supplies of these productive factors is relatively fixed and will determine the economy's potential output. In periods of economic slack, rising aggregate demand can increase the economy's output and employment up to the level of potential output, which corresponds with full employment.

In the long run, as the supplies of capital and labor and the level of technology increase, the level of potential output also increases. Over time the steady rise of potential output will define the economy's long-term growth path (called the "trend" growth rate). When aggregate demand is below potential output the economy can grow faster than trend growth, but when the level of aggregate demand reaches the level of potential output, further growth of output will be constrained to the trend growth rate.

Typically the long run growth path is thought to be relatively stable and not greatly affected by recessions and the associated short-term fluctuations in aggregate demand. Over the post-war period, the average annual growth rate of potential output for the United States has been 3.4%, however, since the 1970s it has averaged closer to 3.0%.[24]

Recent analysis by the International Monetary Fund (IMF) examines the question of whether output will return to its pre-crisis trend after the crisis.[25] It examines the medium-term and long-run paths of output after 88 banking crises over the past four decades in a wide range of countries (including both advanced and developing economies). A key conclusion was that seven years after the crisis, output had declined relative to trend by nearly 10% for the average country. But there was considerable variation of outcomes across crisis episodes.

In other words, such crises not only reduce actual output, but also may reduce potential output (the economy's structural and institutional capacity to produce output). In this circumstance, the economy could return to its trend growth rate, but there is unlikely to be a rebound period of above normal growth to quickly return the economy to its pre-crisis potential output and growth path and, in turn, quickly reduce unemployment. This failure to return to the pre-crisis potential output means that the economy bears the burden of a permanent output loss and the large initial increase in the unemployment rate caused by the crisis could persist even as the economy is growing at its trend rate.

The reduction of the post-crisis growth path is found to be the consequence of decreases of approximately equal size in the employment rate, the capital-labor ratio, and productivity. The adverse effect of the financial crisis on the employment rate is thought to arise from an increase in the "structural unemployment rate," hampering the post-crisis economy's ability to accomplish the needed reallocation of labor from sectors that have contracted permanently to sectors that are expanding.

Because the aftermath of the crisis will likely involve sizable changes in the composition of the economy, it likely also increases the mismatch between the skills of the unemployed and the skills demanded in the post-crisis labor market—job vacancies go unfilled for lack of a worker with sufficient skills for the job.[26] Also, labor force participation rates may fall if the crisis is severe enough to substantially increase the numbers of the long-term unemployed, some of whom may become discouraged from searching for a new job. A crisis induced fall of house prices and a rising incidence of mortgages with negative equity will also discourage the geographic mobility of workers who are unable to sell their house.

The adverse impact of a financial crisis on capital accumulation is likely the combined outcome of several factors. Decreased demand for products and heightened uncertainty of potential return dampens the incentive to invest. In addition, the financial crisis could impede the process of financial intermediation for up to several years, as weakened balance sheets, lower collateral values, and elevated risk premiums slow the flow of credit and elevate the real cost of borrowing.

The dampening effect on productivity may occur as higher risk premiums and a generally more cautious approach to spending by businesses diminishes the willingness and ability to finance relatively high-risk projects. Expenditures on research and development are very pro-cyclical and likely to be sharply reduced in times of crisis.

Productivity tends to recover quickly after recessions and thus allow the economy to resume growth at the pre-crisis trend rate. However, the capital and employment losses tend to endure and keep the economy on a lower growth path.

Has the recent financial crisis caused a reduction in the potential output of the U.S. economy and placed it on a lower trend growth path? It is difficult to make a concurrent determination because potential output is not directly observable, and can only be imputed from the economy's actual post-crisis performance. Therefore, a clear determination of such a permanent output loss is some years in the future.

Although the IMF study gives reasons why the financial crisis possibly could have adversely affected the economy's supply-side, the study also finds that there can be some significant mitigating factors that could be particularly relevant for the U.S. economy. First, a high pre-crisis investment share is a good predictor of a large potential output loss. This is a reflection of the high sensitivity of investment to the negative effects of a financial crisis. For the United States there was no sharp increase in investment spending above trend as measured as a share of GDP for the three years prior to the financial crisis, averaging near a typical 16% of GDP.

Second, the IMF study also found that those economies that aggressively apply stimulative fiscal and monetary policies during the crisis tend to have smaller medium-term output losses. As already discussed, the United States has applied quickly and substantially stimulative polices in response to the financial crisis.

Third, countries with fewer labor market rigidities suffered smaller medium-term output losses. U.S. labor markets, as compared to other advanced economies, are relatively free of labor market rigidities, though as mentioned declining house prices may have reduced mobility of some workers who own their own homes.

Policy Responses to Increase the Pace of Economic Recovery

If the pace of private spending proves insufficient to assure a sustained recovery, would further stimulus by monetary and fiscal policy be warranted? One of the important lessons from the Great Depression is to guard against an overly hasty withdrawal of fiscal and monetary stimulus in the fragile early stages of recovering from a deep decline. The removal of fiscal and monetary stimulus in 1937 is thought to have stopped a recovery and caused a slump that did not end until WWII.[27]

The Case for More Fiscal Stimulus

In a recent speech, Lawrence Summers, Assistant to the President for Economic Policy and Director of the National Economic Council, argued that further fiscal stimulus is necessary because the effects of the first stimulus package are now beginning to fade, and because of the prospect that private spending may still lack sufficient vigor to sustain a healthy recovery.[28] The risk, in Summers' view, of not applying further fiscal stimulus is possibly several years of subnormal growth, or worse, dipping into a second recession. Nevertheless, in his speech, Summers also recognized the need for a complementary policy to address the long-term challenge to economic growth of large future budget deficits. In periods of normal economic growth, unconstrained by weak aggregate demand, large budget deficits are thought to increase interest rates, depress investment, and dampen economic growth. He urged Congress to pass a variety of spending measures it is now considering that would inject up $200 billion into the economy.

A recent CBO report examined the potential for various fiscal policy options for increasing economic growth and employment in 2010 and 2020, emphasizing the policies' cost effectiveness as measured by the effects on GDP and employment per dollar of budgetary cost.[29] Recognizing the role of uncertainty, high and low estimates were generated giving a range for the effects. For 2010, the biggest "bang for the buck" came from increasing aid to the unemployed, reducing employers' payroll taxes, and reducing employer payroll taxes for firms that increase their payroll. (Providing an additional one-time social security payment and allowing full or partial expensing of investment costs also had a positive impact). For 2011, the CBO finds the strongest effects would come from providing aid to states for projects other than infrastructure and providing additional refundable tax credits for lower and middle income households.

However, the CBO report also cautioned that despite their beneficial short-run effects, these actions would also add to already large future deficits. Unless future actions were taken to offset the accumulation of additional government debt, future economic growth would tend to be lower than otherwise. However, the scale of economic stimulus now being discussed, while possibly having a sizable effect on aggregate demand in the short run, would have a relatively small effect on the size of the government's long-term debt.

Because the United States faces two macroeconomic problems, two policy responses are, arguably, appropriate: a short-term policy to sustain a cyclical recovery of economic growth and a long-term policy to trim government debt. Conceptually there is no necessary tradeoff between these two objectives. They can be mutually reinforcing: a credible commitment to dealing with the long-term debt problem allays investor uncertainty and increases the near-term incentive to spend, while effectively dealing with the short-term problem of weak aggregate demand puts the economy on a stronger growth path, which boosts tax revenue and eases the long-term debt problem.

Is More Monetary Stimulus Needed?

Could monetary policy do more to put the economy on the path of sustained recovery? First, given that the economy is still weak and inflation only a possible long-term threat, the

Fed has given no indication that it would repeat, the mistake of 1937 and remove liquidity prematurely. The most recent minutes from the Feds policy making body, the Federal Reserve Open Market Committee, indicated that the continued weak state of the economy warranted keeping the federal funds rate, the principal policy rate, low for an extended time. [30]

In regard to added stimulus, policy rates are already near zero and, as noted above, the Fed has already injected a substantial amount of liquidity into the financial system. The problem may not be the level of liquidity, but a substantial impairment of the monetary transmission mechanism that channels liquidity from lenders to borrowers to support current spending. In the aftermath of the financial crisis and recession, the combination of credit strained financial intermediaries and overleveraged borrowers has impeded this transfer of liquidity. In this circumstance monetary policy is often unable to "get the traction" it needs to indirectly stimulate current spending. If economic activity picks up on its own or with the jump start of more fiscal stimulus there is likely sufficient liquidity in the financial system to support a sustained recovery.

The Case against More Fiscal Stimulus

The case against more fiscal stimulus comes in three forms, used separately or in combination; one, no further stimulus is needed; two, fiscal stimulus does not work; and three, stimulus increases the budget deficit, makes the U.S. long-term debt problem worse, and dampens economic growth.[31]

In regard to the need for stimulus, the U.S. economy does have strong recuperative powers and it is possible that private spending and economic growth will soon surge without further fiscal stimulus. Events such as improved consumer confidence, lower energy prices, a more normal flow of credit, or faster growth in the rest of the world could separately or in combination induce stronger spending by households and businesses. However, given the severity of the recent recession and, as outlined above, given the current weakness of private spending and the several economic obstacles that households and businesses will probably continue to face over the near term, there remains a significant risk of sub-normal growth for the next one to two years.

In regard to the ability of fiscal stimulus to boost output and employment, some economists argue that fiscal stimulus only shifts spending, it does not increase spending. In this view, when people see the government running a budget deficit, they anticipate that the government will need to increase taxes in the future to pay of the debt, and increase their current savings to pay for the higher taxes. The increase in saving tends to offset the stimulative effect of the budget deficit.[32] There is little empirical support for this theory, however. Mainstream economic analysis indicates that in circumstances like the present, where the economy's output is likely constrained by insufficient demand, fiscal stimulus can raise the level of output and employment.[33]

In regard to the long-term debt problem, it is true that for an economy operating close to potential output, government borrowing to finance budget deficits will draw down the pool of national saving, leaving less available to support private capital investment. Private investment by business and households in education, housing, research & development, and capital equipment that would have otherwise occurred is in theory "crowded out" through higher interest rates bid up by the government borrowing. If budget deficits divert national saving from private investment, other things equal, future productivity and income growth may be slowed. However, the U.S. economy is currently operating well short of capacity and the risk of such "crowding out" occurring and damaging future economic growth does not seem immediate.[34]

Once the short-term problem of weak demand is solved and the economy has returned to a normal growth path, the appropriate policy response for an economy with a looming debt crisis is fiscal consolidation—cutting deficits. Such a policy would have the benefits of low and stable interest rates, a less fragile financial system, improved investment prospects, and possibly faster long-term growth.

Economic Projections

Given the large deterioration of the balance sheets of households and businesses, the possible reduction of the U.S. economy's level of potential output, and the weakened state of the global economy in the aftermath of the recent financial crisis, projections of the U.S. economy's near-term path carry a high degree of uncertainty. Most forecasts have the U.S. economy on a path of recovery in 2010 and for several years after that. However, there is some variance among forecasters regarding the pace of that recovery.

- The IMF forecasts a relatively slow paced economic recovery by historical standards. Real GDP is projected to advance 3.3% in 2010 and 2.9% in 2011. Weak near-term economic growth is attributed to permanent output losses and impaired growth potential due to a damaged financial system, greater household saving (less consumption spending) needed to rebuild weakened balance sheets, and slow growth of trading partners. The unemployment rate is projected to be 9.6% in 2010 and decrease to 8.3% in 2011.[35]
- CBO forecasts a slightly less vigorous recovery. Real GDP is projected to advance a weak 1.7% in 2010, accelerates to 3.3% in 2011, and the pace quickens to 4.7% in 2012 and 2013. The unemployment rate is projected to remain near 10% in 2010 and above 9% in 2011.[36]
- Global Insight, a private economic forecasting company, projects real GDP to advance at 3.0% in 2010 and 2011. The unemployment rate is projected to be 9.6% in 2010 and 9.0% in 2011.[37]

End Notes

[1] See CRS Report R40007, *Financial Market Turmoil and U.S. Macroeconomic Performance*, by Craig K. Elwell.

[2] Real GDP is the output of goods and services produced in the United States.

[3] Data on GDP is available from the Department of Commerce, Bureau of Economic Analysis, http://www.bea.gov/national/index.htm#gdp.

[4] Data on unemployment and employment available from the Department of Labor, Bureau of Labor Statistics, http://www.bls.gov/.

[5] Data on wealth and financial flows available at the Board of Governors of the Federal Reserve System, http://www.federalreserve.gov/releases/z1/Current/.

[6] See IMF, *World Economic Outlook*, October 2009, Chapter 2, http://www.imf.org/external/ pubs/ft/weo/2009/02/pdf/ c2.pdf.

[7] See CRS Report RL34427, *Financial Turmoil: Federal Reserve Policy Responses*, by Marc Labonte.

[8] See CRS Report R40104, *Economic Stimulus: Issues and Policies*, by Jane G. Gravelle, Thomas L. Hungerford, and Marc Labonte.

[9] Data on spreads found at http://www.bloomberg.com/apps/quote?ticker=.TEDSP%3AIND.

[10] Housing start data reported by U.S. Department of Commerce, Bureau of the Census, New Residential Construction Statistics, May 19, 2010, http://www.census.gov/const/www/newresconsthist.html.

[11] Department of Commerce, Bureau of Economic Analysis, http://www.bea.gov/national/index.htm#gdp.

[12] The long-term growth of aggregate supply is determined by the growth in the supplies of capital and labor and on the growth in production technology used to turn capital and labor into goods and services.

[13] The Congressional Budget Office, The Budget and Economic Outlook: Fiscal Years 2010 to 2020, January 2010, http://www.cbo.gov/ftpdocs/108xx/doc10871/BudgetOutlook2010_Jan.cfm.

[14] Board of Governors of the Federal Reserve System, "Flow of Funds Accounts," Table B.100, June 2010, http://www.federalreserve.gov/releases/z1/Current/z1r-5.pdf.

[15] See Evan Tanner and Yassar Abdih, "Rebuilding U.S. Wealth," *Finance & Development*, IMF, December 2009.

[16] The standard model of consumer spending used in economic analysis assumes that consumers seek to avoid large swings in their living standards over the course of their lifetimes. Thus as incomes rise and fall both in the short and long term, individuals are expected to vary their saving rate in order to minimize the effect on their consumption. If consumers seek to maintain a fairly stable level of consumption over their entire lives, then the level of consumption at any given point in their lives will depend on their current wealth and some expectation about their income over the rest of their lives. See Annamaria Lusardi, Jonathan Skinner, and Steven Venti, "Saving Puzzles and Saving Policies in the United States," National Bureau of Economic Research, Working Paper 8237, April 2001.

[17] See CRS Report R40647, *The Fall and Rise of Household Saving*, by Brian W. Cashell.

[18] U.S. Department of Commerce, Bureau of Economic Analysis, *National Accounts*, Table 5.1, http://www.bea.gov/ national/nipaweb/SelectTable.asp?Selected=N.

[19] Ibid, Table 1.1.5.

[20] Data for Capacity utilization are available at Board of Governors of the Federal Reserve System, *Industrial Production and Capacity Utilization*, Table G17, http://www.federalreserve.gov/releases/g17/.

[21] U.S. Department of Commerce, Bureau of Economic Analysis, *National Economic Accounts*, http://bea.gov/national/ nipaweb/Index.asp.

[22] On global rebalancing, see for example: Oliver Blanchard, "*Sustaining Global Recovery*," International Monetary Fund, September 2009, "Rebalancing," The Economist, March 31, 2010, http://www.imf.org/external/pubs/ft/fandd/ 2009/09/index.htm, and Board of Governors of the Federal Reserve System, Vice-chairman Donald L. Kohn, Speech "Global Imbalances," May 11, 2010, http://www.federalreserve.gov/newsevents/speech/kohn20100511a.htm.

[23] Of course, for these reforms to translate into a shift in China's trade balance, that nation must be willing to allow its' exchange rate to rise relative to the dollar, causing a decrease in the price of foreign goods relative to domestic goods, and exerting downward pressure on China's trade surplus. From July 2005 to February 2009, China abandoned its dollar peg, allowing the yuan to appreciate by 28% (on a real trade-weighted basis). However, faced with weakening export sales due to the global financial crisis China for the last 10 months has re-pegged the yuan to the dollar. China's export-led growth model, relying on a high saving rate (to keep internal demand low) and a low exchange rate pegged to the dollar (to keep external demand high), has been very successful and, despite the possible advantages of reforms to boost domestic demand, it is uncertain whether China would move substantially away from this model.

[24] Ibid, CBO, p.39.

[25] P. Kannan, A. Scott, and M. Terrones (2009), "From Recession to Recovery: How Soon and How Strong?," in World Economic Outlook, pp. 103-138. International Monetary Fund. Also see Furceri, Davide and Annabelle Mourougane, "The Effect of Financial Crisis on Potential Output: New Empirical Evidence from OECD Countries," *Economics Department Working Papers No. 699*, May 2009.

[26] Employment in construction, financial services, and some types of manufacturing may remain depressed for some time, requiring some who lose their jobs in those sectors to seek employment in other sectors.

[27] For further discussion of economic policy during the Great Depression, see Christina D. Romer, "The Nation in Depression," *The Journal of Economic Perspectives*, vol. 7, no. 2 (spring 1993), pp. 19-39.

[28] Lawrence H. Summers, "*Reflections on Fiscal Policy and Economic Strategy*," Speech at the Johns Hopkins School of Advanced International Studies, May 24, 2010. Other economists have also concluded that further stimulus is called for. See, for example, Brad DeLong "The Worst -of-Both-Worlds Fiscal Policy," June 18, 2010, http://delong.typepad.com/sdj/2010/06/worst-of-both-worlds-fiscal-policy.html; and "The Case for More Stimulus" Interview with William Gale of the Brookings Institution, June 2010, http://www.theatlantic.com/business/archive/ 2010/06/the-case-for-more-stimulus/57776/.

[29] CBO, Policies for Increasing Economic Growth and Employment, January 2010, http://www.theatlantic.com/ business/archive/2010/02/heres-why-government-stimulus-does-not-work/36466/.

[30] Board of Governors of the Federal Reserve System, *Federal Open Market Committee*, http://www.federalreserve.gov/ monetarypolicy/fomccalendars.htm

[31] See for example: Derek Thompson, "The Case Against More Stimulus," *The Atlantic*, June 2010, http://www.theatlantic.com/business/archive/2010/06/the-case-against-more-stimulus/57774/, and "Here's Why Fiscal Stimulus Won't Work," *The Atlantic*, February 2010.

[32] This theory is called "Ricardian equivalence." It is named after the nineteenth-century economist David Ricardo who first made the argument. For further discussion see N. Gregory Mankiw, *Principles of Economics* (Ft. Worth, Dryden Press, 1998), p556, and Robert J. Barro, "Are Government Bonds Net Wealth?" *Journal of Political Economy*, vol. 82, no. 6. (November-December, 1974), pp. 1095-1117.

[33] See CRS Report RL31235, *The Economics of the Federal Budget Deficit,* by Brian W. Cashell; Alan J. Auerbach and William G. Gale, "Activist Fiscal Policy to Stabilize Economic Activity," working paper, September 29, 2009, available at http://elsa.berkeley.edu/~auerbach/activistfiscal.pdf; and Robert E. Hall, "By How Much Does GDP Rise If the Government Buys More Output?" *Brookings Papers on Economic Activity*, fall 2009, pp. 183- 250.

[34] For discussion of the long term debt issue see President Obama's *National Commission on Fiscal Responsibility and Reform*, http://www.fiscalcommission.gov/.

[35] IMF, *World Economic Outlook*, July 2010, http://www.imf.org/external/pubs/ft/weo/2010/01/pdf/c2.pdf.

[36] The Congressional Budget Office, *The Budget and Economic Outlook: Fiscal Years 2010 to 2020*, January 2010, http://www.cbo.gov/ftpdocs/108xx/doc10871/BudgetOutlook2010_Jan.cfm.

[37] Global Insight, *U.S. Economic Outlook*, April 2010, http://www.ihsglobalinsight.com/.

In: U.S. Economic Recovery and Stimulus Measures
Editor: Jessica D. Saparito
ISBN: 978-1-61209-266-9

Chapter 2

BUSINESS INVESTMENT AND EMPLOYMENT TAX INCENTIVES TO STIMULATE THE ECONOMY

Thomas L. Hungerford and Jane G. Gravelle

SUMMARY

According to the Business Cycle Dating Committee of the National Bureau of Economic Research (NBER), the U.S. economy has been in recession since December 2007. Congress passed and the President signed an economic stimulus package, the American Recovery and Reinvestment Act of 2009 (P.L. 111-5), in February 2009. The $787 billion package included $286 billion in tax cuts to help stimulate the economy. Among the tax reductions, many were tax incentives directed to business. The preliminary estimate of fourth quarter real gross domestic product (GDP) growth is 5.9%; the unemployment rate, a lagging indicator, averaged 9.6% in the third quarter and 10.0% in the fourth quarter of 2009. Federal Reserve Chairman Ben Bernanke expects the economy to continue growing at a modest pace, but predicts that bank lending will remain constrained and the job market will remain weak into at least 2010. To further assist unemployed workers, help business, and stimulate housing markets, Congress passed the Worker, Homeownership, and Business Assistance Act of 2009 (P.L. 111-92). The Obama Administration has advocated further business tax incentives to spur investment and employment, especially for small business. The House and Senate passed the Hiring Incentives to Restore Employment (HIRE) Act, which includes an employment tax credit. The President signed the act into law on March 18, 2010.

The two most common measures to provide business tax incentives for new investment are investment tax credits and accelerated deductions for depreciation. The evidence, however, suggests that a business tax subsidy may not necessarily be the best choice for fiscal stimulus, largely because of the uncertainty of its success in stimulating aggregate demand. If such subsidies are used, however, the most effective short-run policy is probably a temporary investment subsidy. Permanent investment subsidies may distort the allocation of investment in the long run.

Employment and wage subsidies are designed to increase employment directly by reducing a firm's wage bill. The tax system is a frequently used means for providing employment subsidies. Most of the business tax incentives for hiring currently under discussion are modeled partially on the New Jobs Tax Credit (NJTC) from 1977 and 1978. Evidence provided in various studies suggests that incremental tax credits have the potential of increasing employment, but in practice may not be as effective in increasing employment as desired. There are several reasons why this may be the case. First, jobs tax credits are often complex and many employers, especially small businesses, may not want to incur the necessary record-keeping costs. Second, since eligibility for the tax credit is determined when the firm files the annual tax return, firms do not know if they are eligible for the credit at the time hiring decisions are made. Third, many firms may not even be aware of the availability of the tax credit until it is time to file a tax return. Lastly, product demand appears to be the primary determinant of hiring.

According to the Business Cycle Dating Committee of the National Bureau of Economic Research (NBER), the U.S. economy has been in recession since December 2007.[1] Congress passed and the President signed an economic stimulus package, the American Recovery and Reinvestment Act of 2009 (P.L. 111-5), in February 2009. The $787 billion package included $286 billion in tax cuts to help stimulate the economy. Among the tax reductions, many were tax incentives directed to business. The estimated revenue losses of the business tax incentives are $40 billion for FY2009, $36 billion for FY2010, and $6 billion for FY2009-FY2019 (because of estimated revenue gains in the out years). The business tax incentives included a temporary expansion of the work opportunity tax credit, a temporary increase of small business expensing, a temporary extension of bonus depreciation, and a five-year carryback of 2008 net operating losses for small businesses.

The preliminary estimate of fourth quarter real gross domestic product (GDP) growth is 5.9%; the unemployment rate, a lagging indicator, averaged 9.6% in the third quarter and 10.0% in the fourth quarter of 2009. Federal Reserve Chairman Ben Bernanke expects the economy to continue growing at a modest pace, but predicts that bank lending will remain constrained and the job market remain weak into at least 2010.[2] To further assist unemployed workers, help business, and stimulate housing markets, Congress passed the Worker, Homeownership, and Business Assistance Act of 2009 (signed by the President on November 6, 2009, P.L. 111-92).

Many observers have advocated further business tax incentives to spur investment and employment. Recent op-ed contributors have proposed tax credits to encourage businesses to hire.[3] The Obama Administration has proposed tax incentives for small businesses to encourage investment and hiring. The House and Senate passed the Hiring Incentives to Restore Employment (HIRE) Act, which includes an employment tax credit. The President signed the act into law on March 18, 2010.

THE STATE OF THE ECONOMY

The need for tax incentives to boost economic activity depends on the state of the economy. One measure that has tracked economic activity fairly well in the past is the Federal Reserve Board's industrial production index, which is used by NBER in its determination of the economy's turning points.[4] **Figure 1** and **Figure 2** show the monthly industrial production index for four past recessions and the current recession. The index is followed from the beginning of each recession (month 0 in the figures) and for the next 36 months.[5] **Figure 1** compares the trend in the industrial production index for the previous two recessions (the 1990-1991 recession and 2001 recession) with the current recession (the dashed line). The previous two recessions lasted for eight months according to NBER; the industrial production index in both cases started to track upward eight months after the recession started.[6] In the current recession, however, the industrial production index was still declining eight months after the recession started and continued to trend downward for the next 10 months.

Figure 2 compares the current recession with the 1973-1975 and 1981-1982 recessions. The latter recessions lasted for 16 months according to NBER and the industrial production index bottomed out at the end of each recession.[7] The trend in index for the current recession appears to approximately track the trend over the other two recessions. In the current recession, the index declined between December 2007 and May 2009, before turning up. The data on real GDP growth and industrial production suggest that economic activity (that is, output) may have begun increasing in May or June 2009. The tax incentives to enhance economic activity being discussed, however, do not target output. Rather they target investment and employment.

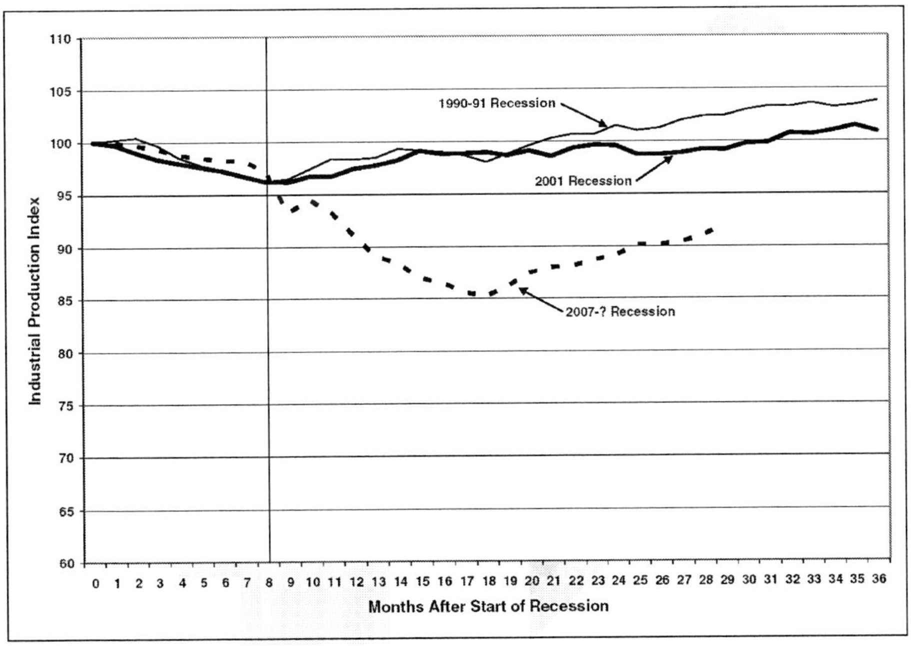

Source: CRS analysis of Federal Reserve Board data.

Figure 1. Industrial Production Index: 1990-1991, 2001, and Current Recession.

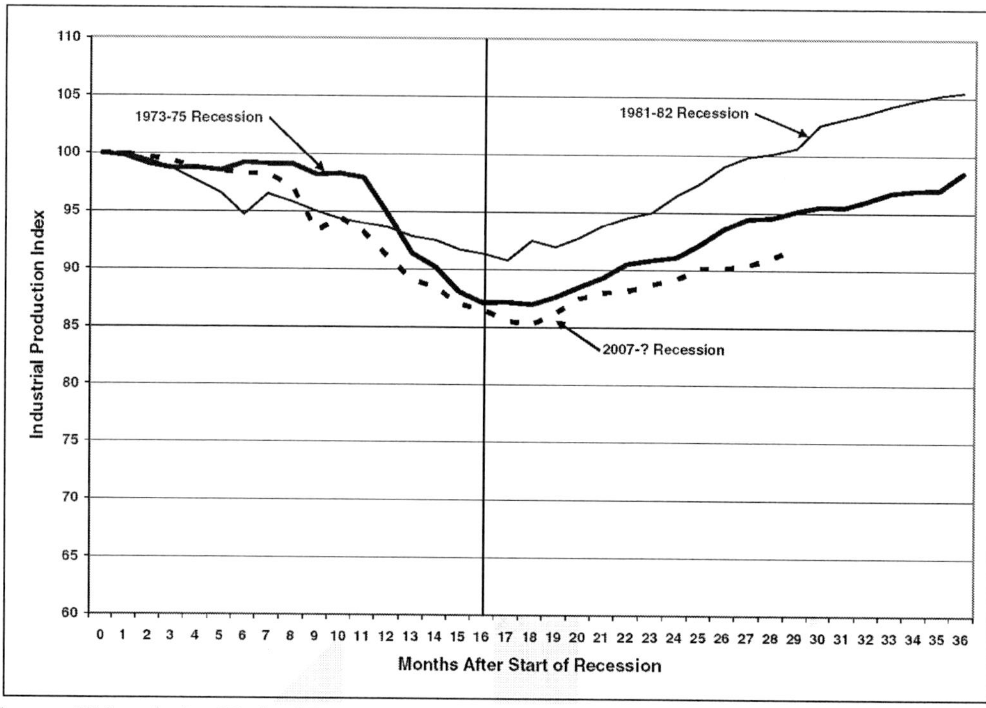

Source: CRS analysis of Federal Reserve Board data.

Figure 2. Industrial Production Index: 1973-1975, 1981-1982, and Current Recession.

Investment

Investment spending by firms tends to decrease in a recession. **Figure 3** displays the quarterly growth rates for real nonresidential gross investment (i.e., business investment) for the quarter in which the recession started and the subsequent 10 quarters for five recessions. Each recession is different, but generally by the third quarter after the start of the recession real investment growth is negative and remains negative for the next four quarters. During the current recession, the decline in real investment spending was particularly severe in the fourth and fifth quarters compared to the other four recessions.

Not all gross investment is used to add to the capital stock; some is used to replace worn-out capital goods (i.e., consumption of fixed capital or depreciation). In 2008, about 75% of gross investment spending replaced the value of worn-out fixed assets (this percentage has varied between 57% and 83% over the past 40 years); the other 25% increased the capital stock. The consumption of fixed assets as a percentage of gross nonresidential investment stood at 60% in 1970; it increased by 15 percentage points between 1970 and 2008 (reaching 83% in 2003). Overall, net nonresidential investment as a percentage of GDP has been trending downward—falling from 4.1% in 1970 to 3.0% in 2008.

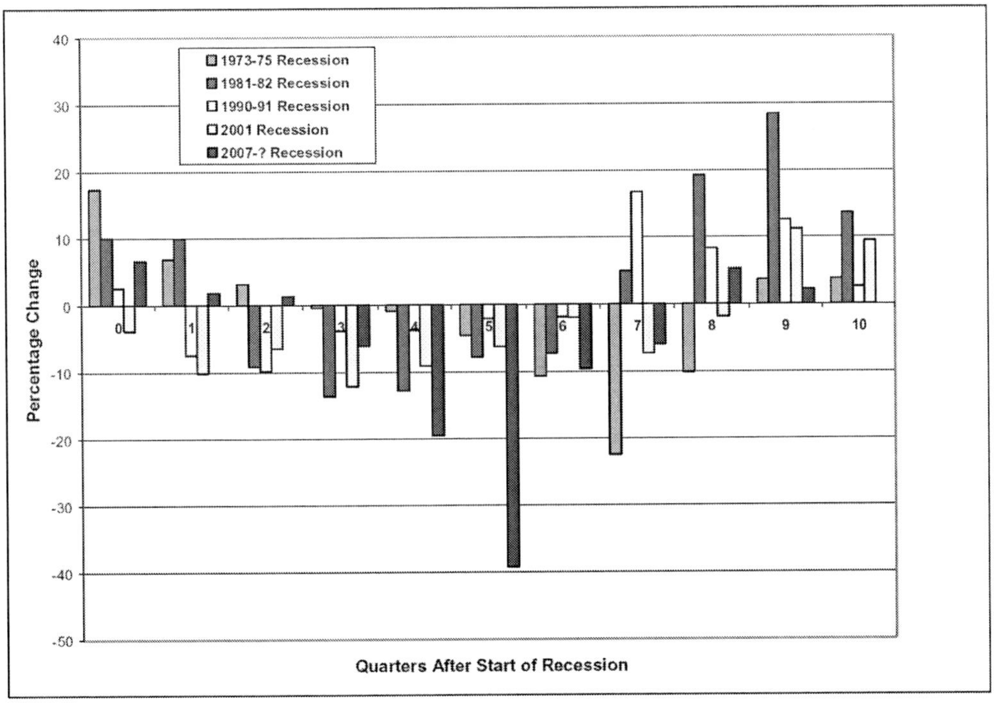

Source: CRS analysis of Bureau of Economic Analysis data.

Figure 3. Real Investment Growth in Five Recessions.

Employment

Employment has fallen in every month since the recession began in December 2007. **Figure 4** and **Figure 5** show employment for the first month of the recession and the subsequent 36 months for the current recession and four other recessions. Employment is shown as an employment index (i.e., as the percentage of employment in the first month of the recession). Employment typically lags the recovery in output by a few months in part because employers are likely to restore the hours worked by employees still on their payrolls before recalling those laid off or hiring new workers.

The current recession is compared with the previous two recessions—the 1990-1991 and 2001 recessions—in **Figure 4**. Although the previous two recessions were relatively mild and short (lasting for eight months), employment levels were either stagnant (the 1990-1991 recession) or declining (the 2001 recession) for several months after the end of the recession. For example, employment hit bottom 21 months after the 2001 recession ended. In the current recession, employment levels declined slightly over the first nine months of the recession and then fell sharply over the next 12 months. By January 2010, employment stood at 94% of the December 2007 employment level.

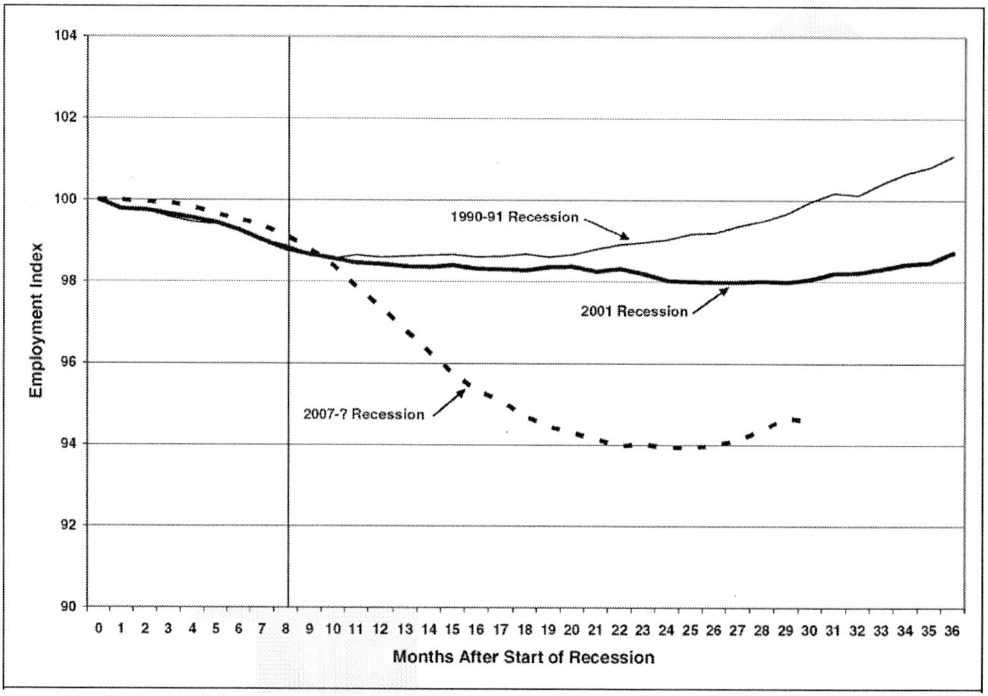

Source: CRS analysis of Bureau of Labor Statistics data.

Figure 4. Employment Levels During the 1990-1991, 2001, and Current Recessions.

Figure 5 compares the employment levels during the current recession with employment levels during the 1973-1975 and 1981-1982 recessions. These latter two recessions were relatively deep and prolonged—lasting for 16 months. For these two recessions, the employment level began increasing within a month or two after the end of the recession (the end of these recessions is denoted by the vertical line in the figure). In the current recession, employment levels were continuing downward 25 months after the recession began.

Weakness in the labor market is further indicated by the proportion of the labor force who have been unemployed for at least six months (the long-term unemployed). **Figure 6** displays the monthly unemployment and long-term unemployment rates since 1948. The long-term unemployment rate has generally tracked the unemployment rate over the business cycle. Over a business cycle, the long-term unemployment rate is at its lowest point at or near the beginning of a recession and then reaches a peak a few months after the end of the recession (typically within six to eight months). Like the unemployment rate, the long-term unemployment rate is a lagging indicator—the labor market does not begin to recover from a recession until some time after the official end of the recession. After the 1990-1991 and 2001 recessions, however, the long-term unemployment rate did not reach its peak until 15 and 19 months, respectively, after the recession ended. The long-term unemployment rate is currently higher than at any time over the past 62 years—in June 2010, 4.4% of the labor force or about 46% of the unemployed had been out of work for six months or more.

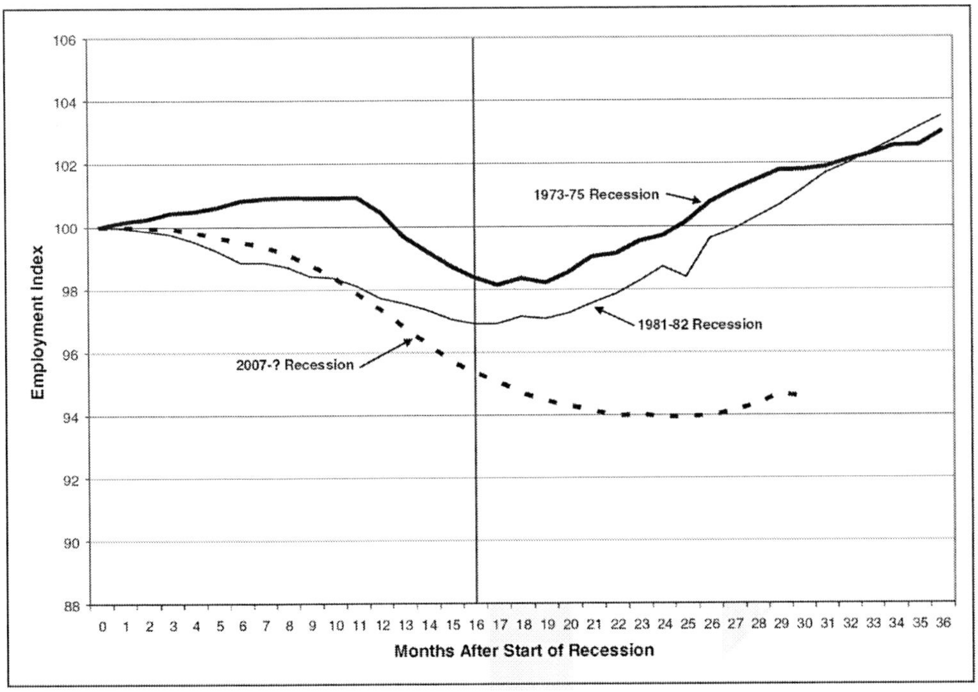

Source: CRS analysis of Bureau of Labor Statistics data.

Figure 5. Employment Levels During the 1973-1975, 1981-1982, and Current Recessions.

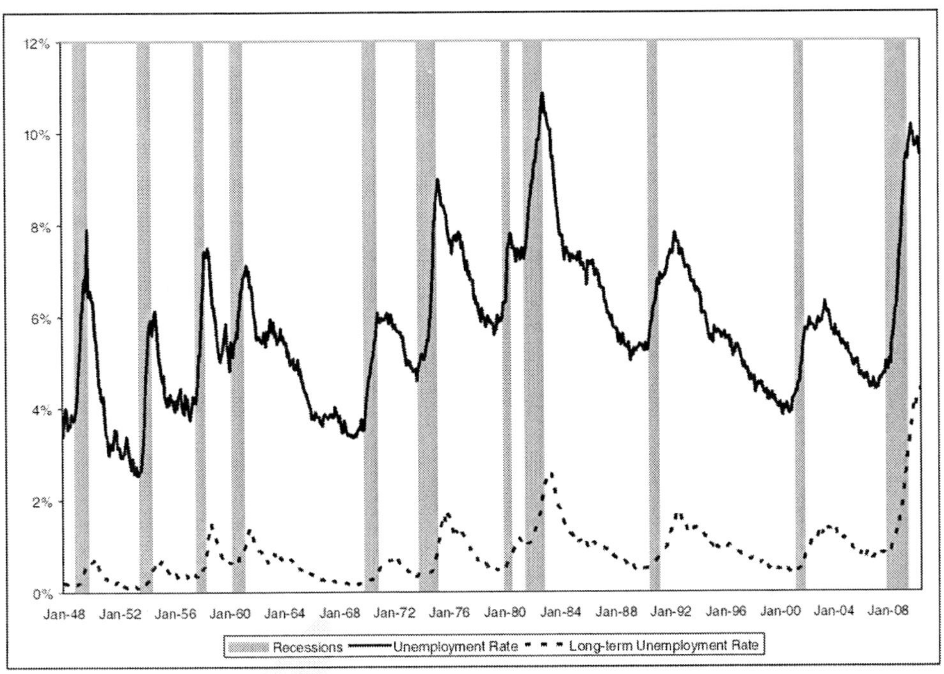

Source: CRS analysis of Bureau of Labor Statistics data.

Figure 6. Unemployment Rate and Long-Term Unemployment Rate.

Investment Subsidies

The two most common measures to provide tax incentives for new investment are investment tax credits and accelerated deductions for depreciation. Investment tax credits provide for a credit against tax liability for a portion of the purchase price of assets and are often proposed as a counter-cyclical or economic stimulus measure. Accelerated depreciation speeds up the rate at which the cost of an investment is deducted.

The investment tax credit was originally introduced in 1962 as a permanent subsidy, but it came to be used as a counter-cyclical device. It was temporarily suspended in 1966-1967 (and restored prematurely) as an anti-inflationary measure; it was repealed in 1969, also as an anti-inflationary measure. The credit was reinstated in 1971, temporarily increased in 1975, and made permanent in 1976. After that time, the credit tended to be viewed as a permanent feature of the tax system. At the same time, economists were increasingly writing about the distortions across asset types that arose from an investment credit. The Tax Reform Act of 1986 moved toward a system that was more neutral across asset types and repealed the investment tax credit while lowering tax rates.

Accelerated depreciation tends not to be used for counter-cyclical purposes. At least one reason for not using accelerated depreciation for temporary, counter-cyclical purposes is because such a revision would add considerable complexity to the tax law if used in a temporary fashion, since different vintages of investment would be treated differently. An investment credit, by contrast, occurs the year the investment is made and, when repealed, only requires firms with carry-overs of unused credits to compute credits. An exception to the problem with accounting complexities associated with accelerated depreciation is partial expensing (that is, allowing a fraction of investment to be deducted up front and the remainder to be depreciated). This partial expensing approach also is neutral across all assets it applies to, but the cash flow effects are more concentrated in the present (and revenue is gained in the future). A temporary partial expensing provision, allowing 30% of investments in equipment to be expensed over the next two years, was included in H.R. 3090 in 2002 and expanded to 50% and extended through 2004 in tax legislation enacted in 2003. It expired in 2004. The Economic Stimulus Act of 2008 (P.L. 110-185) included temporary bonus depreciation for 2008, which was extended for 2009 by the American Recovery and Reinvestment Act of 2009 (ARRA; P.L. 111-5). The Obama Administration recently proposed 100% expensing for qualified capital investments through the end of 2011.

The extent to which these business tax breaks are a successful counter-cyclical stimulus hinges on the effectiveness of investment subsidies in inducing spending. It is difficult to determine the effect of a business tax cut and the timing of induced investment. A business tax cut is aimed at stimulating investment largely through changes in the cost (or price) of capital. If there is little marginal stimulus or if investment is not responsive to these price effects in the short run, then most of the cut may be saved: either used to pay down debt or paid out in dividends, although some of the latter might eventually be spent after a lag. That is, if a tax cut simply involved a cash payment to a firm, most of it might be saved, particularly in the short run. Business tax cuts (of most types) also have effects on rates of return that increase the incentive to invest, and it is generally for that reason that investment incentives have been considered as counter-cyclical devices. Investment incentives through expensing for small businesses, however, are usually phased-out. As a result, these provisions produce a disincentive to investment over the phase-out range.[8] Consequently, the overall incentive effect is ambiguous.

Empirical Evidence on the Effectiveness of Investment Incentives

Despite attempts to analyze the effect of the investment tax credit, considerable uncertainty remains. Time series studies of aggregate investment using factors such as the tax credit (or other elements that affect the tax burden on capital or the "price" of capital) as explanatory variables tended to find little or no relationship.[9] A number of criticisms could be made of this type of analysis, among them the possibility that tax subsidies and other interventions to encourage investment were made during periods of economic slowdown. A recent study using micro data found an elasticity (the percentage change in investment divided by the percentage change in the user cost of capital) for equipment of -0.25.[10] A widely cited study by Cummins, Hassett, and Hubbard used panel data and tax reforms as "natural experiments" and found effects that suggest a price elasticity of -0.66 for equipment.[11] Although the second estimate is higher, both are considered inelastic (less than a unitary elasticity) implying that induced spending is less than the cost.

This last estimate is a higher estimate than had previously been found and reflects some important advances in statistical identification of the response. Yet, it is not at all clear that this elasticity would apply to stimulating investment in the aggregate during a downturn when firms have excess capacity. That is, firms may have a larger response on average to changes in the cost of capital during normal times or times of high growth, when they are not in excess capacity. Certainly, one might expect the response to be smaller in low growth periods.

An additional problem is that the timing of the investment stimulus may be too slow to stimulate investment at the right time. If it takes an extensive period of time to actually plan and make an investment, then the stimulus will not occur very quickly compared to a cut in personal taxes that stimulates consumption immediately. Indeed, the stimulus to investment could even occur during the recovery when it is actually undesirable.

There is some evidence that the temporary bonus depreciation enacted in 2002 had little or no effect on business investment. A study of the effect of temporary expensing by Cohen and Cummins at the Federal Reserve Board found little evidence to support for a significant effect.[12] They suggested several potential reasons for a small effect. One possibility is that firms without taxable income could not benefit from the timing advantage. In a Treasury study, Knittel confirmed that firms did not elect bonus depreciation for about 40% of eligible investment, and speculated that the existence of losses and loss carry-overs may have made the investment subsidy ineffective for many firms, although there were clearly some firms that were profitable that did not use the provision.[13] Cohen and Cummins also suggested that the incentive effect was quite small (largely because depreciation already occurs relatively quickly for most equipment), reducing the user cost of capital by only about 3%; that planning periods may be too long to adjust investment across time; and that adjustment costs outweighed the effect of bonus depreciation. Knittel also suggested that firms may have found the provision costly to comply with, particularly because most states did not allow bonus depreciation.

A recent study by House and Shapiro found a more pronounced response to bonus depreciation, given the magnitude of the incentive, but found the overall effect on the economy was small, which in part is due to the limited category of investment affected and the small size of the incentive.[14] Their differences with the Cohen and Cummins study reflect in part uncertainties about when expectations are formed and when the incentive effects occur.

Cohen and Cummins also reported the results of several surveys of firms, where from 2/3 to over 90% of respondents indicated bonus depreciation had no effect on the timing of investment spending. Overall, bonus depreciation did not appear to be very effective in providing short-term economic stimulus.

There are reasons to expect that tax incentives for equipment might have limited effects in stimulating investment in the short-run, primarily because of planning lags and because of the slowness of changing the technology of production. Essentially, there are two reasons that firms may increase investment. First, they may expect output to increase. This response, called the accelerator, is a result of other forces that increase aggregate demand thus requiring making more of the same type of investment (along with hiring more workers). The second reason is that the cost of investment has fallen. Part of this effect may be an output effect since the overall cost of investment is smaller, output can be sold at a lower price with an expectation that sales will rise in the future. Also part of this effect has to do with encouraging more use of capital relative to labor.

This analysis suggests that a business tax subsidy may not necessarily be the best choice for fiscal stimulus, largely because of the uncertainty of its success in stimulating aggregate demand. If such subsidies are used, however, the most effective short-run policy is probably a temporary investment subsidy. Permanent investment subsidies may distort the allocation of investment in the long run.

Direct Effects of Investment Incentives on Employment

The objective of investment subsidies is to increase spending which, in turn, should lead to increased employment (first in the capital goods manufacturing sector, and then in the economy as a whole through multiplier effects). Investment subsidies could also, however, have a direct effect on employment within the firm receiving the subsidy because they change relative prices.

Capital and skilled labor (i.e., more educated workers) tend to be complements, that is, they are used together in the production process.[15] Consequently, increasing the amount of capital tends to increase the demand for skilled labor. Furthermore, capital and unskilled labor (i.e., less-educated workers) tend to be substitutes. Thus, increasing investment could reduce the demand for less-skilled labor. These labor market effects could show up in one of two ways: changes in wages or employment levels. Unfortunately, there are no studies estimating the direct impact of investment incentives on employment.

One study examined the effect of investment subsidies on the prices of capital goods and wages of workers in the capital goods producing industry.[16] Goolsbee found that benefit of investment tax incentives generally went to the producers of capital equipment through higher capital prices and somewhat higher wages for workers in the capital goods industry. Overall, it appears that investment incentives could reduce the demand of less-educated workers (a group with a relatively high unemployment rate), and increase the demand for highly educated workers (a group with a relatively low unemployment rate) and workers in capital goods producing industries. It is not clear, however, whether these effects would occur in a slack economy.

EMPLOYMENT SUBSIDIES

Employment and wage subsidies are designed to increase employment directly by reducing a firm's wage bill. A firm's wage bill for labor includes wages and salaries paid to employees, the cost of fringe benefits (e.g., health insurance and pensions), hiring costs, and taxes paid such as the employer's share of the payroll tax.[17] These subsidies can take many forms. For example, earnings or time spent working can be subsidized. Furthermore, the subsidies can be incremental or non-incremental—that is, new hires are subsidized or all workers are subsidized. The subsidies can be targeted to certain groups of workers such as disadvantaged individuals, or can be available for any worker.

The tax system is a frequently used means for providing employment subsidies. Currently, the Work Opportunity Tax Credit (WOTC), a nonrefundable credit, is available to employers who hire individuals from 11 targeted disadvantaged groups.[18] Another example of an employment tax credit is the New Jobs Tax Credit (NJTC) from 1977 and 1978. It was an incentive to business to hire employees in excess of a base amount.

Most of the business tax incentives for hiring currently under discussion are modeled somewhat on the NJTC. The NJTC was an incremental jobs tax credit in that the employer had to increase the Federal Unemployment Tax Act (FUTA) wage base above at least 102% of the FUTA wage base in the previous year. The credit was 50% of the increase in the FUTA wage base (the wage base consisted of wages paid up to $4,200 per employee). The employer's income tax deduction for wages, however, was reduced by the amount of the credit. Consequently, the effective maximum credit for each new employee ($2,100 minus the additional tax due from the reduced deduction) ranged from $1,806 for taxpayers in the 14% tax bracket to $630 for taxpayers in the 70% tax bracket. Furthermore, the total credit could not exceed $100,000, which in effect limited the size of the subsidized employment expansion at any one firm to 47. The credit was nonrefundable but could be carried back for three years and forward for seven years.

Empirical Evidence on the Effectiveness of Employment Subsidies

Employment and wage subsidies have been analyzed since at least the 1930s, but few of the analyses include empirical estimates of the effects of the subsidies. In an early theoretical analysis of a nonincremental wage subsidy, Arthur Pigou concluded that a wage subsidy could increase employment but "in practice it is probable that the application of such a system would be bungled."[19] Nicholas Kaldor, however, in another theoretical analysis, argued that a temporary incremental wage subsidy to deal with cyclical unemployment could be very effective.[20] In a more recent theoretical analysis, Richard Layard and Stephen Nickell also argue that a temporary incremental wage subsidy could be effective in increasing employment when unemployment is high.[21]

In the United States, employment subsidies have often been offered through the tax system. Two major tax programs to subsidize employment that have been evaluated are the New Jobs Tax Credit (NJTC) and the Targeted Jobs Tax Credit (TJTC); the TJTC was a targeted hiring subsidy that was replaced by the WOTC. The NJTC was explicitly designed to be a counter-cyclical employment measure to boost employment after the 1973-1975 recession.

The NJTC was enacted in May 1977 at a time when the economy had begun to recover from the recession and was already growing. The credit was incremental in that it applied only to employment greater than 102% of the previous year's employment level. For each new eligible worker hired, a firm received a tax credit of 50% of wages paid up to $4,200 (the maximum gross credit for each new employee, therefore, was $2,100). The credit had an aggregate $110,000 cap so that the majority of benefits went to small firms. Once the cap was reached, the firm received no subsidy for hiring additional workers. Thus very large firms whose employment grew substantially more than 2% may not have had a marginal incentive. In addition, the credit was allowed against income tax liability and firms without adequate tax liability were not able to use all (or in some cases, any) of the credit.

The first evaluation of the NJTC used responses from a federal survey of for-profit firms. Jeffrey Perloff and Michael Wachter compared employment growth of firms that knew about the tax credit to firms that did not know about the credit.[22] They find that employment at the firms with knowledge of the credit grew about 3% faster than at the other firms. They note, however, that only 34% of the firms knew about the tax credit and these firms were probably not randomly drawn—it is possible that the firms most likely to hire workers were also more likely to seek out tax benefits. They caution that their results may overstate the NJTC's employment effect.

A second evaluation by John Bishop focused on the employment effects of the NJTC in the construction and distribution industries.[23] Bishop's key explanatory variable is the proportion of firms in the industry that knew about the tax credit. He estimates that the NJTC was responsible for 150,000 to 670,000 of the 1,140,000 increase in employment in these industries. The estimated effect, however, varies dramatically from industry to industry and sometimes from one empirical specification to another for the same industry. The results of both Perloff and Wachter, and Bishop suggest that the NJTC may have been somewhat successful in increasing employment, but showing a relationship between knowledge of the NJTC and employment gains does not mean that one caused the other.

Not all evaluations of the NJTC were positive. Robert Tannenwald analyzed data from a survey of private firms in Wisconsin and concludes that the NJTC did not live up to expectations.[24] He estimates that the per job cost of the NJTC was greater than public service employment programs.

Over half of the firms that did not expand employment in response to the tax credit said that consumer demand for their product determines the level of employment.[25] Some firms reported they were reluctant to take advantage of the tax credit because of its complexity.

Emil Sunley argues that there was a gap between the time of the hiring decision and the time eligibility for the credit was determined.[26] He notes that because the capital stock is essentially fixed in the short-run, an increase in employment will only come about because of an increase in product demand. Furthermore, it automatically favors firms that are already growing, which could increase geographic differentials in job creation.

A report on the NJTC commissioned by Congress from the Department of Labor and the Department of Treasury also was skeptical of the effectiveness of the subsidy.[27] In a mail survey, only about a third of firms knew about the credit (although these firms covered 77% of employees). About 20% both knew about the credit and qualified for it (covering 58% of employees). However, when firms were asked, only 2.4% of firms indicated that they made a conscious effort to hire because of the subsidy. Similar effects were found in a survey of the National Federation of Independent Businesses (NFIB), which covers smaller employers. Their survey results indicated that from 1.4% to 4.1% of employers were affected by the subsidy.

The Labor/Treasury study also raised questions about the studies by Perloff and Wachter, and by Bishop. They noted that the former study used data for 1977 and the credit was not enacted until May 1977. They questioned the latter author's lack of tests for significance of the wage variable. In addition, since the credit came at a time when the economy was already growing, it is possible that the credit may have shifted employment from one sector to another rather than increased aggregate employment.

Evaluation of other employment tax credit programs also yield mixed results.[28] The Targeted Jobs Tax Credit (TJTC) provided a wage subsidy to firms for hiring eligible workers (e.g., welfare recipients, economically disadvantaged youth, and ex-offenders). One study by Kevin Hollenbeck and Richard Willke found that the TJTC improved employment outcomes for nonwhite youth but not for other eligible individuals.[29] Bishop and Mark Montgomery estimate that the TJTC induced some new employment, but at least 70% of the tax credits were claimed for hiring workers who would have been hired even in the absence of the tax credit.[30] Dave O'Neill concludes that programs targeted to narrow socioeconomic groups are unlikely to "achieve the desired effect of significantly increasing the employment level of the target group."[31]

Taken together, the results of the various studies suggest that incremental tax credits have the potential of increasing employment, but in practice may not be as effective in increasing employment as desired. There are several reasons why this may be the case. First, jobs tax credits are often complex (so as to subsidize new jobs rather than all jobs) and many employers, especially small businesses, may not want to incur the necessary record-keeping costs. Second, since eligibility for the tax credit is determined when the firm files the annual tax return, firms do not know if they are eligible for the credit at the time hiring decisions are made. Third, many firms may not even be aware of the availability of the tax credit until it is time to file a tax return. Additionally, the person making the hiring decision is often unaware of tax provisions and the tax situation of the firm. Lastly, product demand appears to be the primary determinant of hiring.

Current Proposals

The Obama Administration has proposed a $5,000 business tax credit against payroll taxes for every net new employee they hire in 2010; the credit would have a $500,000 aggregate cap per firm. In addition, small businesses that increase wages or expand hours would get a credit against added payroll taxes. The proposals try to overcome some of the limitations of the NJTC. For example, the proposal would allow firms to claim the credits on a quarterly rather than an annual basis. All firms should qualify for the tax credit since it is allowed against payroll taxes rather than income taxes (over half of all firms were not eligible for the full 1977-1978 NJTC because of insufficient income tax liability). The credit would also be available for nonprofits and startups would be eligible for half the credit. The Administration estimates that this proposal would cost $33 billion.

Senators Baucus and Grassley (the chairman and ranking minority member of the Senate Finance Committee, respectively) proposed the Hiring Incentives to Restore Employment (HIRE) Act on February 11, 2010. Their proposal includes two tax incentives for hiring and retaining unemployed workers. This proposal was enacted in the Hiring Incentives to Restore Employment (HIRE) Act (P.L. 111-147), which was signed by the President on March 18, 2010. It is estimated that the tax incentives would cost $13 billion over 10 years.

The first tax incentive is forgiveness of the 2010 payroll tax (6.2% of the worker's earnings) for qualified workers hired in 2010 after enactment of the proposal. A qualified worker is an individual who was unemployed for at least 60 days and does not replace another worker at the firm unless the replaced worker left voluntarily or for cause. Verifying that these conditions are met could be unenforceable or prohibitively expensive to enforce. Furthermore, an employer cannot take advantage of both the payroll tax forgiveness and WOTC; consequently, employers may hire the long-term unemployed rather than individuals from other disadvantaged groups. Firms with no or little income tax liability (including nonprofits) would be eligible for the payroll tax forgiveness and the benefits would be received on a quarterly rather than annual basis.

The second tax incentive is a business credit for retention of newly hired qualified workers. Employers would be allowed a $1,000 business tax credit for each qualified worker who remains employed for 52 weeks at the firm. Since this is an income tax credit, the employer would not receive the benefits of retaining workers until they file their 2011 income returns in early 2012.

Furthermore, firms with little or no tax liability (including nonprofits) cannot take full advantage of this incentive since the credit is nonrefundable.[32]

Another recent proposal for a job creation tax credit is also modeled partially on the NJTC and, like the Administration's proposal, tries to correct some of the flaws that may have limited the effectiveness of the NJTC. [33] The credit would be equal to 15% of additional taxable payroll (i.e., payroll subject to Social Security taxes) in 2010 and to 10% of additions to taxable payroll in 2011. This tax credit would be refundable so both unprofitable firms and non-profits can take advantage of the credit. Furthermore, the benefits of the credit would be received on a quarterly basis rather than annually when the firm files an income tax return. Bartik and Bishop estimate that the tax credit could create 2.8 million jobs in 2010 and 2.3 million jobs in 2011. They further estimate that the budgetary cost would be no more than $15 billion per year. Their estimates assume a labor demand elasticity of 0.3, which indicates that a 10% reduction in the cost of labor would increase employment by 3%. Their estimates did not rest on a study of the 1977-1978 credit, but rather predicted the effect on jobs based on a central tendency labor demand elasticity.[34] They also estimate that if the labor demand elasticity were 0.15, then 1.4 million jobs would be created in 2010 and 1.1 million jobs in 2011. Note that this estimate is a general demand elasticity, and might not necessarily be as high during a recession, when business is slack.[35]

CONCLUDING REMARKS

The evidence suggests that investment and employment subsidies are not as effective as desired in increasing economic activity, especially employment. Economic theory indicates that a deficit-financed fiscal stimulus designed to increase aggregate demand would have the maximum impact on employment in the short-term. Such policies could include increases in federal government spending for goods and services, federal transfers to state and local governments, and tax cuts for low and middle income taxpayers. The short-term benefits of higher deficits, however, could be outweighed by the long-term costs if deficits are not reduced when unemployment falls. Additional fiscal stimulus that increases the deficit arguably should be considered in the context of a 2009 deficit that was larger relative to the size of the economy than all but a handful of previous wartime years. The 2009 deficit is not sustainable in the long run in the sense that deficits of that size would cause the national debt to continually rise relative to output—eventually investors will refuse to continue financing it because they no longer believe that the government would be capable of servicing it.

End Notes

1 NBER defines a recession as a "significant decline in economic activity spread across the economy, lasting more than a few months" (http://www.nber.org/cycles/cyclemain.html).

2 Ben S. Bernanke, "On the Outlook for the Economy and Policy," speech at the Economic Club of New York, November 16, 2009, available at http://www.federalreserve.gov/newsevents/speech/bernanke20091116a.htm.

3 See, for example, Mark Zandi, "Help Small Businesses Hire Again," *New York Times*, November 3, 2009, p. A35; Robert Pozen, "Give Credit to Create Jobs-But Only Where It's Due," *Financial Times*, November 4, 2009, p. 11; and Charles E. Schumer and Orrin G. Hatch, "A Payroll Tax Break for Jobs," *New York Times*, January 26, 2010, p. A23.

4 The production index measures real output in the manufacturing, mining, and electric and gas utilities industries. See http://www.federalreserve.gov/releases/g17/About.htm.

5 The index is rescaled so that it equals 100 in the month the recession started.

6 The end of the 1990-1991 and 2001 recessions is denoted by the vertical line in the figure.

7 The end of the 1973-1975 and 1981-1982 recessions is denoted by the vertical line in the figure.

8 See CRS Report RL31852, *Small Business Expensing Allowance: Current Status, Legislative Proposals, and Economic Effects*, by Gary Guenther.

9 A summary of this early literature can be found in several sources. For a non-technical summary, see Jane G. Gravelle, *The Economic Effects of Taxing Capital Income,* Cambridge, MIT Press, 1994, pp. 118-120.

10 Robert S. Chirinko, Steven M. Fazzarri, and Andrew P. Meyer, "How Responsive is Business Capital Formation to its User Cost? An Exploration with Micro Data?" *Journal of Public Economics* vol. 74 (1999), pp. 53-80.

11 Jason G. Cummins, Kevin A. Hassett, and R. Glen Hubbard, "A Reconsideration of Behavior Using Tax Reforms as Natural Experiments." *Brookings Papers on Economic Activity*, 1994, no. 1, pp. 1-72.

12 Darryl Cohen and Jason Cummins, *A Retrospective Evaluation of the Effects of Temporary Partial Expensing*, Finance and Economics Discussion Series 2006-19, Federal Reserve Board, Washington, D.C. April 2006. They compared investment increases for shorter lived and longer lived assets (longer lived assets received a larger incentive) and investment closer to expiration to test the effects.

13 Matthew Knittel, *Corporate Response to Bonus Depreciation: Bonus Depreciation for Tax Years 2002-2004*, U.S. Department of Treasury, Office of Tax Analysis Working Paper 98, May 2007.

14 Christopher House and Matthew Shapiro, "Temporary Investment Tax Incentives: Theory with Evidence from Bonus Depreciation," *American Economic Review*, vol. 98, no. 3 (June 2008), pp. 737-768.

15 See Daniel S. Hamermesh, *Labor Demand* (Princeton, NJ: Princeton University Press, 1993), pp. 110-122.

16 Austan Goolsbee, "Investment Tax Incentives, Prices, and the Supply of Capital Goods," *Quarterly Journal of Economics*, vol. 113, no. 1 (February 1998), pp. 121-148.

17 Labor costs are a deductable business expense for income tax purposes.

18 The American Recovery and Reinvestment Act of 2009 (ARAA; P.L. 111-5) temporarily added two new groups: unemployed veterans and disconnected youth. The other nine groups include welfare recipients, ex-felons, and

summer youth among others. This tax credit expires on August 31, 2011. See CRS Report RL30089, *The Work Opportunity Tax Credit (WOTC)*, by Linda Levine for more information.

[19] Arthur C. Pigou, *The Economics of Welfare*, 4th ed. (London: MacMillan and Co., 1932), p. 704.

[20] Nicholas Kaldor, "Wage Subsidies as a Remedy for Unemployment," *Journal of Political Economy*, vol. 44, no. 6 (December 1936), pp. 721-742.

[21] P.R.G. Layard and S.J. Nickell, "The Case for Subsidizing Extra Jobs," *Economic Journal*, vol. 90, no. 357 (March 1980), pp. 51-73.

[22] Jeffrey M. Perloff and Michael L. Wachter, "The New Jobs Tax Credit: An Evaluation of the 1977-78 Wage Subsidy Program," *American Economic Review, papers and proceedings*, vol. 69, no. 2 (May 1979), pp. 173-179.

[23] John Bishop, "Employment in Construction and Distribution Industries: The Impact of the New Jobs Tax Credit," in *Studies in Labor Markets*, ed. Sherwin Rosen (Chicago: University of Chicago Press, 1981), pp. 209-246.

[24] Robert Tannenwald, "Are Wage and Training Subsidies Cost-Effective? Some Evidence from the New Jobs Tax Credit," *New England Economic Review*, September/October 1982, pp. 25-34.

[25] For example, one firm reported that "orders determine levels of hiring, not tax gimmicks" (Tannenwald, p. 31).

[26] Emil M. Sunley, "A Tax Preference in Born: A Legislative History of the New Jobs Tax Credit," in *The Economics of Taxation*, ed. Henry J. Aaron and Michael J. Boskin (Washington: Brookings Institution, 1980), pp. 391-408.

[27] Departments of Labor and Treasury, *The Use of Tax Subsidies for Employment*, A Report to Congress, Washington, May 1986.

[28] For a summary of other studies examining the TJTC, see CRS Report 95-981E, *The Targeted Jobs Tax Credit, 1978-1994*, by Linda Levine, which is available on request from the authors.

[29] Kevin M. Hollenbeck and Richard J. Willke, *The Employment and Earnings Impacts of the Targeted Jobs Tax Credit*, Upjohn Institute, Staff Working Paper 91-07, Kalamazoo, MI, February 1991.

[30] John H. Bishop and Mark Montgomery, "Does the Targeted Jobs Tax Credit Create Jobs at Subsidized Firms?" *Industrial Relations*, vol. 32, no. 3 (Fall 1993), pp. 289-306.

[31] Dave M. O'Neill, "Employment Tax Credit Programs: The Effects of Socioeconomic Targeting Provisions," *Journal of Human Resources*, vol. 17, no. 3 (Summer 1982), p. 449.

[32] Unused credits can be carried forward to future tax years but cannot be carried back to past years.

[33] Timothy J. Bartik and John H. Bishop, *The Job Creation Tax Credit*, Economic Policy Institute Briefing Paper, October 20, 2009, http://www.epi.org/publications/entry/bp248/.

[34] See Daniel L. Hamermesh, *Labor Demand* (Princeton University Press: Princeton, NJ, 1993), for a survey: Hamermesh suggests a midpoint elasticity of 0.3 on p. 92.

[35] Even with the elasticities discussed, only 10% to 30% of the subsidy cost would be reflected in additional wages for a nonincremental subsidy. With an elasticity of e, $dL/L = (-e)\ dW/W$, where L is labor, dL is the change in labor, W is the wage and dW is the change in wage. Thus for the addition to the wage bill ((W)(dL)), $(W)(dL) = (-e)(dW)(L)$. At a subsidy rate of s, $dW = -sW$ and the cost of the subsidy is sWL, Thus additional wages, esWL divided by the cost equals e, the elasticity. The Congressional Budget Office (CBO) estimated the impact of a reduction in the employer's share of the payroll tax which is a nonincremental subsidy. CBO estimates that reducing the employer share of payroll taxes would increase output by $0.40 to $1.30 per dollar of total budgetary cost. This effect is relatively large compared to other policies and not consistent with the elasticities. CBO did not model the payroll tax holiday as an increase in labor demand as did Bishop and Bartik; nor did they model it in the same way they model investment subsidies (as an increase in the demand for capital goods). Rather, they treated it largely as leading directly to a price reduction, similar to a sales tax holiday. The theoretical and empirical justifications for this approach, however, are not clear. See Congressional Budget Office, *Policies for Increasing Economic Growth and Employment in 2010 and 2011*, January 2010.

In: U.S. Economic Recovery and Stimulus Measures
Editor: Jessica D. Saparito
ISBN: 978-1-61209-266-9

Chapter 3

UNEMPLOYMENT AND ECONOMIC RECOVERY

Linda Levine

SUMMARY

Although the economy has begun growing again, it may be a while before the unemployment rate shows steady improvement. The unemployment rate is considered a lagging indicator, meaning that its ups and downs happen some time after the ups and downs of other indicators of economic activity. For example, more than a year elapsed before the unemployment rate trended downward following the end of the 1990-1991 and 2001 recessions. This led the two to be labeled jobless recoveries. By contrast, after four earlier recessions the unemployment rate began a sustained decline within four to five months.

Unemployment often does not fall appreciably when economic growth first picks up because some firms may have underutilized labor that they kept on their payrolls during the recession to avoid incurring costs related to layoffs and rehiring. At the end of a recession as demand increases, some firms may initially be able to increase production without adding workers by raising the productivity of the labor on hand. But once the labor on hand has been fully utilized, output will grow at the growth rate of productivity until firms add workers. As an economic expansion progresses, output growth will be determined by the combined rates of productivity and labor force growth. If output growth exceeds the growth rate of productivity, then employment will rise. If employment growth exceeds the labor force growth rate, then the unemployment rate will fall.

Just as the time it takes for the unemployment rate to begin falling after a recession has varied, the speed at which it falls has varied. After nine of the past 10 contractions, it took at least eight months for the unemployment rate to fall by one full percentage point. Of the 10, the fastest decline occurred after the expansion that ended in October 1949 when the unemployment rate measured 7.9%. In one year's time, it dropped by 3.7 percentage points to 4.2%. The slowest decline occurred after the recession that ended in November 2001 when the unemployment rate was 5.5%, the lowest rate recorded at the start of any expansion. About 3½ years elapsed (June 2005) before the unemployment rate fell just one-half of a percentage point. In contrast, the expansion that followed the July 1981-November 1982 contraction began with the highest unemployment rate of the postwar period at 10.8%. In that case, it took only eight months for the unemployment rate to fall more than one percentage point.

From a policy perspective, what matters for a sustainable reduction in the unemployment rate is the growth rate of potential output. Potential output is a measure of the economy's capacity to produce goods and services when resources (e.g., labor) are fully utilized. The rate of growth of potential gross domestic product (GDP) is a function of the growth rate of potential productivity and the labor supply when the economy is at full employment. If, as recently estimated, the growth rate of potential output is as low as 2% to 2.4%., then real economic growth would not have to be much above that to yield a declining unemployment rate. How much it is above that range will determine the speed with which the unemployment rate declines during the recovery from the recession that began in December 2007.

This report examines the relationship between economic growth and the unemployment rate to anticipate possible future developments.

INTRODUCTION

By many accounts, the economic contraction that began in December 2007 is already over.[1] The increase in real gross domestic product (GDP) in the third quarter of 2009, and GDP growth having remained positive thereafter, lends support to that view. Growth in GDP (i.e., the output of goods and services) is a key measure that the Business Cycle Dating Committee uses to officially designate the beginning and ends of recessions.

What may concern some policymakers as much or even more than whether the "Great Recession" has ended, however, is the outlook for the unemployment rate. Although the economy has been growing again, it may be a while before the unemployment rate begins to decline steadily. The rate may even continue rising for some time after the beginning of an expansion. The unemployment rate is considered a lagging indicator, meaning that its ups and downs happen some time after the ups and downs of other broad indicators of economic activity.[2]

Not only might the unemployment rate be slow to fall at the beginning of an economic expansion, its rate of decline, or whether it declines at all, is likely to depend on the rate of GDP growth. It is possible for there to be above-zero real economic growth that is insufficient to prevent continued increases in the unemployment rate. This report examines the relationship between economic growth and the unemployment rate to anticipate possible future developments.

ECONOMIC GROWTH AND THE UNEMPLOYMENT RATE

In the short run, the relationship between economic growth and the unemployment rate may be a loose one. One reason that unemployment may not fall appreciably when economic growth first picks up is that some firms may have underutilized labor. Laying off workers when times are bad and rehiring them as conditions improve has costs. Therefore, up to a point, firms may be willing to pay for more workers than they need to satisfy the depressed demand for their goods and services. As a result, at the end of a recession as demand increases, some firms may, at first, be able to increase production without adding workers. In other words, firms may be able to increase their output by raising the productivity of the labor on hand, which yields a temporary boost in measured labor productivity above its longer-run trend rate of growth.

Once the labor on hand is fully utilized, output will grow no faster than the rate of growth of labor productivity until the firm begins to add workers. As the economic expansion progresses, output growth will be determined by the combined rates of growth of the labor supply and labor productivity. As long as growth in total output exceeds the rate of growth of labor productivity, then employment will rise. If employment growth is more rapid than growth in the labor force, then the unemployment rate will fall.

Over the longer run, there tends to be a link between changes in the rates of real economic growth and unemployment. This stable long-run relationship between the two economic variables was most famously pointed out in the early 1960s by economist Arthur Okun, which is why it is commonly referred to as "Okun's Law."[3] It has been included in a list of "core ideas" that are widely accepted in the economics profession.[4]

The key to the relationship between the rate of economic growth and the unemployment rate is the rate of growth of what economists refer to as "potential output." In brief, potential output is an unobservable measure of the capacity of the economy to produce goods and services when the available resources, such as labor and capital, are fully utilized. The rate of growth of potential output is a function of the rate of growth of potential productivity and the labor supply when the economy is at full employment. When the unemployment rate is high, as it is now, then actual GDP falls short of potential GDP.

Labor's contribution to output is determined by the hours worked by employed members of the labor force. This, in turn, depends on the size of the population, the share of the population that is in the labor force, and the share of the labor force that is actually employed.

In the absence of productivity growth, as long as each new addition to the labor force is employed, growth in total output will just equal the growth in the labor force. If the rate of output growth falls below the rate of growth of the labor force, then there will not be enough new jobs created to accommodate all of the new job seekers. The proportion of the labor force that is employed will fall, and the unemployment rate will rise. If growth in output exceeds the rate of growth in the labor force, some of the new jobs created by employers to satisfy the rising demand for goods and services will be filled by drawing down the pool of unemployed labor.[5]

As productivity increases over time it takes fewer and fewer workers to produce a given quantity of goods and services. If growth in output just equals the growth rate of the labor force in the presence of productivity growth, then more people will be entering the labor force than are needed to produce a given amount of output. The share of the labor force that is employed will fall, and the unemployment rate will rise. Only as long as the growth in output exceeds the combined growth rates of the labor force and productivity will the unemployment rate fall in the long run. Knowing what that rate is might be useful to policymakers.

Even when GDP is growing rapidly enough to create jobs fast enough to push the unemployment rate down, it may still take time to match jobs and job seekers. If the new jobs being created require substantially different skills from those jobs that have disappeared, then it may be difficult for displaced workers to get rehired. Some of those job seekers may have skills that are easily transferred from one job to another and thus may not experience long-term unemployment. Those with skills that have become outmoded or are less applicable in those industries that are expanding may have more difficulty finding new work. The more of a mismatch in skills there is between new jobs and job seekers, the longer it will take for displaced workers to find new jobs.[6]

Limits to geographical mobility may also account for some of the mismatches in the labor market. There are costs, both monetary and emotional, associated with pulling up stakes and moving to another part of the country to get a new job. It may also be the case that the further removed a job prospect is, geographically, the less likely it is that a job seeker will even hear about it. This may be especially relevant in areas where job losses are permanent, such as seems to be happening in segments of the motor vehicle industry and other industries that are in decline due in part to heightened foreign competition.

Figure 1 shows the long-run relationship between real economic growth and changes in the unemployment rate. Each point in the graph refers to a calendar quarter and indicates a pair of observations. The first observation of each pair is the percentage change in real GDP over the previous four quarters (shown on the horizontal scale). The second observation of each pair is the percentage point change in the civilian unemployment rate over the same period (shown on the vertical scale). The downward sloping line indicates the estimated statistical relationship between the two series over the interval shown.[7] Where it crosses the zero line indicates, approximately, the rate of real economic growth necessary to keep the unemployment rate from either rising or falling. Above that growth rate, the unemployment rate tended to fall, and below that growth rate, the unemployment rate tended to rise.

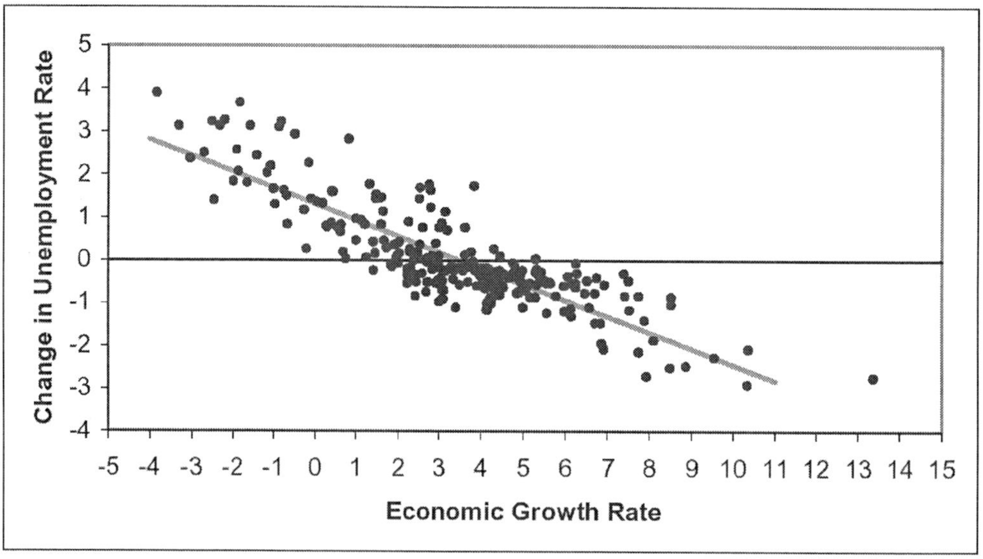

Source: Department of Commerce, Bureau of Economic Analysis; Department of Labor, Bureau of Labor Statistics.

Figure 1. Real Economic Growth Rate (%) and Percentage Point Changes in the Unemployment Rate, 1949 – 2009.

This analysis of the long-run relationship between economic growth and changes in the unemployment rate is relatively simple. There are certainly other economic factors to take into account, in addition to more sophisticated statistical techniques. Nonetheless, over an extended period of time, there is evidently a strong link between the real GDP growth rate and changes in the unemployment rate. Based on the estimate of the relationship between the two variables over the entire period shown in **Figure 1**, real economic growth of about 3.5% was associated with a stable unemployment rate. Thus, in the long run, a one percentage point difference in the real GDP growth rate has historically led to a 0.4 percentage point change in the unemployment rate. In other words, an annual increase in real output of 4.5% is expected to result in a decline in the unemployment rate of 0.4 percentage points.

There are times, however, when the long-run relationship temporarily breaks down or weakens. A change in the rate of growth of productivity in the short run can cause the economic growth rate and the unemployment rate to change in the same direction. In 1993, for example, the economic growth rate fell to 2.7% from 3% in 1992 and the unemployment rate fell to 6.9% from 7.5%. The reason was a decline in productivity growth in 1993 after a brief surge in the previous year.[8] Another surge in the rate of productivity growth occurred in 2009, which explains the unemployment rate's increasing to a much greater extent than would have been expected by Okun's law.[9] Instead of the small anticipated increase, the unemployment rate rose by almost four percentage points from 5.8% in 2008 to 9.3% in 2009.

Depending on possible changes in the productivity growth rate, GDP growth might not have to be above 3.5% now to push down the unemployment rate. Between 1949 and 2000, the civilian labor force grew at an average annual rate of 1.6%. More recently, that growth rate has slowed and is projected to continue to do so as a result of the aging of the baby-boom generation.[10] Between 2000 and 2009, the annual rate of growth of the labor force was 0.9%.[11]

Although the near-term growth rate of the labor force may be known with some degree of confidence, predicting productivity growth is difficult. Economists have identified three time periods that correspond with three different trend rates of growth in productivity.[12] Between 1947 and 1973, output per hour of labor grew at an annual rate of 2.8%. Between 1973 and 1995, labor productivity grew at a 1.4% rate. Between 1995 and 2009, labor productivity grew at a 2.6% annual rate.[13]

To get the unemployment rate to fall, economic growth will likely have to exceed the sum of the recent rates of labor force and productivity growth. This would seem to indicate that, if recent trends continue, sustained economic growth above 3.5% may be necessary to push down the unemployment rate.

Even after GDP growth picks up, however, experience suggests it may be some time before the unemployment rate steadily declines. Suppose that two successive monthly declines is taken as the beginning of a meaningful downward trend in the unemployment rate.[14] **Table 1** shows how long it has taken following the end of each of the past 10 economic contractions for that trend to begin. After the end of the 1990-1991 and 2001 contractions, for example, it was well over a year before there was a clear downward trend in the unemployment rate. This led the two to be labeled jobless recoveries. By contrast, after the end of four earlier recessions the unemployment rate began a steadily decline within four to five months.

Table 1. Time in Months between the End of Economic Contractions and Two Successive Monthly Declines in the Unemployment Rate

Date of End of Contraction	Months Following End of ContractionUntil There Were Two Successive Declines
October 1949	4
May 1954	6
April 1958	5
February 1961	9
November 1970	11
March 1975	4
July 1980	2
November 1982	5
March 1991	17
November 2001	21

Source: National Bureau of Economic Research; Department of Labor, Bureau of Labor Statistics.

Just as the time it takes for the unemployment rate to begin coming down has varied, the rate at which it falls has varied as well. Each of the lines in **Figure 2** shows the percentage point change in the unemployment rate following the end of each of the past 10 economic contractions. In nine of those 10 instances, it took at least eight months for the unemployment rate to fall by one full percentage point. The slowest decline occurred after the recession that ended in November 2001 when the unemployment rate stood at 5.5%, the lowest unemployment rate recorded at the start of an expansion. About 3½ years elapsed (June 2005) before the unemployment rate fell *one-half* of a percentage point. In contrast, the expansion that followed the July 1981-November 1982 downturn began with the highest unemployment rate of the postwar period (10.8%). In that case, it took only eight months for the unemployment rate to fall more than one percentage point (to 9.4%).

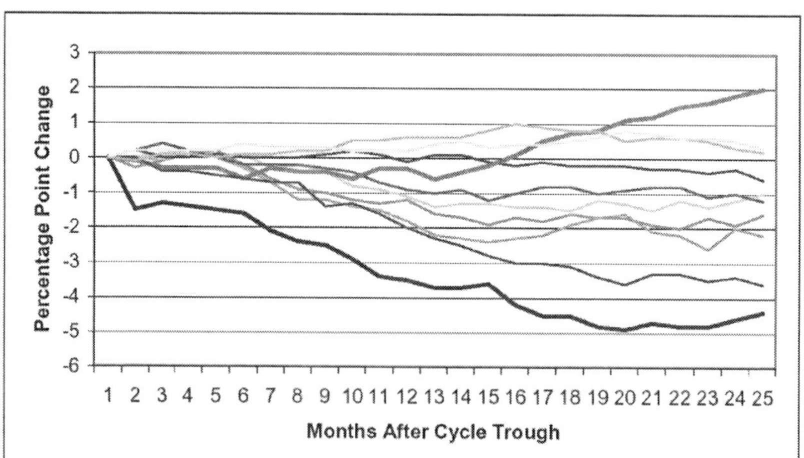

Source: National Bureau of Economic Research; Department of Labor, Bureau of Labor Statistics.

Figure 2. Percentage Point Change in the Unemployment Rate in the First Two Years of Each of the Past 10 Economic Recoveries.

Similarly, the two thickest lines in **Figure 2** show the wide range of possible outcomes. The top line represents the two years following the July 1980 business cycle trough, which ended with an unemployment rate of 9.8%—two percentage points *higher* than it was at the trough. In that case, the expansion only lasted a year and another contraction began in July 1981. (It is for that reason that the two recessions of the early 1980s are sometimes referred to as a double-dip recession.) The bottom line shows the two years following the October 1949 business cycle trough, which ended with the unemployment rate 4.4 percentage points *lower* than it had been at the trough.

THE OUTLOOK

From a policy perspective, what matters for the sustainable reduction of the unemployment rate is what the growth rate of potential output will be in the future. According to estimates by economist Robert J. Gordon, potential output has grown at an average annual rate of 3.4% since 1875.[15] Gordon doubts, however, that growth in potential GDP will be that rapid over the next 20 years. He argues that the acceleration in productivity growth of the late 1990s was temporary. He examines economy-wide productivity rather than just that for the private business sector and finds that productivity growth slowed between 2004 and 2008 because the gains from information technology investments were beginning to diminish. His assumption of slower productivity growth along with expected declines in the growth rate of the labor force led him to project a 2.4% rate of growth in potential output over the next 20 years. If that view is correct, then over the long run, real economic growth in excess of 2.4% would be likely to yield a declining rate of unemployment.

Economists Susanto Basu and John G. Fernald also examined the current outlook for growth in potential output.[16] They point out that there has been a significant decline in household net worth during the most recent contraction. That drop in wealth will likely make it more difficult to afford leisure time or to make down payments on purchases of durable goods like automobiles. Consequently, the supply of labor may be larger in the near term than it might otherwise have been, and that would tend to temporarily raise growth in the labor force and potential output. At the same time, they expect that disruptions in financial markets will tend to constrain growth in potential output over the near term because of higher risks associated with investment spending. Those factors tend to offset and mainly serve to emphasize how uncertain estimates of growth in potential output can be.

Weidner and Williams examined the relationship between real economic growth and the strength of past recoveries. They estimate that potential output growth was comparatively rapid during the initial expansions of the 1960s through 1980s (at 3.6%). In contrast, potential output was much more moderate (2.5%) during the first two years of recovery from the 1990-1991 and 2001 recessions. The economists estimate potential GDP growth at the outset of the recovery from what is commonly being referred to as the "Great Recession" will be a more sluggish 2.1%, "likely reflecting the low prevailing rate of labor force growth."[17] If they are correct, real economic growth greater than 2.1% would likely produce a falling unemployment rate.

The Congressional Budget Office (CBO) publishes projections of growth in potential output. In its August 2010 economic outlook, CBO projects that potential output of the overall economy will grow at an average annual rate of 2.1% between 2010 and 2014, rising to a 2.4% rate of increase between 2015 and 2020.[18] CBO's projected average annual growth rate of potential GDP was a higher 2.7% over the 2002-2009 period. The different estimates for the three periods chiefly reflects CBO's diminishing projection over time of potential growth of the labor force. In terms of the unemployment rate in the near term, CBO expects it will average 9.5% in 2010 and 9.0% in 2011. The unemployment rate is projected to gradually fall thereafter to 8.1% in 2012, 6.6% in 2013, and 5.3% in 2014.

In conclusion, if the current rate of growth in potential output is as low as 2% to 2.4%, then real economic growth would not have to be much above that to yield a declining unemployment rate. How much it is above that range will determine the speed with which the unemployment rate declines during the recovery from the recession that began in December 2007.

End Notes

[1] For example, in October 2009, the National Association for Business Economics released the results of a survey of 44 professional forecasters, the "vast majority" of whom felt that the recession was already over. See http://www.nabe.com/publib/macsum.html.

[2] As discussed in CRS Report R40798, *Unemployment and Employment Trends Before and After the End of Recessions*, by Linda Levine, the unemployment rate did not peak until two to four months after the end of four postwar recessions and not until nine to 18 months after the end of three recessions.

[3] Using real-time data from the late 1940s through early 1960s that would have been available to Okun, Knotek estimated that real output growth of 4% was consistent with a stable unemployment rate, which means that faster output growth usually coincided with a decreasing unemployment rate whereas output growth below 4% usually coincided with an increasing unemployment rate. See Edward S. Knotek, "How Useful is Okun's Law?," Federal Reserve Bank of Kansas City, *Economic Review*, fourth quarter 2007, available at http://www.kansascityfed.org/ PUBLICAT/ECONREV/PDF/4q07Knotek.pdf.

[4] Alan Blinder, "Is There A Core of Practical Macroeconomics That We Should All Believe?," *American Economic Review*, vol. 87, no. 2, May 1997.

[5] If there is considerable slack in the economy, as is now the case, this does not pose a problem, but once unemployment reaches relatively low levels then the increased demand for labor is more likely to be satisfied by rising wages than by higher levels of employment and there may be a risk of accelerating inflation. CBO estimated, in 2008, that the rate close to which that becomes a risk (which is referred to as the nonaccelerating inflation rate of unemployment or NAIRU) may have been as low as 5%. At current levels of unemployment, the risk of accelerating wages and inflation would seem low. See Robert Arnold, "Reestimating the Phillips Curve and the NAIRU," Congressional Budget Office, Working Paper 2008-06, August 2008.

[6] For more information see CRS Report R41179, *Long-Term Unemployment and Recessions*, by Gerald Mayer and Linda Levine.

[7] Using ordinary least squares.

[8] David Altig, Terry Fitzgerald, and Peter Rupert, "Okun's Law Revisited: Should We Worry about Low Unemployment?," Federal Reserve Bank of Cleveland, *Economic Commentary*, May 15, 1997, available at http://www.clevelandfed.org/research/commentary/1997/0515.htm.

[9] Mary Daly and Bart Hobijn, "Okun's Law and the Unemployment Surprise of 2009," Federal Reserve Bank of San Francisco, *Economic Letter*, March 8, 2010, available at http://www.frbsf.org/public ations/economics/letter/2010/ el2010-07.html.

[10] Mitra Toossi, "Labor Force Projections to 2018: Older Workers Staying More Active," *Monthly Labor Review*, November 2009.

[11] Calculated by CRS from data published by the Bureau of Labor Statistics.

[12] For example, see J. Bradford DeLong, Productivity Growth in the 2000s, National Bureau of Economic Research Macroeconomics Annual, vol. 17 (2000), and CRS Report RL34677, *Productivity Growth: Trends and Prospects*, by Brian W. Cashell.

[13] As measured by changes in output per hour of the nonfarm private business sector. Calculated by CRS from data published by the Bureau of Labor Statistics.

[14] This may not be a rigorous definition, other standards could be used. See **Figure 2** to appreciate the time it takes for the unemployment rate to decline substantially after the end of an economic contraction.

[15] Robert J. Gordon, "The Slowest Potential Output Growth in U.S. History: Measurement and Interpretation," presented at the Center for the Study of Innovation and Productivity at the Federal Reserve Bank of San Francisco, November 2008, available at http://www.frbsf.org/csip/research/200811_Gordon.pdf.

[16] Susanto Basu and John G. Fernald, "What Do We Know and Not Know About Potential Output?," Federal Reserve Bank of San Francisco, Working Paper, March 2009, available at http://www.frbsf.org/publications/economics/papers/ 2009/wp09-05bk.pdf.

[17] Justin Weidner and John C. Williams, "The Shape of Things to Come," Federal Reserve Bank of San Francisco, Economic Letter, May 17, 2010, available at http://www.frbsf.org/publications/economics/letter/2010/el2010-15.html.

[18] Congressional Budget Office, *The Budget and Economic Outlook: An Update*, August 2010, available at http://www.cbo.gov/ftpdocs/117xx/doc11705/08-18-Update.pdf.

In: U.S. Economic Recovery and Stimulus Measures
Editor: Jessica D. Saparito
ISBN: 978-1-61209-266-9

Chapter 4

JOB GROWTH DURING THE RECOVERY

Linda Levine

SUMMARY

Congress in recent years passed a number of bills intended in part to jump-start a recovery in the labor market from the recession that began in December 2007. Policymakers are interested in how employment has responded to stimulus measures to determine how effective the legislation has been and to decide whether additional job creation legislation is warranted.

One way to assess the extent of recovery in the labor market since the passage of stimulus legislation is to compare employment data from the end of the recession in June 2009 with more recent data gathered in surveys that the government regularly conducts. Accordingly, to determine if and how much job growth has occurred thus far in the recovery, this report examines the change in the number of jobs over the June 2009-August 2010 period. (August 2010 was the latest month for which data were available at the time of the report's preparation.) To provide historical context, the results are compared with job growth at a comparable point (14 months) from the start of the prior 10 recoveries of the postwar period. Data for August 2010 are compared with December 2007, as well, to discern how close the number of jobs has come to the level at the recession's onset, and to provide historical context, the results are compared with job growth at a comparable point (32 months) from the start of the prior 10 recessions. Lastly, employment data by job and individual characteristics in December 2007, June 2009, and August 2010 are analyzed to ascertain how different sectors and demographic groups have fared in recent years.

A "jobless recovery" has been underway since the recession's end in June 2009. That is to say, the number of jobs at private and public sector employers generally decreased between June 2009 and August 2010. After falling in the second half of 2009, overall employment rose through May 2010 partly as a result of the Census Bureau hiring workers temporarily to help conduct the decennial count of the population. Total employment subsequently resumed declining, driven in part by state and local governments laying off workers in an effort to address budget shortfalls. In contrast, after decreasing for six months from the recession's end, the number of jobs in the private sector (i.e., excluding federal, state and local government) began to steadily increase in January 2010. Despite this recent job growth, there were fewer jobs at private sector firms in August 2010 than at the recession's end.

Employment rebounded faster during almost all of the prior 10 recoveries of the postwar period. At a comparable point in the business cycle (14 months into the current recovery as of August 2010), the number of jobs overall and in the private sector exceeded their levels at the start of eight earlier recoveries. The exceptions are the two recoveries that immediately preceded the current one (i.e., the recoveries that followed the 1990-1991 and 2001 recessions).

Two of the industry groups hardest hit by the recession—construction and manufacturing—have continued to lose jobs during the recovery, although at a lower rate than during the recession. Some of the states with the most depressed housing markets as well as manufacturing-dependent states have experienced relatively large decreases in total employment (Arizona, California, Florida, Indiana, Michigan, Nevada, Ohio). Smaller job losses among women than men during the recession partly are explained by construction and manufacturing having predominantly male workforces. Larger job losses among women than men during the recovery partly are explained by women's substantial presence in the occupations (e.g., teachers) that account for much of local and state government workforces.

Congress in recent years passed a number of bills intended in part to jump-start a recovery in the labor market from the recession that began in December 2007. One of the bills, the American Recovery and Reinvestment Act of 2009 (P.L. 111-5), requires the Council of Economic Advisers and executive branch agencies to estimate the number of jobs dependent on some or all of the act's provisions. The methodologies they have used to estimate the number of jobs created or maintained have been criticized, however.[1] Moreover, ARRA is not the only job creation bill enacted into law.[2] Congress did not include a requirement to estimate job growth associated with the Hiring Incentives to Restore Employment (HIRE) Act of 2010 (P.L. 111-147), for example. Policymakers nonetheless remain interested in the labor market's response to these measures to help Members decide how well the legislation is working and whether additional job creation legislation is warranted.

One way to assess the extent of recovery in the labor market since the passage of stimulus legislation is to compare employment data from the recession's end (i.e., the trough of the business cycle) in June 2009 with more recent data gathered in surveys that the government regularly conducts. Accordingly, to determine the extent of job growth thus far in the recovery, this report examines the number of jobs from the trough of the business cycle to August 2010 (the latest month for which data were available at the time of the report's preparation). To provide historical context, the results are compared with job growth at a comparable point (14 months) from the start of the prior 10 recoveries of the postwar period. Data for August 2010 are compared with December 2007, as well, to discern how close the number of jobs has come to its level at the recession's onset (i.e., the peak of the business cycle), and to provide historical context, the results are compared with job growth at a comparable point (32 months) from the start of the prior 10 recessions. Lastly, seasonally adjusted employment data that are available by job and individual characteristics in December 2007, June 2009, and August 2010 are analyzed to ascertain how different sectors and demographic groups have fared in recent years.

JOB GROWTH OVERALL AND IN THE PRIVATE SECTOR

The Business Cycle Dating Committee at the National Bureau of Economic Research announced that the 11th recession of the postwar period ended in June 2009, but job growth typically does not commence until a recovery has been underway for some time. The usual length of time before an upward trend in employment began following the end of the prior 10 recessions was four months. After the end of the two shallow recessions that immediately preceded the 2007-2009 recession, however, sustained job growth across all nonfarm employers did not begin until 12 months into the recovery from the 1990-1991 recession and until 22 months into the recovery from the 2001 recession.[3] Initially, some had hoped that the deep 2007-2009 recession would be followed by a strong rebound such as occurred after the severe 1973-1975 and 1981-1982 recessions. But, neither these nor the other U.S. recessions of the postwar period were precipitated by a financial crisis. The evidence from other countries that experienced recessions caused by financial crises instead suggests a slow recovery for the United States.[4]

At 14 months into the recovery that began in June 2009, sustained job growth in the total nonfarm economy has not yet begun. As shown in **Figure 1**, the number of jobs on employers' payrolls fell during the second half of 2009. Overall employment then rose through May 2010, before resuming its decline through August. The brief period of job growth earlier in 2010 was fueled in part by the Census Bureau's usual practice of temporarily hiring workers to help conduct the decennial count of the U.S. population.

Employment in the nonfarm private sector (i.e., excluding federal, state and local government)—which accounts for more than four of every five jobs in the labor market—has exhibited a consistently positive trend during 2010. Data from the U.S. Bureau of Labor Statistics (BLS) monthly survey of employers in the nonfarm economy show that the number of jobs in private industry has been steadily increasing since January 2010. Thus far in 2010, then, private sector firms increased the size of their payrolls by almost 750,000 jobs.

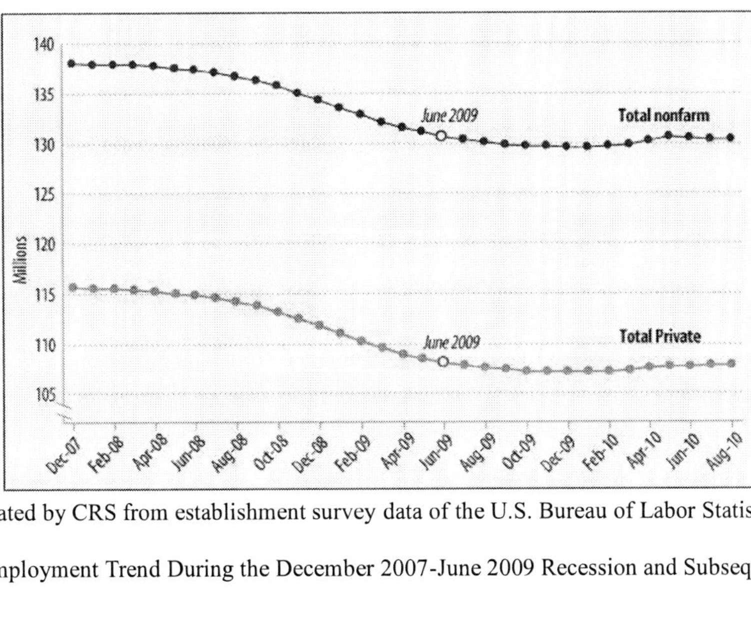

Source: Created by CRS from establishment survey data of the U.S. Bureau of Labor Statistics.

Figure 1. Employment Trend During the December 2007-June 2009 Recession and Subsequent Recovery.

Employment rebounded faster during almost all of the prior 10 recoveries of the postwar period. At a comparable point in the business cycle (14 months into the current recovery as of August 2010), the number of jobs overall and in the private sector exceeded their levels at the start of eight earlier recoveries. The exceptions are the two recoveries that immediately preceded the current one. At 14 months into the recovery from the 1990-1991 recession, the number of jobs overall exceeded the number at the recovery's outset but the number of private sector jobs did not. At 14 months after the end of the 2001 recession, both total and private sector employment were lower than at the recovery's start—by 0.5% and 0.9%, respectively. Hence the phrase "jobless recovery" came into common usage. It is also being applied to the current recovery because total employment decreased by 0.3%, and private industry employment decreased by 0.2%, between June 2009 and August 2010. (See **Table 1**.) The *less* sluggish pace of the current recovery compared to 14 months into the recovery from the 2001 recession may be related to differences in the stimulus legislation enacted to mitigate the two recessions.[5]

The last two columns of **Table 1** show how much employment must increase from its depressed level in August 2010 to recoup all the jobs lost since the beginning of the latest recession in December 2007. Total nonfarm employment at 32 months from the recession's start was 7.6 million jobs (5.5%) below its pre-recession level. Employment at private sector firms in August 2010 was farther below its level at the recession's outset (7.7 million jobs, 6.7%).

In contrast, total and private sector employment at 32 months from the start of all prior postwar recessions exceeded or more nearly approached their pre-recession levels. All jobs lost during each of eight recessions were fully recouped by 32 months from their outset. Compared to August 2010's 5.5% shortfall from total nonfarm employment in December 2007, the number of jobs was closer to its cyclical peak at 32 months from the start of two recessions: overall employment at 32 months from the beginning of the 1990-1991 recession was 1.1% below its level at the recession's outset; at the same point following the 2001 recession's start, total employment was 1.7% lower. Compared to August 2010's 6.7% shortfall from private sector employment in December 2007, the number of jobs was closer to its cyclical peak at 32 months from the start of the same two recessions: private sector employment at 32 months from the start of the 1990-1991 recession was 1.5% below its level at the recession's outset; at the same point following the 2001 recession's start, it was 2.6% lower.

Some have looked to the 2001 recession and subsequent jobless recovery, when the rate of increase in productivity growth also uncharacteristically rose, to gauge how long it might be before all jobs lost since December 2007 are recouped. The rate of increase in productivity growth usually does not rise during recessions, but it did so during and for some years after the 2001 recession; it has done so again during and after the 2007-2009 recession.[6] (An increasing productivity growth rate enables businesses to produce the same amount of goods and services with fewer workers.) [7] After the annual rate of change in nonfarm business productivity had diminished to a decade-low of 0.9% in 2006, it measured 3.5% in 2009. BLS data show the productivity growth rate continued to accelerate in the first and second quarters of 2010 (at annual increases of 6.3% and 3.7%, respectively). Partly due to similarly high rates of increase it took 47 months (until February 2005) from the 2001 recession's start before all job losses were recouped and 50 months (until May 2005) before private sector job losses were recouped. The greater stimulus measures enacted by Congress to mitigate the impact of the deeper 2007-2009 recession may have contributed to the less sluggish ongoing recovery in the labor market compared to the recovery from the 2001 recession. If these measures also were to mitigate most of the greater job losses incurred during the 2007-2009 recession compared to the 2001 recession, then by early 2012, about four years from the December 2007 onset of the latest recession, employment may return to its pre-recession level. But, as previously mentioned, the 2007-2009 recession was precipitated by a financial crisis, from which a recovery is especially difficult according to the experiences of other countries.

Some within the public policy community also believe the increase since earlier in the decade in offshoring of jobs historically performed in the United States may be a factor in addition to accelerating productivity growth that has sapped the strength of job growth in recent years.[8] This perspective arguably contributed to Congress's support for a Buy America provision in the ARRA to increase demand for goods manufactured in the United States. Although not expressly intended as an offshoring measure, a tax provision in the HIRE Act encourages firms to maintain and expand their U.S. employment.

JOB CHARACTERISTICS

The idea that offshoring may have slowed the pace of U.S. job growth differs from the contention that certain industries' percentages of national employment will not return to their shares at the recession's outset. Some suggest that the latest recession, like the 2001 recession, was accompanied by a substantial reallocation of labor across sectors because many of the jobs lost in recent years may reflect the permanent downsizing of certain industries due to such factors as globalization and technological among other innovations. As a result, workers displaced during the recession may endure unusually long spells of unemployment while they search for new jobs in faster-growing industries. However, no consensus has yet been reached among economists about whether displacement during recent recessions has involved an increase in structural vis-à-vis cyclical unemployment.[9] The remainder of this section of the report will analyze recent changes in employment by industry.

The two industries that accounted for almost one of every two jobs lost during the latest recession have had markedly different experiences during the recovery. Construction firms cut payrolls by 1.5 million jobs, and manufacturers by 1.9 million jobs, out of a total of 7.3 million nonfarm jobs lost between December 2007 and June 2009. Both industry groups have continued to shed jobs since then, but construction has been recovering much more slowly than manufacturing. Manufacturers lost 130,000 jobs (a 0.9% decrease) during the first 14 months of the recovery, whereas construction lost 418,000 jobs (a 6.9% decrease). As a result, one of every four construction jobs and one of every seven manufacturing jobs at employers in December 2007 did not exist in August 2010. Expressed another way, the construction industry must gain almost 1.9 million jobs and the manufacturing industry over 2.0 million jobs to return to their levels at the recession's outset. (See the last two columns of **Table 1**.)

Table 1. Employment Change During the 2007-2009 Recession and the Ensuing Recovery by Industry (numbers in thousands)

Industry	Number of Jobs			Employment Change					
				During the Recession, Dec. 2007-June 2009		During the Recovery, June 2009-Aug. 2010		Since the Recession's Start, Dec. 2007-Aug. 2010	
	Dec. 2007	June 2009	Aug. 2010[a]	Number	Percentage	Number	Percentage	Number	Percentage
All nonfarm industries	137951	130640	130311	-7311	-5.3	-329	-0.3	-7640	-5.5
All private nonfarm industries	115574	108075	107870	-7499	-6.5	-205	-0.2	-7704	-6.7
Goods-producing sector	21956	18503	18031	-3453	-15.7	-472	-2.6	-3925	-17.9
Mining and logging	739	692	741	-47	-6.4	49	7.1	2	0.3
Construction	7491	6029	5611	-1462	-19.5	-418	-6.9	-1880	-25.1
Manufacturing	13726	11782	11679	-1944	-14.2	-103	-0.9	-2047	-14.9
Private service-providing sector	93618	89572	89839	-4046	-4.3	267	0.3	-3779	-4.0
Wholesale trade	6038	5613	5592	-425	-7.0	-21	-0.4	-446	-7.4
Retail trade	15566	14546	14434	-1020	-6.6	-112	-0.8	-1132	-7.3
Transportation and warehousing	4549	4223	4179	-326	-7.2	-44	-1.0	-370	-8.1
Utilities	557	561	553	4	0.7	-8	-1.4	-4	-0.7
Information	3023	2797	2714	-226	-7.5	-83	-3.0	-309	-10.2
Financial activities	8227	7742	7576	-485	-5.9	-166	-2.1	-651	-7.9
Professional and business services	18051	16453	16714	-1598	-8.9	261	1.6	-1337	-7.4
Education and health services	18559	19165	19611	606	3.3	446	2.3	1052	5.7
Leisure and hospitality	13535	13105	13124	-430	-3.2	19	0.1	-411	-3.0
Other services	5514	5367	5343	-147	-2.7	-24	-0.4	-171	-3.1
Government	22377	22565	22441	188	0.8	-124	-0.5	64	0.3

Source: Calculated by CRS from U.S. Bureau of Labor Statistics' establishment survey data.

Notes: The establishment survey is asked of nonfarm employers and covers all employees on their payrolls.

a. Data for August 2010 are preliminary. The establishment survey revises initial monthly estimates twice (in the immediately succeeding two months) after they have been published to improve the data series by incorporating additional information that was not available at the time of their initial publication.

The bursting of the housing bubble led to those who worked for residential builders and for specialty trade contractors in residential construction to be the hardest-hit groups within the construction industry. Employment in residential building construction fell by 259,000 jobs (28.9%) during the recession and by 64,100 jobs (10.1%) during the recovery thus far, according to BLS data. Similarly, employment at specialty trade contractors in residential construction fell by 551,400 jobs (25.4%) during the recession and by 93,900 jobs (5.8%) during the recovery.

Some of the states with the weakest housing markets have experienced comparatively large cutbacks in employment of the industry's mostly blue-collar work force. In Nevada and Arizona, for example, employment in the construction industry (i.e., residential and nonresidential building construction, heavy and civil engineering construction, and specialty trades contractors) was about halved between December 2007 and August 2010. BLS data by state also show that in California and Florida there were over one-third fewer construction jobs in August 2010 than in December 2007.

Within manufacturing, the problems at General Motors, Chrysler, and motor vehicle parts suppliers were so grave during the recession that the Bush and Obama Administrations chose to provide them with financial assistance.[10] The industry's employment, like that of a few other manufacturers (i.e., primary and fabricated metal products, food, plastics and rubber products), has subsequently increased. After employment at motor vehicle and parts manufacturers fell by 326,100 jobs (34.2%) between December 2007 and June 2009, it then rose by 56,100 jobs (9.0%).[11] Temporary programs enacted by Congress to increase demand for vehicles (e.g., "cash for clunkers," P.L. 111-32, enacted in June 2009) likely led automakers and their parts suppliers to subsequently recall from layoff their predominantly blue-collar workforce to rebuild depleted inventories.[12] Nonetheless, one of four jobs at motor vehicle and parts manufacturers when the recession started did not exist 32 months later in August 2010.

Manufacturing-dependent states tend to be especially vulnerable to economic downturns, a time during which consumers and businesses usually postpone buying costly long-lasting products in particular (e.g., household appliances, cars, farm and construction machinery). Manufacturing industries also are sensitive to weakened global demand and impaired access to credit, such as has occurred in recent years. More than one in 10 employees in Indiana, Michigan, Mississippi, Ohio, and Wisconsin worked for durable goods manufacturers in 2006, the last full year before the onset of the recession.[13] Three of the five states—Michigan, Indiana, and Ohio—recorded among the largest decreases in nonfarm employment during the recession (9.8%, 7.2%, and 6.9%, respectively).[14]

A third industry group that incurred many of the recession's job losses is professional and business services. (See **Table 1**.) More than one-fifth of all jobs lost during the recession occurred at firms that provide professional and business services (e.g., accounting, computer, and other professional-technical services; and administrative support services). Temporary help agencies accounted for one-half of the 1.6 million decrease in employment at professional and business services providers between December 2007 and June 2009.[15] Unlike the two industries hardest hit by the recession—construction and manufacturing—employment in professional and business services grew since the recovery began. The employment rebound at professional and business services providers largely was due to a 358,500 job gain at temporary help agencies, which outweighed losses elsewhere in the industry group. When companies are unsure of a recovery's robustness they typically prefer to temporarily hire employees from the help industry rather than commit themselves to hiring permanent employees.

Retail trade is another industry group in which a sizeable share of the recession's job losses occurred. The decrease of over 1 million jobs at such firms as automobile dealers, clothing and accessories stores, department stores, furniture and home furnishings stores, and building material and garden supply stores accounted for 14% of all jobs lost between December 2007 and June 2009. Retail employment continued to contract during the recovery (0.8% or 112,000 jobs), albeit at a fraction of the pace that occurred during the recession (6.6% or 1.0 million jobs). Nonetheless, one of every 14 jobs at retail establishments in December 2007 no longer existed in August 2010. Put differently, retail employment must expand by more than 1.1 million jobs to return to its cyclical peak (see the last two columns of **Table 1**).

Despite the recession having been precipitated by a financial crisis, employment conditions within the financial activities industry group have varied greatly. Almost one of every five job losses in financial activities during the recession and ensuing recovery occurred among real estate agents and other employees of the real estate industry.[16] Employment declined by 86,800 (5.8%) in the real estate industry as the housing market collapsed between December 2007 and June 2009, and by another 31,700 (2.3%) through August 2010 as conditions in the housing market continued to be a drag on the economy. At 32 months into the recovery, the real estate industry had 118,500 (7.9%) fewer jobs than at the recession's outset. In contrast, the number of jobs at securities brokers, securities and commodity contracts brokers and exchanges, and other investment firms, which is linked to non-residential uses of credit, decreased by 6.6% compared to the private sector average of 6.7% between December 2007 and August 2010. The decline in employment has been even milder at commercial banks, savings institutions, and credit unions (3.9%) through August 2010. But job losses at consumer finance providers that do not accept deposits (e.g., credit card issuers, automobile financiers) and at firms that engage in activities related to credit intermediation (e.g., mortgage and nonmortgage loan brokers, check cashing and money order providers, credit card processors) have been quite steep (16.4%).

Government and utilities are the only two industry groups that gained jobs during the recession but lost jobs during the recovery thus far. The increase in government employment during the recession occurred at the federal, state, and local levels. Federal employment was higher in August 2010 than at the recession's end in June 2009, despite the Census Bureau letting go workers in 2010 that it had hired to assist the agency while it conducted the decennial population count.[17] The decrease in government employment overall since the recovery began has occurred in state government, excluding education, and in local government. Congress was motivated by the fiscal problems of state and local governments to include assistance for them in the American Recovery and Reinvestment Act (P.L. 111-5) enacted in February 2009, and in the Education Jobs and Medicaid Funding bill (P.L. 111-226) enacted in August 2010.

Table 2. Employment Change During the 2007-2009 Recession and the Ensuing Recovery by Gender, Age, Race, Ethnicity, and Educational Attainment (numbers in thousands)

	Number of Employed Persons[a]			Employment Change					
				During the Recession, Dec. 2007-June 2009		During the Recovery, June 2009-Aug. 2010		Since the Recession's Start, Dec. 2007-Aug. 2010	
Characteristic	Dec. 2007	June 2009	Aug. 2010	Number	Percentage	Number	Percentage	Number	Percentage
Gender									
Men	78239	73727	73454	-4512	-5.8	-273	-0.4	-4785	-6.1
Women	67934	66311	65642	-1623	-2.4	-669	-1.0	-2292	-3.4
Age									
16-19	5829	4943	4373	-886	-15.2	-570	-11.5	-1456	-25.0
20-24	13722	12745	12838	-977	-7.1	93	0.7	-884	-6.4
25-34	31599	29996	30318	-1603	-5.1	322	1.1	-1281	-4.1
35-44	34072	31706	30584	-2366	-6.9	-1122	-3.5	-3488	-10.2
45-54	34749	33611	33104	-1138	-3.3	-507	-1.5	-1645	-4.7
55 and older	26218	27119	28069	901	3.4	950	3.5	1851	7.1
Race or ethnicity									
White	119914	115102	114470	-4812	-4.0	-632	-0.5	-5444	-4.5
Black	15988	15048	14967	-940	-5.9	-81	-0.5	-1021	-6.4
Hispanic	20465	19609	20002	-856	-4.2	393	2.0	-463	-2.3
Educational attainment									
Less than high school	11317	10449	10165	-868	-7.7	-284	-2.7	-1152	-10.2
High school or equivalent	36787	34719	34373	-2068	-5.6	-346	-1.0	-2414	-6.6
Some college/AA	34969	33786	33850	-1183	-3.4	64	0.2	-1119	-3.2
Bachelor's or advanced degree	43616	43367	43582	-249	-0.6	215	0.5	-34	-0.1

Source: Created by CRS from U.S. Bureau of Labor Statistics' data from the Current Population Survey.

Notes: The survey of households provides data for all workers (including the self-employed, private household workers, and unpaid family workers) in all sectors of the economy (i.e., farm and nonfarm) aged 16 and older, except for educational attainment data which relate to workers aged 25 and older.

a. Data are subject to revision each January based on updated population controls from the Census Bureau. The population controls are used to weight survey sample results to reflect the civilian noninstitutional population.

Individual Characteristics

The employment trends of women and men over the course of a business cycle are related in part to their differing employment distributions by industry. From the start of the latest recession in December 2007 until August 2010, women lost jobs at almost half the rate of men (3.4% and 6.1%, respectively). (See **Table 2.**) The gender difference is due largely to men accounting for more than seven out of 10 employees in the recession-wracked construction and manufacturing industries, which continued to shed jobs during the recovery.[18] Although women and men lost jobs throughout the period, women went from losing fewer jobs than men during the recession (1.6 million and 4.5 million, respectively) to losing more jobs than men during the recovery (669,000 and 273,000, respectively). In this instance, the relatively greater presence of women in the occupations that populate local governments in particular (e.g., teachers) likely worked against them.[19] As previously discussed, employment in local and state governments, excluding education, decreased during the recovery after having posted gains during the recession.

The oldest and youngest workers have had very different experiences since December 2007. As shown in **Table 2**, persons aged 55 and older enjoyed job growth not only during the recovery but also during the recession. The seniority that usually comes with age appears to have worked to their advantage. Not surprisingly, given the industry distribution of employment discussed above, older women have reported even greater job growth than older men.

In contrast, the employer practice of "last hired, first fired" operated to the disadvantage of the youngest workers. Employment decreased more precipitously among 16- to 19-year-olds than any other age group. One in four jobs held by teenagers at the start of the recession had disappeared by August 2010; this was true for girls and boys alike. Black teens suffered steeper job losses than white teens: employment of black 16- to 19-year-olds dropped 32.6% whereas employment of white teenagers fell 23.0% between December 2007 and August 2010.[20]

Employment among black workers, regardless of age, has fallen to a greater degree than among white workers. As shown in **Table 2**, employment of black workers was 6.4% less in August 2010 than in December 2007 whereas employment of white workers was 4.5% less. Employment decreased to a greater extent among black than white workers during the recession (5.9% and 4.0%, respectively). When teenagers are excluded and the data for black and white workers aged 20 and older are further disaggregated by gender, adult black men lost jobs at the highest rate during the recession (8.4%) compared with adult white men (5.2%), adult black women (2.7%) and adult white women (1.7%).[21] Employment of black and white workers aged 16 and older continued to decline during the recovery, but at a much slower rate (0.5%). When teenagers are excluded and the data for black and white workers aged 20 and older are further disaggregated by gender, adult black women lost jobs at a higher rate than adult white women (1.1% and 0.5%, respectively) during the recovery whereas adult black men experienced job growth at a higher rate than adult white men (1.2% and 0.2%, respectively).

Hispanics, who can be of any race, experienced job growth during the recovery after their employment fell at about the average rate for all workers during the recession. (See **Table 2.**) The employment of Hispanic workers is fairly quickly returning to its level at the start of the recession. Some might regard this as surprising because, according to BLS data, one in four workers in the construction industry were of Hispanic origin in 2006, the last full year before the recession's onset. However, Hispanics also comprised over one in five workers in the accommodation and food services industry in that year. The industry is part of the leisure and hospitality group which, as shown in **Table 1**, was one of only three industry groups in which employment fell during the recession but then rose during the recovery. Additionally, leisure and hospitality experienced among the lowest rates of job loss during the recession.

The lower a worker's educational attainment, the worse they typically fared between December 2007 and August 2010. As shown in **Table 2**, employment over the 32-month period decreased by 10.2% among workers without a high school diploma, 6.6% among those with a high school diploma, 3.2% among those with some college or an associate degree, and by 0.1% among those with a bachelor's or advanced diploma. The two educational attainment groups that experienced job growth thus far in the recovery are workers with some college or an associate degree and those with a bachelor's or advanced diploma.

End Notes

[1] For information on the methodology utilized to develop job creation estimates related to the ARRA see CRS Report R40080, *Job Loss and Infrastructure Job Creation Spending During the Recession*, by Linda Levine.

[2] For information on stimulus legislation see CRS Report R41006, *Unemployment: Issues and Policies*, by Jane G. Gravelle, Thomas L. Hungerford, and Marc Labonte.

[3] CRS Report R40798, *Unemployment and Employment Trends Before and After the End of Recessions*, by Linda Levine.

[4] CRS Report R41332, *Economic Recovery: Sustaining U.S. Economic Growth in a Post-Crisis Economy*, by Craig K. Elwell, pp. 11-12.

[5] The Economic Growth and Tax Relief Reconciliation Act of 2001 (P.L. 107-16) was passed to speed the recovery from the 2001 recession by amending the Internal Revenue Code. For information on the stimulus approaches included in legislation to mitigate the effects of the 2007-2009 recession (e.g., income tax relief, infrastructure spending, assistance to state and local governments) see CRS Report R41006, *Unemployment: Issues and Policies*, by Jane G. Gravelle, Thomas L. Hungerford, and Marc Labonte.

[6] Bob McTeer, "Productivity and the Job Market," *New York Times*, December 3, 2008, available at http://economix.blogs.nytimes.com/2008/12/03/productivity-and-the-job-market/.

[7] For information on productivity growth in the short- and long-run, see CRS Report RL34677, *Productivity Growth: Trends and Prospects*, by Brian W. Cashell.

[8] For additional information see CRS Report RL32292, *Offshoring (a.k.a. Offshore Outsourcing) and Job Insecurity Among U.S. Workers*, by Linda Levine, pp. 1-9.

[9] CRS Report R41179, *Long-Term Unemployment and Recessions*, by Gerald Mayer and Linda Levine.

[10] CRS Report R40003, *U.S. Motor Vehicle Industry: Federal Financial Assistance and Restructuring*, coordinated by Bill Canis.

[11] Calculated by CRS from BLS establishment survey data.

[12] CRS Report R40654, *Accelerated Vehicle Retirement for Fuel Economy: "Cash for Clunkers,"* by Brent D. Yacobucci and Bill Canis.

[13] Calculated by CRS from BLS establishment survey data.

[14] The four states previously mentioned as having experienced very large decreases in construction jobs because of conditions in their housing markets recorded large decreases in total employment as well. Employment in Nevada was 11.6% lower in June 2009 than in December 2007; in Arizona, 10.0% lower; Florida, 8.9% lower; and in California, 7.3% lower.

[15] Calculated by CRS from BLS establishment survey data.

[16] Calculated by CRS from BLS establishment survey data.

[17] In the *Employment Situation—August 2010*, BLS noted that the number of temporary workers hired for Census 2010 peaked in May 2010 at 564,000. By August, their number had fallen to 82,000.

[18] According to data from the BLS establishment survey, women comprised just 28.7% of employment across all manufacturing industries and just 20.4% of employment in the residential building construction industry in 2006, the last full year before the latest recession began.

[19] According to data from the BLS establishment survey, women comprised 59.3% of employment in local government overall and 68.3% of employment in local government's education function in 2006, the last full year before the latest recession began. Also in that year, women were 51.8% of all state government employees.

[20] Calculated by CRS from BLS data from the Current Population Survey.

[21] Ibid.

In: U.S. Economic Recovery and Stimulus Measures
Editor: Jessica D. Saparito
ISBN: 978-1-61209-266-9

Chapter 5

JOB LOSS AND INFRASTRUCTURE JOB CREATION SPENDING DURING THE RECESSION

Linda Levine

SUMMARY

After the long economic expansion that characterized much of the current decade, the nation entered its 11th postwar recession in December 2007. The size of job losses and the comparison to the Great Depression intensified congressional interest in passing legislation early in 2009 aimed at encouraging job creation and warding off further cuts in employment.

To mitigate all but one recession since the 1960s, Congress chose to increase federal spending on public works (i.e., infrastructure). Public works expenditures traditionally have gone to certain types of construction activities (e.g., building highways and bridges, dams and flood control structures), which indirectly increase demand in industries that supply their products to construction firms (e.g., sand and gravel mines, heavy equipment manufacturers). Today, the definition of infrastructure has been expanded to include green economic activities (commonly referred to as green jobs), which include industries that utilize renewable resources (e.g., electricity generated by wind), produce energy-efficient goods and services (e.g., mass transit), and install energy-conserving products (e.g., retrofitting buildings with thermal-pane windows).

A question that typically arises during congressional consideration of economic stimulus legislation is which approach produces the most bang for the buck. In the instant case, this means how many jobs might be supported by federal expenditures on traditional and green infrastructure projects. Once stimulus legislation is signed into law, the focus of Congress customarily turns to estimates of the number of jobs that result as federal funds are allocated to specific activities. Therefore, after briefly examining the trend in employment since the recession's onset, the report turns to an in-depth look at estimates of job creation, including the limitations of the methodology often used to derive them and the difficulties associated with developing job estimates for green infrastructure in particular.

The report closes with a review of what is known to date about the number of jobs supported by infrastructure spending and other provisions in the American Recovery and Reinvestment Act (ARRA, P.L. 111-5). Section 1512 requires entities that receive ARRA appropriations from federal agencies, totaling approximately $271 billion, to include in quarterly reports to the agencies the number of direct jobs created or maintained as a result. Section 1513 requires the Council of Economic Advisers (CEA) to report quarterly on the effect of ARRA provisions on employment and other economic indicators. The CEA's reports are the most comprehensive because they contain estimates of not only jobs supported by ARRA appropriations but also of jobs associated with other parts of the act (e.g., unemployment and health insurance benefits, state fiscal relief, and tax provisions). The CEA has estimated that ARRA might have increased aggregate employment above what it otherwise would have been by 1.0-1.1 million jobs in the third quarter of 2009, 1.7-1.9 million jobs in the fourth quarter of 2009, 2.2-2.8 million jobs in the first quarter of 2010, and 2.5-3.6 million jobs in the second quarter of 2010.

After the long economic expansion that characterized much of the current decade, the nation entered its 11th postwar recession in December 2007. It was not until November 2008, however, that the Business Cycle Dating Committee of the National Bureau of Economic Research announced that a substantial and widespread decline in economic activity had begun a year earlier. As part of its announcement, the committee noted that it "views the payroll employment measure, which is based on a large survey of employers, as the most reliable comprehensive estimate of employment. This series [the CES] reached a peak in December 2007."

The committee's announcement intensified congressional interest in passage of legislation aimed at encouraging creation of new jobs and warding off further loss of jobs. So, too, did comments equating the recession to the Great Depression. (See CRS Report R40655, *The Labor Market During the Great Depression and the Current Recession.*) This, in turn, sparked the interest of some policymakers in the job creation programs of the Depression period. (See CRS Report R41017, *Job Creation Programs of the Great Depression: the WPA and the CCC.*)

To mitigate all but one recession since the 1960s, Congress chose to increase federal expenditures on infrastructure (public works), thereby directly raising demand for goods and services to offset the reduced demand of consumers. (See CRS Report 92-939, *Countercyclical Job Creation Programs.*) But, there are a number of issues associated with using spending on public works to quickly create jobs during a recession. (See CRS Report R40107, *The Role of Public Works Infrastructure in Economic Stimulus.*)

When Congress considers spending on infrastructure to help stimulate a flagging economy, "how many jobs are created" is a commonly asked question. After first briefly examining trends in employment since the latest recession began, this report focuses on job creation estimates available in late 2008 associated with increased spending on traditional and so-called green infrastructure, placing a heavy emphasis on explaining the methodology often used to derive them and the difficulties associated with developing estimates for green economic activities in particular.

Once stimulus legislation is signed into law, the focus of Congress customarily turns to estimates of the number of jobs that result as federal funds are allocated to specific activities. In the case of the American Recovery and Reinvestment Act (ARRA, P.L. 111-5), which was enacted in early 2009, Congress included language requiring entities that receive ARRA appropriations from federal agencies to report the number of jobs created or maintained as a result and requiring the Council of Economic Advisers to report on the employment and other economic effects of ARRA provisions. The report closes with a review of what is known to date about the number of jobs associated with the stimulus act.

NET JOB LOSS

Total nonfarm employment declined steadily between December 2007 and October 2009, falling from 137,951,000 to 129,633,000. The great majority of this 8,318,000 job loss occurred after November 2008. Despite a small uptick in employment from October to November 2009, the number of jobs on employer payrolls fell the following month. Private and public employers typically have increased aggregate employment since then, however, with the number of jobs in July 2010 preliminarily rising to 130,470,000.

As is typical during economic downturns, employees in the goods-producing sector (mining, construction, manufacturing) have been the most adversely affected. Workers in the sector's construction industry began experiencing job losses even before the economy-wide downturn began.

Employment in the service-providing sector most recently peaked in December 2007, when the recession began. Some service-providing industries—education and health services—have continued to add workers. But, job losses elsewhere in the sector have far outweighed their gains. The financial activities industry began to lose jobs before the advent of the economy-wide downturn. This mirrors the above-mentioned trend in construction employment in part because real estate is a component of financial activities and it, like construction, has been hurt by the collapse of the housing market. Other components of financial activities, such as brokerage firms that packaged high-risk mortgages and the investors (e.g., banks) that purchased them, have been negatively affected by the housing market downturn as well.

Despite the widely expressed belief that the recession ended sometime in the third quarter of 2009, the pattern following the end of the prior 10 postwar recessions suggests that an uninterrupted rebound in jobs will not be immediate. According to a CRS analysis, in all but one of these recessions,

> the number of jobs on employer payrolls fluctuated for months.... Sustained job growth occurred within three to five months of the start of seven recoveries. In sharp contrast, steady job growth did not commence until March 1992—12 months after the July 1990–March 1991 recession ended—and not until September 2003—22 months after the March–November 2001 recession ended.[1]

INFRASTRUCTURE SPENDING AND JOB CREATION ESTIMATES

When in response to a recession Congress has acted to create jobs by raising demand for goods and services through increased federal spending, it often has chosen to direct the funds to infrastructure (public works) activities. Other means of direct countercyclical job creation—public service employment, fiscal relief to state governments, and employment tax credits—have been relied on much less often.[2]

Historically, public works has been synonymous with heavy and civil construction activities (e.g., road and bridge building, flood control structures and dam building). Today, it includes green economic activities or so-called green jobs. Although numerous studies on the emerging green economy have been released in the last several years, no consistent definition of green jobs exists at present. Green jobs seemingly are those in and related to industries that utilize renewable resources to produce their outputs (e.g., energy generated by wind, solar, and geothermal technologies) and jobs in and related to industries that produce energy-efficient goods (e.g., Energy Star appliances) and services (e.g., mass transit).[3] For this reason, the following discussion focuses on what is known about the job-generating impact of infrastructure spending broadly defined.

The section below begins with an in-depth examination of how job creation estimates usually are developed. The focus then narrows to look at two models that can be used to calculate the number of jobs nationwide dependent upon demand in the construction industry among others, and one model that can be used to calculate the number of jobs by state dependent on the construction industry among other industries. The section ends by reviewing the difficulties that researchers encounter in estimating the number of jobs supported by expenditures on green economic activities and the consequent caution that should be taken when utilizing these estimates in particular.

Job Creation Estimates: What Are They?

Interest in how many jobs are created by a particular type of economic activity has surfaced when the economy is in a downturn and policymakers seek to compare the relative advantages of different stimulus options. It also has arisen when policymakers want to know the impact of shifting expenditures from one federal budget category to another (e.g., away from defense and towards social services programs). Unless there is an *increase* in total spending, however, the number of jobs in the labor market would remain largely unchanged.[4]

Although there are other bases upon which to develop estimates of the number of jobs created by a given economic activity, an input-output (I-O) model of the economy often is utilized due to its cost-effectiveness.[5] An I-O model describes the interrelationships between industries in the production process, showing how the dollar value of a sale is distributed across industries at a particular point in time. It thus reflects how much of the purchased product comes from final and supplier industries. An I-O table might show, for example, the dollar value of roof trusses produced by the veneer, plywood, and engineered wood products manufacturing industry and the dollar value of bricks produced by the clay product and refractory manufacturing industry used by the construction industry to erect residential buildings.

The output requirements from each industry must then be converted to employment requirements. Employment requirements are derived from productivity estimates for each industry at a particular point in time. The total employment requirement associated with a given type of final demand (e.g., a water reuse program) is the employment in the industry producing the final product or service and in the supplier industries. In other words, it is an approximation of both the direct and indirect employment dependent upon/supported by the economic activity. It commonly is expressed as the number of jobs per billion dollars of expenditures valued in a particular year's dollars.

Like an I-O table, an employment requirements table is a matrix of hundreds of columns and rows. Each column displays the number of jobs supported in each of the industry rows by an expenditure of one billion dollars in the column industry. For example, one billion dollars spent in the construction industry supports (direct) employment in the various components of that industry (e.g., residential and commercial building, highway and bridge building) and (indirect) employment in the many industries that supply their goods and services to the construction industry (e.g., asphalt shingle manufacturing, fabricated metal bridge section manufacturing). An employment requirements table thus permits estimation of the varying impact of an expenditure on different industries and the varying impact of different kinds of expenditures.

Some Caveats

I-O models freeze technology and productivity at a particular point in time. Thus, the job-generating potential of an economic activity undertaken today could differ from that of an earlier period if there were technological and productivity improvements in the intervening years. Similarly, the estimates often are stated in terms of the number of jobs created for every billion dollars of expenditures, but a billion dollars spent in one year could buy less (or more) than a billion dollars spent in another year depending on changes in price levels over time.

There also could be differences in estimated versus actual job creation because I-O models assume that resources are unlimited. If, for example, the economy was performing at a fairly high level with plants operating near full capacity and with fairly few workers unemployed, the actual number of new jobs might fall short of the estimate due to capital and labor constraints. This is less likely to matter during a broad-based economic downturn.

Further, I-O tables do not necessarily differentiate between imported and domestically produced goods. As a consequence, the domestic employment impact of expenditures might be overstated to the extent that inputs are imported. Similarly, I-O tables typically do not express employment in terms of full-time equivalents (i.e., both full-time and part-time jobs are counted equally). Thus, programs which draw upon industries that rely relatively more on part-time workers (e.g., retail trade) might appear to create more jobs than programs that draw to a greater extent on industries employing relatively more full-time workers (e.g., manufacturing).

The Multiplier Effect

A more comprehensive estimate of the number of jobs created by a particular type of economic activity has three components:

- the number of jobs directly attributable to the activity,
- the number of jobs indirectly attributable to the activity, and
- the number of jobs induced throughout the economy as a result of the activity.

Induced jobs are those dependent upon the purchases of persons in direct and indirect jobs. For example, workers who are directly or indirectly employed as the result of a highway construction program might spend some portion of their wages in their communities at grocery stores, auto repair shops, and movie theaters.

Estimates of induced jobs or the multiplier are considered tenuous. To calculate the multiplier effect, one must estimate how much of the additional money earned by directly and indirectly employed workers will likely be spent versus saved. The actual number of jobs created by this added spending will further depend on economic conditions (e.g., the availability of labor, the inflation rate). As a result, there are widely varying estimates of the multiplier effect and those job creation studies that include induced employment utilize different multipliers.

Job Estimates and Construction Spending

The Federal Highway Administration

Perhaps the most widely known estimate of the employment impact of federal spending on our nation's roads comes from the Federal Highway Administration (FHWA). Although the FHWA twice updated its 1997 analysis, which estimated that $1 billion of federal-aid highway expenditures plus a $250 million state match supported 47,575 jobs, some proponents of stimulating job growth through increased federal spending on infrastructure continue to use this figure. The most recent update by the FHWA to 2007 indicates that a $1.25 billion expenditure on highway construction consisting of $1 billion from the federal government and $250 million from state government could support 34,779 jobs. If a state match is not required, "then $1 billion in Federal funds supports 27,800 jobs."[6] The jobs number has decreased over time in part because of increases in the price of inputs, such as asphalt and diesel fuel.

The FHWA breaks down the estimate of 27,822 jobs per billion dollars of federal spending on highways as follows:

- 9,536 construction-oriented jobs (i.e., jobs at construction companies working on the projects and at businesses that provide direct inputs to the projects such as asphalt, concrete, and guard rails);
- 4,324 jobs in supporting industries (i.e., employment at firms that provide inputs to the industries directly providing the materials and equipment utilized in highway construction such as producers of sheet metal who supply the manufacturers of guard rails); and
- 13,962 induced jobs (i.e., jobs throughout the economy dependent upon consumer expenditures from the wages of workers in "construction-oriented" and "industry-supporting" jobs).

Thus, induced jobs account for one-half of the total estimate.

The FHWA notes one caveat about I-O analysis in addition to those mentioned above; that is, the job estimate "utilizes the national average mix of construction materials and labor inputs. Specific projects and local utilization ratios will alter the estimated number of jobs supported."[7] For example, a different combination of materials and number of workers might be required for road resurfacing projects compared to bridge building or commuter rail projects.

The FHWA also states that

> [t]he employment figures have recently been used as a justification for including highway spending in an economic stimulus package. But with the exception of short-term resurfacing and preservation projects, highway funds spend out slowly, with only 27% of a project, on average, outlaying in the first year.[8]

BLS Employment Requirements Table

In recognition of the fact that "people want to assess the impact on employment of different policies or actions," the U.S. Bureau of Labor Statistics (BLS) makes available electronically free-of-charge to the public the employment requirements tables it develops as part of its employment projections program.[9] I-O and employment requirements tables developed and utilized by others often are proprietary and not made widely available.

The employment requirements tables are based on the official I-O tables for the nation that the U.S. Bureau of Economic Analysis (BEA) develops every five years. BLS takes the latest national I-O table available from BEA—in this case, 1997—and updates it to reflect more recent production and distribution technologies. It then utilizes the updated I-O table and recent labor productivity data to develop an employment requirements table. The employment requirements table referenced in this report reflects 2006 technologies of production and distribution as well as labor productivity. It is the table that was available in late 2008 when this report was first released.[10]

The BLS employment requirements table provides information for the construction industry as a whole. The construction industry, according to the North American Industry Classification System, is composed of three major subdivisions:

- construction of buildings (residential and nonresidential),
- heavy and civil engineering construction (highway, street, and bridge construction; utility system construction; construction of flood control structures, dams, and hydroelectric power generation facilities), and
- specialty trade contractors (foundation, structure, and building exterior contractors; building equipment contractors; building finishing contractors).

Some 11,768 jobs are directly and indirectly dependent upon $1 billion of spending on construction. A majority of the jobs are in the construction industry itself (i.e., 6,925 direct jobs).

The figure from the BLS employment requirements table for construction expenditures (11,768) is somewhat lower than the direct and indirect jobs figure for highway expenditures from the FHWA (13,860). Potential explanations for the disparity include differences in industry definition, data sources, method of updating the model, and time period.

The employment requirements available from BLS do not break out other types of construction that have been discussed as part of a federal job creation package (e.g., public school construction). BLS formerly conducted surveys to estimate full-time year-long employment associated with a variety of different construction activities, including new schools, hospitals, water and sewer facilities, roads, mass transit, and maintenance and repair construction. The survey information was last updated a few decades ago, however.

BEA's Regional Input-Output Modeling System (RIMS II)

From its Regional Input-Output Modeling System (RIMS II), the BEA produces estimates by geographic area of the employment, earnings, and output dependent on additional spending in hundreds of different industries. [11] For a fee to most parties, BEA utilizes either the 1997 benchmark I-O for the nation or the 2006 annual I-O for the nation adjusted by 2006 data from its regional economic accounts to provide these estimates at the subnational level.[12]

As shown in **Table 1**, the number of jobs directly and indirectly supported by an expenditure of $1 billion in the construction industry in a given state ranges widely. The main reason for the disparity in job creation estimates is that each state has a different mix of industries within its borders. As a consequence, one state varies from the next in its capacity to supply all the intermediate goods needed to carry out construction projects. A secondary explanation is that earnings vary by state.

Table 1. Number of Direct and Indirect Jobs by State Dependent on an Expenditure of $1 Billion in the Construction Industry

State	Number of Jobs	State	Number of Jobs
Alabama	15,851	Montana	16,127
Alaska	11,009	Nebraska	13,946
Arizona	12,238	Nevada	11,459
Arkansas	15,306	New Hampshire	12,374
California	12,289	New Jersey	11,118
Colorado	12,575	New Mexico	14,279
Connecticut	10,709	New York	10,106
Delaware	9,518	North Carolina	15,555
District of Columbia	1,874	North Dakota	13,500
Florida	13,127	Ohio	14,391
Georgia	14,224	Oklahoma	16,232
Hawaii	11,614	Oregon	13,184
Idaho	15,860	Pennsylvania	12,390
Illinois	11,916	Rhode Island	10,767
Indiana	13,747	South Carolina	15,319
Iowa	14,330	South Dakota	15,316
Kansas	13,625	Tennessee	14,556
Kentucky	15,039	Texas	12,985
Louisiana	13,731	Utah	14,692
Maine	15,988	Vermont	14,883
Maryland	10,687	Virginia	12,085
Massachusetts	10,714	Washington	12,171
Michigan	13,354	West Virginia	13,834
Minnesota	12,998	Wisconsin	13,673
Mississippi	15,357	Wyoming	13,091
Missouri	13,241	United States	14,315

Source: Prepared by CRS from RIMS II estimates supplied by the BEA Regional Product Division in 2008.

Job Estimates and Green Infrastructure Spending

Estimating the number of jobs dependent upon green infrastructure activities presents a greater challenge than estimates related to infrastructure projects as traditionally defined. The basis for most data collection by U.S. statistical agencies is the North American Industry Classification System (NAICS). It currently does not identify separately so-called green industries (e.g., those that utilize renewable resources to produce their outputs, those that manufacture goods which minimize energy use). For example, the NAICS disaggregates the electric utility industry into hydroelectric, fossil fuel, nuclear, and other power generation, transmission, and distribution. Such renewable sources of energy production as wind, solar, and biomass are not uniquely recognized; they are included in the "other" category. If harnessing the wind to produce electricity and plant material to produce biofuel requires a substantially different mix of inputs than relying on coal and gasoline, for example, the conventional I-O model does not seem well-suited as a basis for estimating the number of jobs supported by these green activities. Similarly, within NAICS, the construction industry does not have a unique category for retrofitting (e.g., installing additional insulation, fluorescent lighting, or energy-efficient heating and air-conditioning systems). Retrofitting likely requires a combination of inputs from supplier industries that differs from the mix for the top-to-bottom construction of buildings, once again making use of conventional I-O models problematic.

This recognized difficulty generally is either not mentioned, or how it is dealt with is not described, in the analyses of green job creation. One study, commissioned by the Center for American Progress and discussed in more detail below, does address the problem. The researchers explain that because "the U.S. government surveys and accounts that are used to construct the input-output tables do not specifically recognize wind, solar, biomass, building retrofitting, or new mass transit as industries in their own right," they created synthetic industries by combining parts of industries for which data are available. The researchers provided an example in the case of the biomass "industry:" they constructed it by combining farming, forestry, wood products, and refining industries; then they "assigned relative weights to each of these industries in terms of their contributions to producing biomass products."[13]

Further complicating the matter is the context and manner in which estimates of green jobs generally are presented. Studies often develop employment projections based on differing sets of assumptions and time horizons. For example, the number of direct and indirect jobs some 10 or more years in the future supported by an assumed increase in the demand for energy that is met by an assumed shift during the projection period from coal to wind and geothermal power generation. Some reports also include induced employment, but this is not always made clear. In addition, some analyses relate to a particular state. Their results may not be generalizeable to other areas because state economy's have different mixes of industries and may not be able to provide any or all of the inputs for a particular green output. Additionally, the assumptions and methodologies underlying the job creation estimates often are not clearly articulated, which makes thoughtful review of the results very difficult.

It should be noted that many of the studies by green economy proponents that were available when Congress was crafting stimulus legislation had not been conceived for the purpose of quickly stabilizing or increasing the number of jobs in the nation or in industries particularly hard hit by the recession. Job creation estimates from two organizations that proposed broad-based green economy strategies intended in part to stimulate the deteriorating labor market are briefly described below.

- The September 2008 report, *Green Recovery: A Program to Create Jobs and Start Building a Low-Carbon Economy*, was commissioned by the Center for American Progress (a research and educational institute). It represents an acceleration of a 10-year program included in a 2007 report (*Capturing the Energy Opportunity: Creating a Low-Carbon Economy*). The 2008 report's authors at the Department of Economics and Political Economy Research Institute (University of Massachusetts-Amherst), who relied on I-O analysis, estimate that almost 2 million jobs (935,200 direct jobs, 586,000 indirect jobs, and 496,000 induced jobs) could be created or preserved by a two-year $100 billion "green economic recovery program." Of the $100 billion total, $46 billion would be in the form of federal spending for such activities as public building retrofits, mass transit and freight rail expansion, and smart electrical grid development. Much of the remainder would be in the form of tax credits to encourage businesses and homeowners to retrofit commercial and residential buildings. The authors acknowledge that not all of the green activities can contribute equally to a short-term green economic recovery program. Some ... strategies are clearly capable of delivering within a year, while others will require as long as two years to be implemented.[14]
- In December 2008, the Apollo Alliance (a coalition of labor, environmental, business and community leaders) proposed *The Apollo Economic Recovery Act*. It is an initial step toward achievement of a 10-year $500 billion program to create 5 million green-collar jobs, which had been released in September 2008. The new initiative calls for federal spending of about $50 billion to create or maintain more than 650,000 direct jobs and 1.3 million indirect jobs. The derivation of these job creation figures is not always clear, appearing to rely much of the time on spending-to-jobs relationships estimated by other organizations. The proposed allocation of federal funds and associated job estimates include $10 billion to improve the efficiency and reliability of the electric transmission grid (131,000 direct and indirect jobs), $8 billion to repair roads and bridges (278,000 direct and indirect jobs), and $8 billion to encourage localities to replace aging buses and trains with U.S.-made clean-energy vehicles (37,600 direct jobs in vehicle manufacturing and 167,000 indirect jobs).

Measuring Jobs Supported by Spending Provisions in the American Recovery and Reinvestment Act

While crafting the American Recovery and Reinvestment Act (ARRA), Congress was concerned about timely tracking of the number of jobs whose creation or maintenance results from the legislation. The 111th Congress therefore addressed this matter in bill language much more than prior Congresses had in countercyclical job creation legislation.

Job Reporting by Recipients of ARRA Appropriations

At Title XV—Accountability and Transparency of Division A—Appropriations Provisions, P.L. 111-5 requires entities that receive ARRA appropriations from federal agencies (e.g., grant, loan, or contract recipients; states) to include in their quarterly reports to the agencies estimates of the number of direct jobs created and retained by infrastructure projects, for example.[15] Recipients of recovery funds were required to make their first submission of the required information in October 2009. Federal agencies are required to post the contents of these and subsequent reports on websites 30 days after the end of each calendar quarter. The Office of Management and Budget (OMB) was directed to provide guidance to help recipients prepare the reports, including the development of job estimates. The act further charged the Congressional Budget Office (CBO) and the Government Accountability Office (GAO) with commenting on the job estimates contained in the reports within 45 days after their submission to federal agencies.

Based on the self-reporting of recipients of ARRA appropriations, 633,342 jobs were saved or retained through September 30, 2009. Because the notion of a retained (saved) job caused consternation in some quarters, OMB revised its guidance issued in June 2009. According to that guidance, upon which the aforementioned job figure was based, Congress' reference in ARRA to a job retained meant "an existing position that would not have been continued to be filled were it not for Recovery Act funding."[16] In response to feedback from GAO, among others, OMB revised its guidance on jobs saved so that recipients no longer will have "to make a subjective judgment on whether a given job would have existed were it not for the Recovery Act. The updated guidance [issued in December 2009] ... defines jobs created or retained as those funded ... by the Recovery Act."[17] Based on this definition, recipients reported that 608,311 jobs were funded by ARRA in the fourth quarter of 2009. Another 682,370 jobs were created or saved at ARRA recipients in the first quarter of 2010.[18]

Job Estimation by the Council of Economic Advisers

Title XV of P.L. 111-5 additionally tasked the Council of Economic Advisers (CEA) with submitting quarterly reports to the Committees on Appropriations on the effect of ARRA-provisions on employment and other economic indicators. The CEA's mandate thus extends well beyond the above-described reporting requirements, which apply only to $271 billion in direct government investment spending out of a total of $787 billion.[19]

The first quarterly report of the CEA was issued in September 2009. Based on two different estimating procedures, it found that ARRA might have added some one million jobs to employer payrolls in August 2009 compared to what employment would have been in the absence of the legislation.[20]

As noted above, CBO was charged in ARRA with commenting on the number of jobs created or saved as a result of direct government purchases of goods and services, grants and loans to private entities, and grants to states and localities. Although it did so in *Estimated Impact of the American Recovery and Reinvestment Act on Employment and Economic Output as of September 2009*, CBO went further to provide a broader estimate than can be gleaned from the reports of primary and secondary recipients of more than $25,000 from appropriations in ARRA; it is an estimate more comparable to that of the CEA. Based upon information provided by macroeconomic models and historical relationships, CBO estimated that ARRA's tax cuts and outlay increases that occurred through September 2009 increased the number of people employed by between 600,000 and 1.6 million compared to the employment level without the law. The CEA's estimate of 1.0-1.1 million additional jobs as of August 2009, discussed in the preceding paragraph, falls within the range estimated by CBO.

In its second quarterly report, released in January 2010, the CEA estimated the effect of ARRA on employment through December 2009. It found that the stimulus law might have raised year-end employment by about 1.7–1.9 million jobs above what it otherwise would have been.[21] Similarly, CBO estimated in its report covering the fourth quarter of 2009 that ARRA's policies might have increased the number of people employed by 1.0–2.1 million.[22]

The CEA's third quarterly report, released in April 2010, showed ARRA's employment effect through March 2010. It estimated that the law might have raised employment by 2.2–2.8 million jobs above what it otherwise would have been as of the first quarter of 2010.[23] Similarly, CBO estimated in its report covering the first quarter of 2010 that ARRA's policies might have increased the number of people employed by 1.2–2.8 million.[24]

The fourth quarterly ARRA jobs report of the CEA covering the second quarter of 2010 was released on July 14. Based on the two methods utilized by the CEA, ARRA might have increased employment compared to what it otherwise would have been in the quarter by between 2.5 million and 3.6 million jobs. Using its macroeconomic model, the CEA further estimated the effect on aggregate employment of public investment outlays under ARRA, which include clean energy generation and efficiency; human capital (e.g., Pell grants, K-12 schools excluding the State Fiscal Stabilization Fund); transportation infrastructure (air, sea, highway) and transit; health care delivery and technology; and building construction. Public investment outlays might have increased total employment by over 627,000 jobs in the first quarter of 2010, and by over 800,000 jobs in the second quarter of the year.[25]

End Notes

[1] CRS Report R40798, *Unemployment and Employment Trends Before and After the End of Recessions*, by Linda Levine.

[2] CRS Report 92-939, *Countercyclical Job Creation Programs*, by Linda Levine.

[3] Related jobs include, for example, those in industries that manufacture wind turbines and install thermal-pane windows.

[4] Small differences in the total number of jobs could occur at the same spending levels if the economic activities to (from) which funds were being shifted were more (less) capital-intensive, for example.

[5] Another basis for estimating the impact of policy and other changes on the economy is conducting surveys. According to the U.S. Bureau of Economic Analysis (BEA), the advantage of the I-O approach to making impact estimates is the accessibility of the data sources required to develop the I-O model.

[6] U.S. Department of Transportation, Federal Highway Administration, *Employment Impacts of Highway Infrastructure Investment*. Available from author upon request.

[7] Ibid.

[8] Ibid.

[9] U.S. Bureau of Labor Statistics, *Layout and Description for 201-order Employment Requirements Tables*, Washington, DC, December 2007, p. 3, http://stats.bls.gov/emp/empind4.htm.

[10] BLS in late 2009 released an employment requirements table updated to reflect 2008 technologies of production and distribution as well as labor productivity. It is available at http://stats.bls .gov/emp/ep_data_emp_requirements.htm.

[11] For additional information on RIMS II see BEA, *Regional Multipliers: A User Handbook for the Regional Input-Output Modeling System*, http://www.bea.gov/scb/pdf/regional/perinc/meth/rims2.pdf.

[12] More specific detail by industry is available from the 1997 benchmark I-O than from the annual I-O. Therefore, Table 1 (Number of Direct and Indirect Jobs Per $1 Million of Output Produced by the Water, Sewage and Other Systems Industry) in CRS Report R40107, *The Role of Public Works Infrastructure in Economic Stimulus*, was drawn from the 1997 benchmark I-O because the 2006 annual I-O provides data only for the utilities industry as a whole.

[13] Robert Pollin, Heidi Garrett-Peltier, and James Heintz, et al., *Green Recovery: A Program to Create Good Jobs and Start Building a Low-Carbon Economy*, Center for American Progress, Washington, DC, September 2008, p. 20, http://www.americanprogress.org.

[14] Robert Pollin, Heidi Garrett-Peltier, and James Heintz, et al., *Green Recovery: A Program to Create Good Jobs and Start Building a Low-Carbon Economy*, Center for American Progress, Washington, DC, September 2008, p. 5, http://www.americanprogress.org.

[15] Recipients of ARRA funds awarded to the Department of Transportation (DOT) are subject to Section 1512's job reporting requirement. Separately, at Section 1201, Congress required the DOT to estimate the direct, indirect, and total jobs created by transportation projects funded under ARRA. The DOT estimates thus are akin to the estimates for the entire bill that the CEA produces.

[16] OMB, *Implementing Guidance for the Reports on Use of Funds Pursuant to the American Recovery and Reinvestment Act*, M-09-21, June 22, 2009, available at http://www.whitehouse.gov/omb/assets memoranda_ fy2009/ m09-21.pdf.

[17] OMB, *Updated Guidance on the American Recovery and Reinvestment Act—Data Quality, Non-Reporting Recipients, and Reporting of Job Estimates*, M-10-08, December 18, 2009. See Part 2 of http://www.recovery.gov/ FAQ/recipient/Documents/m10-08%20Updated%20Guidance%2012182009.pdf.

[18] http://www.recovery.gov/Pages/home.aspx.

[19] The remaining ARRA funds fall into five categories: individual income tax cuts, a patch for the alternative minimum tax, investment incentives, aid to people directly hurt by the recession (e.g., unemployment insurance), and fiscal relief for state governments.

[20] Council of Economic Advisers, *The Economic Impact of the American Recovery and Reinvestment Act of 2009, First Quarterly Report,* September 10, 2009.

[21] Council of Economic Advisers, *The Economic Impact of the American Recovery and Reinvestment Act of 2009, Second Quarterly Report*, January 13, 2010.

[22] Congressional Budget Office, *Estimated Impact of the American Recovery and Reinvestment Act on Employment and Economic Output From October 2009 Through December 2009*, February 2010.

[23] Council of Economic Advisers, *The Economic Impact of the American Recovery and Reinvestment Act of 2009, Third Quarterly Report*, April 14, 2010.

[24] Congressional Budget Office, *Estimated Impact of the American Recovery and Reinvestment Act on Employment and Economic Output From January 2010 Through March 2010*, May 2010.

[25] Council of Economic Advisers, *The Economic Impact of the American Recovery and Reinvestment Act of 2009, Fourth Quarterly Report*, July 14, 2010.

In: U.S. Economic Recovery and Stimulus Measures
Editor: Jessica D. Saparito
ISBN: 978-1-61209-266-9

Chapter 6

FINANCIAL TURMOIL: FEDERAL RESERVE POLICY RESPONSES

Marc Labonte

SUMMARY

The Federal Reserve (Fed) has been central in the policy response to the financial turmoil that began in August 2007. It has sharply increased reserves to the banking system through open market operations and lowered the federal funds rate and discount rate on several occasions. Since December 2008, it has allowed the federal funds rate to fall close to zero. As the crisis deepened, the Fed's focus shifted to providing liquidity directly to the financial system through new policy tools. Through new credit facilities, the Fed first expanded the scale of its lending to the banking system and then extended direct lending to non-bank financial firms. The latter marked the first time since the Great Depression that firms that are not banks or members of the Federal Reserve System have been allowed to borrow directly from the Fed. After the crisis worsened in September 2008, the Fed began providing credit directly to markets for commercial paper and asset-backed securities. All of these emergency facilities had expired by the end of June 2010, but central bank liquidity swap lines were reopened in May 2010 in response to the crisis in Greece. The Fed also provided emergency assistance to Bear Stearns, AIG, and Citigroup over the course of the crisis; the Fed still holds assets from and loans to AIG and assets from Bear Stearns.

These programs resulted in an increase in the Fed's balance sheet of $1.4 trillion at its peak in December 2008, staying relatively steady since then. The Fed's authority and capacity to lend is bound only by fears of the inflationary consequences, which have been partly offset by additional debt issuance by the Treasury. High inflation has not materialized yet because most of the liquidity created by the Fed is being held by banks as excess reserves, but after the economy stabilizes, the Fed may have to scale back its balance sheet rapidly to avoid it. Asset sales could be disruptive, but the Fed has argued that it can contain inflationary pressures through the payment of interest on bank reserves, which it was authorized by Congress to do in 2008.

The statutory authority for most of the Fed's recent actions is based on a clause in the Federal Reserve Act to be used in "unusual or exigent circumstances." All loans are backed by collateral that reduces the risk of losses. Any losses borne by the Fed from its loans or asset purchases would reduce the income it remits to the Treasury, making the effect on the federal budget similar to if the loans were made directly by Treasury. It is highly unlikely that losses would exceed its other income and capital, and require revenues to be transferred to the Fed from the Treasury. To date, the Fed's crisis activities have increased its net income.

Two policy issues raised by the Fed's actions are issues of systemic risk and moral hazard. Moral hazard refers to the phenomenon where actors take on more risk because they are protected. The Fed's involvement in stabilizing Bear Stearns, AIG, and Citigroup stemmed from the fear of systemic risk (that the financial system as a whole would cease to function) if they were allowed to fail. In other words, the firms were seen as "too big (or too interconnected) to fail." The Fed regulates member banks to mitigate the moral hazard that stems from access to government protections. Yet Bear Stearns and AIG were not under the Fed's regulatory oversight because they were not member banks.

Some Members of Congress have expressed concern that certain details of the Fed's lending activities are kept confidential. H.R. 4173 adds conditions to the Fed's emergency lending authority, removes most GAO audit restrictions, and requires disclosure of the identities of borrowers with a delay. It also changes the Fed's role in the financial regulatory system (see CRS Report R40877, *Financial Regulatory Reform: Systemic Risk and the Federal Reserve*).

INTRODUCTION

On August 9, 2007, liquidity abruptly dried up for many financial firms and securities markets. Suddenly some firms were able to borrow and investors were able to sell certain securities only at prohibitive rates and prices, if at all. The "liquidity crunch" was most extreme for firms and securities with links to subprime mortgages, but it also spread rapidly into seemingly unrelated areas.[1] The Federal Reserve (Fed) was drawn into the liquidity crunch from the start. On August 9, it injected unusually large quantities of reserves into the banking system to prevent the federal funds rate from exceeding its target. In a series of steps between September 2007 and December 2008, the Fed reduced the federal funds rate from 5.25% to a target range of 0% to 0.25%.

It has been observed that the most unusual aspect of the crisis is its persistence over time. Over that time, the Fed has aggressively reduced the federal funds rate and the discount rate in an attempt to calm the waters. When this proved not to be enough, the Fed greatly expanded its direct lending to the financial sector through several new lending programs, some of which can be seen as adaptations of traditional tools and others which can be seen as more fundamental departures from the status quo.[2]

The Fed's decision to assist specific troubled financial institutions sparked controversy. In March 2008, the Fed helped the investment bank Bear Stearns avoid bankruptcy, even though Bear Stearns was not a member bank of the Federal Reserve system (because it was not a depository institution), and, therefore, not part of the regulatory regime that accompanies membership.[3] At the same time, it created two lending facilities for other non-bank primary dealers. In September, the investment bank Lehman Brothers filed for bankruptcy (it did not receive emergency government assistance), and the financial firm American International Group (AIG), which was also not a member bank, received a credit line from the Fed in order to meet its obligations. (Additional aid to AIG was extended on three subsequent occasions.) The Fed then began directly assisting the markets for commercial paper and asset-backed securities. More recently, the Fed and federal government has guaranteed losses on assets owned by Citigroup. This marked the first time in more than 70 years that the Fed had lent to non-members, and it did so using emergency statutory authority (Section 13(3) of the Federal Reserve Act).[4] The Dodd-Frank Wall Street Reform and Consumer Protection Act (H.R. 4173) adds conditions to the Fed's emergency lending authority. The House passed the conference report for H.R. 4173 on June 30, 2010, and the Senate passed the conference report on July 15, 2010.

In September 2008, the housing government-sponsored enterprises (GSEs) Fannie Mae and Freddie Mac were taken into conservatorship by the government. On November 25, 2008, the Fed announced that it would make large-scale purchases of the direct obligations and mortgage-backed securities (MBS) issued by the housing GSEs.

As financial conditions have improved in 2009, the Fed's focus, in turn, has shifted from stabilizing financial markets to stabilizing the housing market. As fewer financial firms have accessed Fed lending facilities, direct assistance has been replaced on the Fed's balance sheet by purchases of debt and MBS issued by the housing GSEs. This has kept relatively constant the overall amount of liquidity the Fed has provided to the economy. The Fed purchased about $175 billion of GSE debt and $1.25 trillion of MBS by the spring of 2010. Most emergency facilities were allowed to expire in February 2010, but the central bank liquidity swap lines were reopened in May 2010 to provide dollar liquidity to foreign countries needed as a result of the economic crisis in Greece.

One of the original purposes of the Federal Reserve Act, enacted in 1913, was to prevent the recurrence of financial panics. To that end, the Fed has been given broad authority over monetary policy and the payments system, including the issuance of federal reserve notes as the national currency. Because this authority is delegated from Congress, the Fed's actions are subject to congressional oversight. Although the Fed has broad authority to independently execute monetary policy on a day-to-day basis, questions have arisen as to whether the unusual events of recent months raise fundamental issues about the Fed's proper role, and what role Congress should play in assessing those issues. S. 896, which was signed into law on May 20, 2009 (P.L. 111-22), allows Government Accountability Office (GAO) audits of a limited subset of Fed emergency activities. H.R. 4173 removes most GAO audit restrictions, calls for a GAO audit of emergency actions, and requires disclosure of the identities of borrowers with a delay.[5]

H.R. 4173 also made comprehensive changes to the financial regulatory system. The Fed's role in prudential regulation, consumer protection regulation, payment system regulation, and systemic risk regulation was modified by this legislation. CRS Report R40877, *Financial Regulatory Reform: Systemic Risk and the Federal Reserve*, analyzes the effects of this legislation on the Fed's role in the regulatory system.

This report reviews the Fed's actions since August 2007 and analyzes the policy issues raised by those actions.

TRADITIONAL TOOLS

The Fed, the nation's central bank, was established in 1913 by the Federal Reserve Act (38 Stat. 251). Today, its primary duty is the execution of monetary policy through open market operations to fulfill its mandate to promote price stability and maximum employment. Besides the conduct of monetary policy, the Federal Reserve has a number of other duties: it regulates financial institutions and consumer financial products, issues paper currency, clears checks, collects economic data, and carries out economic research. Prominent in the current debate is one particular responsibility: to act as a lender of last resort to the financial system when capital cannot be raised in private markets to prevent financial panics. The next two sections explain the Fed's traditional tools, open market operations and discount window lending, and summarize its recent use of those tools.

Open Market Operations and the Federal Funds Rate

Open market operations are carried out through the purchase and sale of U.S. Treasury securities in the secondary market to alter the reserves of the banking system.[6] By altering bank reserves, the Fed can influence short-term interest rates, and hence overall credit conditions. The Fed's target for open market operations is the federal funds rate, the rate at which banks lend to one another on an overnight basis. The federal funds rate is market determined, meaning the rate fluctuates as supply and demand for bank reserves change. The Fed announces a target for the federal funds rate and pushes the market rate toward the target by altering the supply of reserves in the market through the purchase and sale of Treasury securities.[7] More reserves increase the liquidity in the banking system and, in theory, should make banks more willing to lend, spreading greater liquidity throughout the financial system.

When the Fed wants to stimulate economic activity, it lowers the federal funds target, in what is referred to as expansionary policy. Lower interest rates stimulate economic activity by stimulating interest-sensitive spending, which includes physical capital investment (e.g., plant and equipment) by firms, residential investment (housing construction), and consumer durable spending (e.g., automobiles and appliances) by households. Lower rates would also be expected to lead to a lower value of the dollar, all else equal. A depreciated dollar would stimulate exports and the output of U.S. import-competing firms. To reduce spending in the economy (called contractionary policy), the Fed raises interest rates, and the process works in reverse.

The Fed's actions with regards to open market operations have taken two forms in the crisis. First, a loss of liquidity in the interbank lending market has forced the Fed to inject unusually large volumes of reserves into the market on several occasions since August 2007. These actions have been necessary to maintain the availability of reserves at the existing federal funds target.

Second, the Fed has reduced the federal funds target on numerous occasions over the course of the crisis. On September 18, 2007, the Fed reduced the federal funds target rate by 0.5 percentage points to 4.75%, stating that the change was "intended to forestall some of the adverse effects on the broader economy that might otherwise arise from the disruptions in financial markets." Since then, the Fed has aggressively lowered interest rates several times.

The Fed decides whether to change its target for the federal funds rate at meetings scheduled every six weeks. In normal conditions, the Fed would typically leave the target unchanged or change it by 0.25 percentage points. From September 2007 to March 2008, the Fed lowered the target at each regularly scheduled meeting, by an increment larger than 0.25 percentage points at most of these meetings. It also lowered the target by 0.75 percentage points at an unscheduled meeting on January 21, 2008. Although financial conditions had not returned to normal, the Fed kept the federal funds rate steady from April 30, 2008, until October 9, 2008, when it again reduced the federal funds rate, this time by 0.5 percentage points, to 1.5%. Unusually, this rate reduction was coordinated with several foreign central banks. On December 16, 2008, the Fed established a target range of 0% to 0.25% for the federal funds rate.

Quantitative Easing

Even before December 2008, the Fed began supplying the federal funds market with a greater quantity of bank reserves than needed to reach the federal funds target, a policy that has been described as "quantitative easing."[8] Because the Fed has only one tool, it cannot meet more than one target at once. As long as the Fed was willing to create liquidity on demand, the federal funds rate was unlikely to meet its target. Therefore, after the Fed began focusing on meeting the financial sector's liquidity needs in September, the federal funds rate began undershooting the Fed's target on a regular basis.[9] In December 2008, the Fed began providing so much liquidity that the interest rate target often fell close to zero. The target range of 0% to 0.25% set in December can be seen as an acknowledgment by the Fed that targeting interest rates had been subordinated to the goal of providing ample liquidity to the financial system for the time being. Initially, quantitative easing was implemented through direct lending, but even after that liquidity was no longer sought by financial firms through the Fed's lending facilities, quantitative easing was continued through large purchases of Treasury securities, Agency securities, and Agency mortgage-backed securities in an attempt to continue stimulating the economy.[10] According to one estimate, the Fed purchased 22% of the entire available stock of these assets.[11]

The Discount Window

The Fed can also provide liquidity to member banks (depository institutions that are members of the Federal Reserve system) directly through discount window lending.[12] Discount window lending dates back to the early days of the Fed, and was originally the Fed's main policy tool. (The Fed's main policy tool shifted from the discount window to open market operations several decades ago.) Loans made at the discount window are backed by collateral in excess of the loan value. A wide array of assets can be used as collateral; loans and asset-backed securities are the most frequently posted collateral. Although not all collateral has a credit rating, those that are rated typically have the highest rating.[13] Most discount window lending is done on an overnight basis. Unlike the federal funds rate, the Fed sets the discount rate directly through fiat.

During normal market conditions, the Fed discouraged banks from borrowing at the discount window on a routine basis, believing that banks should be able to meet their normal reserve needs through the market. In 2003, the Fed made that policy explicit in its pricing by changing the discount rate from 0.5 percentage points below to 1 percentage point above the federal funds rate. A majority of member banks do not access the discount window in a typical year. Thus, the discount window has played a secondary role in policymaking to open market operations.

On August 17, 2007, the Fed began reducing the discount rate—about a month before it first reduced the federal funds rate. Since then, the discount rate has been lowered several times, typically at the same time as the federal funds rate. Over that period, the Fed has reduced the spread between the federal funds rate and the discount rate, but kept the spread positive. When the federal funds rate was allowed to fall to zero beginning in December 2008, the discount rate was set at 0.5%. From 1959 to 2007, discount window lending outstanding never surpassed $8 billion, and was usually well below $1 billion. Discount window lending (in the primary credit category) increased from a daily average of $45 million outstanding in July 2007 to $1,345 million in September 2007. Lending continued to increase to more than $10 billion outstanding per day from May 2008, and peaked at $111 billion in October 2008, but was superseded in economic significance by the creation of the "Term Auction Facility" in December 2007. Discount window lending fell steadily throughout 2009, and by mid-2010, it had returned to pre-crisis levels.

New Tools

The Fed's traditional tools are aimed at the commercial banking system, but current financial turmoil has occurred outside of the banking system as well. The inability of traditional tools to calm financial markets since August 2007 has led the Fed to develop several new tools to fill perceived gaps between open market operations and the discount window.[14]

Traditionally, the lender of last resort function has focused on the banking system, and the Fed's relationship with the banking system, encompassing costs and privileges, is prescribed in detail by the Federal Reserve Act. Many of the new facilities are aimed at other parts of the financial system, however, and the Federal Reserve Act is largely silent on the Fed's authority outside the banking system.[15] One exception is the broad emergency authority under Section 13(3) of the Federal Reserve Act, which the Fed has frequently invoked since the financial crisis began.

Term Auction Facility

A stigma is thought to be attached to borrowing from the discount window. In good times, discount window lending has traditionally been discouraged on the grounds that banks should meet their reserve requirements through the marketplace (the federal funds market) rather than the Fed. Borrowing from the Fed was therefore seen as a sign of weakness, as it implied that market participants were unwilling to lend to the bank because of fears of insolvency. In the current turmoil, this perception of weakness could be particularly damaging since a bank could be undermined by a run based on unfounded, but self-fulfilling fears. Ironically, this meant that although the Fed encourages discount window borrowing so that banks can avoid liquidity problems, at first banks were hesitant to turn to the Fed because of fears that doing so would spark a crisis of confidence. To overcome these problems, the Fed created the supplementary Term Auction Facility (TAF) in December 2007.[16]

Discount window lending is initiated at the behest of the requesting institution—the Fed has no control over how many requests for loans it receives. The TAF allows the Fed to determine the amount of reserves it wishes to make available to banks, based on market conditions. The auction process determines the rate at which those funds will be lent, with all bidders receiving the lowest winning bid rate. The winning bid may not be lower than the prevailing federal funds rate. Determining the rate by bid provides the Fed with additional information on how much demand for reserves exists.

Any depository institution eligible for discount window lending can participate in the TAF, and hundreds have accessed it or the discount window at a time since its inception. Auctions through the TAF have been held twice a month beginning in December 2007. The amounts auctioned have greatly exceeded discount window lending, which averages in the hundreds of millions of dollars outstanding daily in normal times and more than $10 billion outstanding since May 2008. The TAF initially auctioned up to $20 billion every two weeks, but this amount was increased on several occasions to as much as $150 billion (and currently up to $125 billion) every two weeks. Loans outstanding under the facility peaked at $493 billion in March 2009, and have fallen steadily since.[17] Like discount window lending, TAF loans must be fully collateralized with the same qualifying collateral. Loans and asset-backed securities are the most frequently posted collateral. Although not all collateral has a credit rating, those that are rated typically have the highest rating. As with discount window lending, the Fed faces the risk that the value of collateral would fall below the loan amount in the event that the loan was not repaid. For that reason, the amount lent diminishes as the quality of the collateral diminishes. Most borrowers borrow much less than the posted collateral.[18]

Loans mature in 28 days—far longer than overnight loans in the federal funds market or the typical discount window loan. (In July 2008, the Fed began making some TAF loans that matured in 84 days.) Another motivation for the TAF may have been an attempt to reduce the unusually large divergence that had emerged between the federal funds rate and interbank lending rates for longer maturities. This divergence, which can be seen as a sign of how much liquidity had deteriorated in spite of the Fed's previous efforts, became much smaller after December 2007. In subsequent periods of market stress, such as September 2008, the divergence reemerged. The evidence on the effectiveness of the TAF in reducing this divergence is mixed.[19]

The TAF program was announced as a temporary program (with no fixed expiration date) that could be made permanent after assessment. Given that the discount rate is set higher than the federal funds rate to discourage its use in normal market conditions, it is unclear what role a permanent TAF would fill, unless the funds auctioned were minimal in normal market conditions. A permanent TAF would seem to run counter to the philosophy governing the discount window that financial institutions, if possible, should rely on the private sector to meet their short-term reserve needs during normal market conditions. The Fed has not held a TAF auction since March 2010.

Term Securities Lending Facility

For many years, the Fed has allowed primary dealers (see box for definition) to swap Treasuries of different maturities or attributes with the Fed on an overnight basis through a program called the System Open Market Account Securities Lending Program to help meet the dealers' liquidity needs. (While all Treasury securities are backed by the full faith and credit of the federal government, some securities are more liquid than others, mainly because of differences in availability.) Securities lending has no effect on general interest rates or the money supply because it does not involve cash, but can affect the liquidity premium of the securities traded. Because the loans were overnight and collateralized with other Treasury securities, there was very little risk for the Fed.

WHAT IS A PRIMARY DEALER?

Primary dealers are about 20 large financial institutions who are the counterparties with which the Fed undertakes open market operations (buying and selling of Treasury securities). Because open market operations are very large, the Fed needs large counterparties to these transactions. To be a primary dealer, an institution must, among other things, meet relevant Basel or SEC capital requirements and maintain a good trading relationship with the Fed.

On March 11, 2008, the Fed set up a more expansive securities lending program for the primary dealers called the Term Securities Lending Facility (TSLF) using emergency authority under Section 13(3) of the Federal Reserve Act. Under this program, up to $75 billion (previously up to $200 billion) of Treasury securities could be lent for 28 days instead of overnight. Loans could be collateralized with private-label MBS with an AAA/Aaa rating, agency commercial mortgage-backed securities, and agency collateralized mortgage obligations.[20] On September 14, 2008, the Fed expanded acceptable collateral to include all investment-grade debt securities. Given the recent drop in MBS and other asset prices, this made the new lending program considerably more risky than the old one. But the scope for losses is limited by the fact that the loans are fully collateralized with a "haircut" (i.e., less money is loaned than the value of the collateral), and if the collateral loses value before the loan is due, the Fed can call for substitute collateral. In addition, most of the collateral that has been posted received a high rating from a credit rating agency.[21] The first auction on March 27 involved $75 billion of securities. In August 2008, the program was expanded to allow the primary dealers to purchase up to $50 billion of options (with prices set by auction) to swap for Treasuries through the TSLF. The TSLF was announced as a temporary facility. In July 2009, the Fed announced that primary dealers could also swap their assets for the Fed's Agency debt securities. Securities lent through all programs peaked at $260 billion on October 1, 2008. Since August 2009, no securities have been borrowed through this facility. The facility expired at the end of January 2010.

By allowing the primary dealers to temporarily swap illiquid assets for highly liquid assets such as Treasuries, "[t]he TSLF is intended to promote liquidity in the financing markets for Treasury and other collateral and thus to foster the functioning of financial markets more generally," according to the Fed.[22] According to research from the New York

Fed, the spreads between repos backed by GSE debt and MBS and repos backed by Treasuries fell from over 1 percentage point before the first TSLF auction to less than 0.2 percentage points by April 2008.[23] Given the timing of the announcement—less than a week before the failure of one of its primary dealers, Bear Stearns—critics have alleged that the program was created, in effect, in an attempt to rescue Bear Stearns from its liquidity problems. As will be discussed below, the Fed would take much larger steps to aid Bear Stearns later the same week.

Emergency Authority under Section 13(3) of the Federal Reserve Act

The Fed has limited authority to assist non-member banks under the Federal Reserve Act. One exception where such authority is granted is under paragraph 3 of Section 13 of the Federal Reserve Act, and the Fed has used it to authorize many of its actions during the crisis. Prior to July 2010, it read,

> In unusual and exigent circumstances, the Board of Governors of the Federal Reserve System, by the affirmative vote of not less than five members, may authorize any Federal reserve bank ... to discount for any individual, partnership, or corporation, notes, drafts, and bills of exchange ... secured to the satisfaction of the Federal Reserve Bank. Provided, that before discounting any such note, draft, or bill exchange ... the Federal reserve bank shall obtain evidence that such individual, partnership, or corporation is unable to secure adequate credit accommodations from other banking institutions.

It is noteworthy that this text allows emergencies to be identified by the Board of Governors and places few limits on what type of institution can receive financial assistance from the Fed or what form that assistance can take. The fact that the authority is justified only by unusual and exigent circumstances suggests that decisions made under 13(3), such as the creation of lending facilities, could not be made permanent under existing authority. Nevertheless, expiration dates were pushed back more than once for some new facilities. In 1991, Section 13(3) was amended to expand the collateral that the Fed could accept to back its lending; this was widely seen as making it easier for the Fed to lend to non-bank financial firms in an emergency. As will be discussed below, on a few occasions in 2008, Section 13(3) has been invoked to lend to an entity that the Fed created so that the entity could purchase private securities.

According to Hackley (1973), only 123 loans to businesses were made using 13(3) authority from 1932 to 1936. Until Bear Stearns, the authority had not been used for non-banks since. (The authority was superseded by Section 13b authority to lend to non-banks; Section 13b was revoked in 1958.) It has been invoked numerous times in 2008, including to authorize the Primary Dealer Credit Facility, the Fed's role in the Bear Stearns merger, and the Fed's extension of credit to AIG. Financial crises can spread quickly, and Section 13(3) makes a prompt response possible. But recent events have demonstrated that it vests the Fed with the ability to make large, wide-ranging financial commitments without congressional approval. It has voluntarily sought and received Treasury approval in each instance, however.

Section 13(3) was amended in October 2008. P.L. 110-343 requires the Fed to report to the House Financial Services Committee and the Senate Banking, Housing, and Urban Affairs Committee on its justification for exercising Section 13(3), the terms of the assistance provided, and regular updates on the status of the loan.

H.R. 4173 requires the Fed to establish policies for lending under 13(3) that ensure that lending programs are broadly available for the purpose of providing liquidity to the financial system, and not used to assist specific firms or failing firms, and that emergency loans are sufficiently secured to protect taxpayers from losses. It also forbids "a program or facility that is structured to remove assets from the balance sheet of a single and specific company." It requires the Fed to seek approval from the Treasury Secretary before establishing a 13(3) program or facility.

For more information, see David Fettig, "The History of a Powerful Paragraph," Federal Reserve Bank of Minneapolis, *The Region*, June 2008; Howard Hackley, *Lending Functions of the Federal Reserve Banks: A History*, May 1973; Walker Todd, "FDICIA's Emergency Liquidity Provisions," *Federal Reserve Bank of Cleveland Review*, Third Quarter 1993, p. 16.

Primary Dealer Credit Facility

On March 16—a day too late to help Bear Stearns—the Fed announced the creation of the Primary Dealer Credit Facility (PDCF), a new direct lending program for primary dealers very similar to the discount window program for depository institutions. Loans are made through the PDCF on an overnight basis at the discount rate, limiting their riskiness. Acceptable collateral initially included Treasuries, government agency debt, and investment grade corporate, mortgage-backed, asset-backed, and municipal securities. On September 14, 2008, the Fed expanded acceptable collateral to include certain classes of equities. Many of the classes of eligible assets can and have fluctuated significantly in value. Fees will be charged to frequent users.

The program was announced as lasting six months, or longer if events warrant. The program is authorized under paragraph 3 of Section 13 of the Federal Reserve Act. The facility was subsequently extended, but allowed to expire at the end of January 2010.

Borrowing from the facility has been sporadic, with average daily borrowing outstanding above $10 billion in the first three months, and falling to zero in August 2008. Much of this initial borrowing was done by Bear Stearns, before its merger with J.P. Morgan Chase had been completed.[24] Loans outstanding through the PDCF peaked at $148 billion during the week of October 1, 2008. Since May 2009, outstanding loans through the PDCF have been zero, because of improvement in the financial system and because the largest investment banks converted into or were acquired by bank holding companies in late 2008, making them eligible to access other Fed lending facilities.

Although the program shares some characteristics with the discount window, the fact that the program was authorized under paragraph 3 of Section 13 of the Federal Reserve Act suggests that there is a fundamental difference between this program and the Fed's normal operations. The Fed is referred to as the nation's central bank because it is at the center of the banking system—providing reserves and credit, and acting as a regulator, clearinghouse, and lender of last resort to the banking system. The privileges for banks that come from belonging to the Federal Reserve system—access to Fed credit—come with the costs of regulation to ensure that banks do not take excessive risks. Although the primary dealers are subject to certain capital requirements, they are not necessarily part of the banking system, and do not fall under the same "safety and soundness" regulatory structure as banks.

Term Asset-Backed Securities Loan Facility

In November 2008, the Fed created the Term Asset-Backed Securities Loan Facility (TALF) in response to problems in the market for asset-backed securities (ABS). According to the Fed, "new issuance of ABS declined precipitously in September and came to a halt in October. At the same time, interest rate spreads on AAA-rated tranches of ABS soared to levels well outside the range of historical experience, reflecting unusually high risk premiums."[25]

Data support the Fed's view: issuance of non-mortgage asset backed securities fell from more than $175 billion per quarter from 2005 through the second quarter of 2007 to $5 billion in the fourth quarter of 2008, according to the Securities Industry and Financial Markets Association (SIFMA). The Fed fears that if lenders cannot securitize these types of loans, less credit will be extended to consumers, and eventually households will be forced to reduce consumption spending, which would exacerbate the economic downturn.

The TALF is intended to stimulate the issuance of new securities backed by pools of the following assets:

- auto loans or leases, including motorcycles, recreational vehicles (including boats), and commercial, rental, and government fleets;
- credit cards, consumer and corporate;
- student loans, private and government guaranteed;
- SBA-guaranteed small business loans;
- business equipment loans, including retail and leases;
- floorplan loans for inventories, including auto dealers;
- mortgage servicing advances;
- commercial mortgages; and
- insurance premium finance loans.

In May 2009, the Fed began accepting legacy commercial mortgage-backed securities (CMBSs). The Fed announced that the TALF may later be expanded to other classes of ABS. In March 2009, the Treasury announced that TALF may be expanded in the future to include private-label residential MBS, and collateralized debt and loan obligations. To date, most TALF loans have been backed by auto, credit card, and student loans.[26]

Rather than purchase ABS directly, the Fed will make non-recourse loans to any private U.S. company or subsidiary with a relationship with a primary dealer to purchase recently issued ABS receiving the highest credit rating, using the ABS as collateral. The minimum loan size will be $10 million. If the ABS lose value, the losses will be borne by the Fed and the Treasury (through the TARP program) instead of by the borrower—an unusual feature for a Fed lending facility. The Fed will lend less than the current value of the collateral, so the Fed would not bear losses on the loan until losses exceed the value of the "haircut" (different ABS receive different haircuts). The loans will have a term of up to three years for most types of assets (and up to five years for some types of assets), but can be renewed. Interest rates will be set at a markup over different maturities of LIBOR or the federal funds rate, depending on the type of loan and underlying collateral.

If the loans are not repaid, the Treasury will bear the first $20 billion in total losses on the underlying collateral, and the Fed will bear any additional losses. Treasury will receive interest in return for bearing this risk. The Treasury's losses will be financed through the Troubled Asset Relief Program (TARP), authorized by P.L. 110-343. In addition, TARP has already loaned the TALF program $100 million to finance initial administrative costs. It was originally proposed that ABS issuers would be subject to TARP's executive compensation restrictions. Subsequently, in a letter to the Special Inspector General for TARP, the General Counsel of the Treasury reasoned that the Fed, not the TALF loan recipients nor the ABS issuers, is the recipient of TARP funds, and so executive compensation restrictions do not apply to TALF.[27]

TALF has some similarities to TARP as it was originally envisioned, with the primary differences being that the Fed is lending to purchase rather than directly purchasing assets, and the assets backing the loans are mostly newly or recently issued as opposed to "troubled" existing assets. Because the Treasury's funds will finance loan losses rather than asset purchases, the $20 billion will support a much larger volume of assets than would be possible through direct purchase via TARP.

In March 2009, Treasury announced a new Public-Private Partnership Investment Program (PPIP) within TARP.[28] Under this program, private investors will receive matching capital from TARP to purchase up to $500 billion to $1 trillion of legacy loans and securities. These legacy securities are defined as existing ABS backed by mortgages and other assets. Treasury has announced that private partners will be able to use loans from TALF (and other sources) to finance the purchase of these legacy securities. In May 2009, the Fed began accepting legacy commercial mortgage-backed securities (CMBSs) as the first class of legacy securities eligible for TALF. PPIP has also turned out to be much smaller than envisioned—as of May 2010, Treasury had pledged a maximum of $30 billion for PPIP-Securities.

The Fed originally announced TALF as a $200 billion program, and Treasury expressed the desire to see it increased to $1 trillion. As it turns out, TALF lending grew slowly after inception, and peaked at $48 billion on March 17, 2010. The low lending totals seem less indicative of the unpopularity of TALF, and more indicative of the continued depressed state of the private securitization market. According to data from SIFMA, non-mortgage ABS issuance rose to $52 billion per quarter in the first two full quarters that TALF was in operation, but fell to $32 billion per quarter in the next two quarters—a far cry from issuance of more than $175 billion per quarter before the crisis. Nevertheless, a review of the program by the Federal Reserve Bank of Dallas argues that TALF should be credited with a decline in ABS spreads against Treasury bonds and a rise in ABS issuance.[29] The facility expired at the end of June 2010 for loans against newly issued CMBS and March 2010 for loans against other assets.

Intervention in the Commercial Paper Market

Many large firms routinely issue commercial paper, which is short-term debt purchased directly by investors that matures in less than 270 days, with an average maturity of 30 days. There are three broad categories of commercial paper issuers: financial firms, non-financial firms, and pass-through entities that issue paper backed by assets. The commercial paper issued directly by firms tends not to be backed by collateral, as these firms are viewed as large and creditworthy and the paper matures quickly.[30]

Individual investors are major purchasers of commercial paper through money market mutual funds and money market accounts. The Securities and Exchange Commission regulates the holdings of money market mutual funds, limiting their holdings to highly rated, short-term debt; thus, investors widely perceived money market mutual funds as safe and low risk. On September 16, 2008, a money market mutual fund called the Reserve Fund "broke the buck," meaning that the value of its shares had fallen below face value. This occurred because of losses it had taken on short-term debt issued by Lehman Brothers, which filed for bankruptcy on September 15. Money market investors had perceived "breaking the buck" to be highly unlikely, and its occurrence set off a run on money market funds, as investors simultaneously attempted to withdraw an estimated $250 billion of their investments—even from funds without exposure to Lehman.[31] This run greatly decreased the demand for new commercial paper. Firms rely on the ability to issue new debt to roll over maturing debt to meet their liquidity needs.

Fearing that disruption in the commercial paper markets could make overall problems in financial markets more severe, the Fed announced on September 19 that it would create the Asset-Backed Commercial Paper Money Market Mutual Fund Liquidity Facility (AMLF). This facility would make non-recourse loans to banks to purchase asset-backed commercial paper. Because the loans were non-recourse, the banks would have no further liability to repay any losses on the commercial paper collateralizing the loan. On October 1, 2008, daily loans outstanding peaked at $152 billion. The AMLF would soon be superseded in importance by the creation of the Commercial Paper Funding Facility, and lending fell to zero in October 2009.[32] The temporary facility was authorized under Section 13(3) of the Federal Reserve Act, and was subsequently extended until the end of January 2010.

Although the creation of the AMLF and the Treasury's temporary guarantee of money market mutual fund deposits had eased conditions in the commercial paper market, the market remained strained. For example, commercial paper outstanding fell from more than $2 trillion outstanding in August 2007 to $1.8 trillion on September 7, 2008, to $1.6 trillion on October 1, 2008. The yield on 30-day, AA-rated asset-backed commercial paper rose from 2.7% on September 8, 2008, to 5.5% on October 7, 2008.

Because of the importance of commercial paper for meeting firms' liquidity needs, the Fed decided to take stronger action to ensure that the market was not disrupted. On October 7, it announced the creation of the Commercial Paper Funding Facility (CPFF), a special purpose vehicle (SPV) that would borrow from the Fed to purchase all types of three-month, highly rated U.S. commercial paper, secured and unsecured, from issuers.[33] The Fed argued that the assurance that firms will be able to roll over commercial paper at the CPFF will encourage private investors to buy commercial paper again. The interest rate charged by the CPFF was set at the three month overnight index swap plus 1 percentage point for secured corporate debt, 2 percentage points for unsecured corporate debt, and 3 percentage points for asset-backed paper. The CPFF can buy as much commercial paper from any individual issuer as that issuer had outstanding in the year to date. Any losses borne by the CPFF would ultimately be borne by the Fed. The Fed has hired the private company PIMCO to manage the SPV's assets. The facility is authorized under Section 13(3) of the Federal Reserve Act, and was subsequently extended until the end of January 2010.

At its peak in January 2009, the CPFF held $351 billion of commercial paper, and has fallen steadily since. Goldman Sachs reports that conditions in commercial paper markets improved significantly after the creation of the CPFF (although they remained worse than before the crisis), and in January 2009, the CPFF was holding far more commercial paper than the total that had been issued since its inception.[34]

The CPFF is notable on several grounds. First, it is the first Fed standing facility in modern times with an ongoing commitment to purchase assets, as opposed to lending against assets. Technically, the Fed is lending against the assets of the SPV, but the SPV was created by the Fed and is controlled by the Fed.[35] Second, in the case of non-financial commercial paper, it is the first time in 50 years that the Fed is providing financial assistance to non-financial firms.[36] (In practice, the Fed has bought very little commercial paper issued by non-financial firms. [37]) Third, in the case of commercial paper that is not asset backed, it is unusual for the Fed (through the SPV) to purchase uncollateralized debt. Indeed, the Federal Reserve Act would seem to rule out the direct purchase of uncollateralized debt.

On October 21, 2008, the Fed announced the creation of the Money Market Investor Funding Facility (MMIFF), and pledged to lend it up to $540 billion. The MMIFF will lend to private sector SPVs that invest in commercial paper issued by highly rated financial institutions. Each SPV will be owned by a group of financial firms and can only purchase commercial paper issued by that group. These SPVs can purchase commercial paper from money market mutual funds and similar entities facing redemption requests to help avoid runs such as the run on the Reserve Fund. The facility expired at the end of October 2009 without ever being used. The Fed's director of the Division of Monetary Affairs reported that money market funds were unwilling to use it because "investors would recognize that leverage would ... intensify their incentive to run."[38]

Mortgage-Backed Securities Purchase Program and Purchase of GSE Obligations

In July 2008, the stock prices of Fannie Mae and Freddie Mac, the housing GSEs, came under increasing pressure, leading to fears that they would be unable to roll over debt and become illiquid. On July 13, 2008, the Fed authorized lending to the housing GSEs, but this authority was not used at that point. On September 7, 2009, Treasury placed the two housing GSEs into conservatorship.[39] On September 19, 2008, the Fed announced that it would purchase debt obligations of Fannie Mae, Freddie Mac, and the Federal Home Loan Banks through open market operations.[40]

On November 25, 2008, the Fed announced it would purchase up to $100 billion of direct obligations (e.g., bonds) issued by these institutions and up to $500 billion of MBS guaranteed by Fannie Mae, Freddie Mac, and Ginnie Mae, a government agency. GSE obligations will be purchased through auctions and MBS will be purchased on the Fed's behalf by private investment managers. Adjustable rate MBS, collateralized mortgage obligations (CMOs), real estate mortgage investment conduits (REMICs), and mortgage derivatives would not be eligible for purchase under the program. Assets purchased under these programs will be held passively and long-term. On March 18, 2009 the Fed announced an increase in the purchase commitment of up to $1.25 trillion in MBS and $200 billion of GSE obligations. In September 2009, the Fed announced that it would complete these purchases by the end of the first quarter of 2010. In November 2009, the Fed announced that it would purchase only $175 billion of Agency debt securities due to limited availability.

The Fed argued that these programs would "reduce the cost and increase the availability of credit for the purchase of houses."[41] Support to mortgage markets through these programs can be seen as indirect and selective, however. The Fed is not providing or purchasing mortgages directly, nor is it purchasing newly issued MBS. By purchasing existing MBS from the secondary market, the price should rise, and that may induce more MBS to be issued. If more MBS are issued, then the increased availability of credit to mortgage markets would be expected to cause mortgage rates to fall. Further, the Fed is accepting MBS issued by GSEs but not by private firms, even though the GSEs have issued more MBS in 2008 than before the crisis started, while private-label issuance has dried up almost entirely, according to data from the Securities Industry and Financial Markets Association. Further, overall mortgage rates have been low during the crisis, but access has been limited to highly qualified lenders. Increasing the demand for GSE-issued MBS and GSE debt would be expected to primarily reduce already low mortgage rates, and increase borrower access only indirectly, at best. Mortgage rates fell noticeably after the Fed announced that the programs had begun, although the amounts of securities purchased by the Fed at that point were small. Subsequently, mortgage rates rose despite the Fed's purchases, presumably because of the economy's improvement. One concern is that mortgage rates could rise after the Fed's purchases are complete, and the housing market will not have recovered by then.

These programs did not require the use of Section 13(3) emergency authority. Transactions involving agency debt are authorized under Section 13(13) and 14b of the Federal Reserve Act. The Fed's programs are similar to two Treasury programs, the GSE MBS Purchase Program and the GSE Credit Facility, already in place. Since the Treasury programs were authorized to provide the GSEs with unlimited financial assistance through the end of 2009, it is not clear why the Fed felt that the Treasury programs needed to be supplemented.[42]

Swap Lines with Foreign Central Banks

In December 2007, the Fed announced the creation of temporary reciprocal currency agreements, known as swap lines, with the European Central Bank and the Swiss central bank.[43] These agreements let the Fed swap dollars for euros or Swiss francs for a fixed period of time. Since September 2008, the Fed has extended similar swap lines to central banks in several other countries. To date, most of the swaps outstanding have been with the European Central Bank and Bank of Japan.[44] In October 2008, it made the swap lines with certain countries unlimited in size. Interest is paid to the Fed on a swap outstanding at the rate the foreign central bank charges to its dollar borrowers. The temporary swaps are repaid at the exchange rate at the time of the original swap, meaning that there is no downside risk for the Fed if the dollar appreciates in the meantime (although the Fed also does not enjoy upside gain if the dollar depreciates). The swap lines are currently authorized through the end of January 2010. Except in the unlikely event that the borrowing country's currency becomes unconvertible in foreign exchange markets, there is no credit risk involved for the Fed. Swaps outstanding peaked at $583 billion in December 2008, and have fallen steadily since.

The swap lines are intended to provide liquidity to banks in non-domestic denominations. For example, many European banks have borrowed in dollars to finance dollar-denominated transactions, such as the purchase of U.S. assets. Normally, foreign banks could finance their dollar-denominated borrowing through the private inter-bank lending market. As banks have become reluctant to lend to each other through this market, central banks at home and abroad have taken a much larger role in providing banks with liquidity directly. But normally banks can only borrow from their home central bank, and central banks can only provide liquidity in their own currency. The swap lines allow foreign central banks to provide needed liquidity in dollars. As such, the swap lines directly benefit foreign borrowers who need access to dollars. But the swap lines indirectly benefit the United States by promoting the use of the dollar as the "reserve" currency, which results in more seigniorage (earnings from currency) for the United States, as well as intangible benefits. Initially, the swap lines were designed to allow foreign central banks to U.S. dollars. In April 2009, the swap lines were modified so that the Fed could access foreign currency to provide to its banks as well; to date, the Fed has not accessed foreign currency through these lines.

The swap lines were ended in February 2010, but reopened with five countries in May 2010 in response to the crisis in Greece.[45] To date, their use in 2010 was much more limited than in 2008 to 2009.

Payment of Interest on Bank Reserves

Banks hold some assets in the form of cash reserves stored in their vaults or in accounts at the Fed to meet daily cash-flow needs and required ratios imposed by the Fed. At times before the federal funds target was reduced to zero in December 2008, the Fed faced conflicting goals—it sought to ensure that banks have enough reserves to remain liquid, but it also sought to maintain its target for the federal funds rate to meet its economic goals. The federal funds rate is the market rate in the private market where a bank with excess reserves lends them overnight to other banks. At times, ensuring that all banks have adequate reserves has resulted in an overall level of reserves in the market that has pushed the federal funds rate below its target. In other words, the only way for the Fed to make sure that each bank has enough reserves has been to oversupply the banking system as a whole with liquidity at the given federal funds target.

To avoid this problem, Congress authorized the Fed to pay interest on bank reserves in the Emergency Economic Stabilization Act of 2008 (H.R. 1424/P.L. 110-343).[46] By setting an interest rate on bank reserves close to the federal funds rate, the Fed would in effect place a floor on the rate. In theory, the federal funds rate would not fall below the interest rate on reserves because banks would rather hold excess reserves to earn interest than lend them out to other banks at a lower interest rate.[47] Paying interest on reserves may also encourage banks to hold more reserves overall, which may somewhat reduce the likelihood that banks will have liquidity problems in the future.

Paying interest on reserves does not encourage banks to increase overall lending to firms and households, however, because it increases the attractiveness of holding reserves. Thus, it is not a policy that stimulates the economy, at least in any direct sense; on the contrary, it prevents the increase in liquidity to banks from stimulating the economy by preventing the federal funds rate from falling.

The interest rate on excess reserves was initially set at 0.75 percentage points less than the federal funds rate. In the short term, paying interest on reserves did not succeed in placing a floor under the federal funds target. Immediately after the Fed began paying interest, the federal funds rate was still falling below the target, and some days was even below the interest rate on reserves. In response, the Fed subsequently reduced the spread between the interest rate on reserves and the federal funds rate, but the actual federal funds rate continued to fall below the target rate.[48] When the Fed reduced the federal funds rate target to a range of 0% to 0.25% in December 2008, it set the interest rate paid on reserves to 0.25%, the high end of the target range. At that point, paying interest on reserves could no longer place a floor under the federal funds rate, the stated rationale for its authorization.

P.L. 110-343 gave the Fed permanent authority to pay interest on reserves. Once financial conditions return to normal, the liquidity benefits from paying interest will be less important (since banks will again be able to meet reserve needs through the federal funds market), and the primary remaining benefit would be a reduction in the volatility of the federal funds rate. The Fed previously intervened in the federal funds market on a daily basis to keep the market rate close to the target, sometimes unsuccessfully. The volatility partly resulted from banks devoting resources to activities that minimize reserves, such as "sweep accounts."

Paying interest on reserves reduces the Fed's profits, and thus reduces its remittances to the Treasury, thereby increasing the budget deficit, all else equal. It can be viewed as a transfer from the federal government to the banks, although in the long run, competition makes it likely that the banks will pass on the benefit to depositors in the form of higher interest paid on deposits. From Congress's perspective, the benefit of a less volatile target rate and less resources spent minimizing reserves would have to be weighed against the lost federal revenue, over time. The decision to pay interest on required, as well as excess, reserves also increases the cost of the policy without any additional benefit to liquidity or reduced volatility (because banks must keep required reserves even if no incentive is offered).

The growth in the Fed's balance sheet has raised concerns about the future implications for inflation. The Fed has argued that paying interest on reserves can help prevent its balance sheet growth from becoming inflationary.[49] It approved "term deposits" of up to six months for bank reserves in April 2010. The interest rate paid by term deposits will be determined by auction.

ASSISTANCE TO INDIVIDUAL FINANCIAL INSTITUTIONS

Over the course of the year, several financial firms that were deemed "too big to fail" received financial assistance from the Fed in the form of loans, troubled asset purchases, and asset guarantees. This assistance went beyond its traditional role of acting as a lender of last resort by providing loans to illiquid but solvent firms.[50] In a joint announcement in March 2009, the Treasury and Fed stated a desire in the long run to transfer assets acquired by the Fed (via the Maiden Lane LLCs) from Bear Stearns and the American International Group (AIG) to the Treasury, but to date have not taken any steps to do so.[51] H.R. 4173 alters Section 13(3) authority in an attempt to prevent assistance to individual firms in the future.

The Fed's Role in the JPMorgan Chase Acquisition of Bear Stearns

The investment bank Bear Stearns came under severe liquidity pressures in early March 2008, in what many observers have coined a non-bank run.[52] On Friday, March 14, 2008, JPMorgan Chase announced that, in conjunction with the Federal Reserve, it had agreed to provide secured funding to Bear Stearns, as necessary. Through its discount window, the Fed agreed to provide $13 billion of back-to-back financing to Bear Stearns via JPMorgan Chase. It was a non-recourse loan, meaning that the Fed had no general claim against JPMorgan Chase in the event that the loan was not repaid and the outstanding balance exceeded the value of the collateral. Bear Stearns could not access the discount window directly because, at that point, only member banks could borrow directly from the Fed. This loan was superseded by the events of March 16, and the loan was repaid in full on March 17, 2008.

On Sunday, March 16, after negotiations between the two companies, the Fed and the Treasury, JPMorgan Chase agreed to acquire Bear Stearns. The Fed agreed to purchase up to $30 billion of Bear Stearns' assets through Maiden Lane I, a new Limited Liability Corporation (LLC) based in Delaware that it created and controls. After the merger was completed, the loan was finalized on June 26, 2008. Two loans were made to the LLC: the Fed lent the LLC $28.82 billion, and JPMorgan Chase made a subordinate loan to the LLC worth $1.15 billion, based on assets initially valued at $29.97 billion.[53] The Fed's loan will be made at an interest rate set equal to the discount rate (2.5% when the terms were announced, but fluctuating over time) for a term of 10 years, renewable by the Fed.[54] JPMorgan Chase's loan will have an interest rate 4.5 percentage points above the discount rate.

Using the proceeds from that loan, the LLC purchased assets from Bear Stearns worth $29.97 billion at marked to market prices by Bear Stearns on March 14, 2008. On its website, the New York Fed gives information on the current fair market value of the assets by type of asset, credit rating of the assets, and geographical location of the underlying assets. At the end of 2008, 44% of the portfolio consisted of agency collateralized mortgage obligations (CMOs), 6% was non-agency CMOs, 18% was commercial loans, 3% was residential loans, 8% was swap contracts, 7% was TBA commitments, and 8% was cash or cash equivalents. More than half of the non-agency CMOs had a credit rating of AAA; about one-fifth had a junk rating. (Agency CMOs are guaranteed by the GSE that issued them, and the Treasury has pledged to maintain the GSE's solvency.)

The CEO of JPMorgan Chase testified that JPMorgan Chase "kept the riskier and more complex securities in the Bear Stearns portfolio.... We did not cherry pick the assets in the collateral pool (for the LLC)."[55] These assets are owned by the LLC, which will eventually liquidate them to pay back the principal and interest owed to the Fed and JPMorgan Chase. The LLC's assets (purchased from Bear Stearns) are the collateral backing the loans from the Fed and JPMorgan Chase. A private company, BlackRock Financial Management, has been hired to manage the portfolio. Neither Bear Stearns nor JPMorgan Chase owes the Fed any principal or interest, nor are they liable if the LLC is unable to pay back the money the Fed lent it. The New York Fed explained that the LLC was created to "ease administration of the portfolio and will remove constraints on the money manager that might arise from retaining the assets on the books of Bear Stearns."[56] JPMorgan Chase and Bear Stearns did not receive the $28.82 billion from the LLC until the merger was completed.[57]

It was announced that the Fed is planning to begin liquidating the assets after two years. The assets will be sold off gradually, "to minimize disruption to financial markets and maximize recovery value."[58] As the assets are liquidated, interest will continue to accrue on the remaining amount of the loan outstanding. Thus, in order for the principal and interest to be paid off, the assets will need to appreciate enough or generate enough income so that the rate of return on the assets exceeds the weighted interest rate on the loans (plus the operating costs of the LLC). **Table 1** shows how the funds raised through the liquidation will be used. Any difference between the proceeds and the amount of the loans is profit or loss for the Fed, not JPMorgan Chase. Because JPMorgan Chase's $1.15 billion loan was subordinate to the Fed's $28.82 billion loan, if there are losses on the total assets, the first $1.15 billion of losses will be borne, in effect, by JPMorgan Chase, however. The interest on the loan will be repaid out of the asset sales, not by JPMorgan Chase. At the end of 2009, the value of the assets had already been written down by over $3.5 billion, exceeding the maximum losses borne by JPMorgan Chase.[59]

The CEO of JPMorgan Chase testified that "we *could* not and *would* not have assumed the substantial risks of acquiring Bear Stearns without the $30 billion facility provided by the Fed" (emphasis in original).[60] The primary risk was presumably that the value of mortgage-related assets would continue to decline. Had the transaction been crafted as a typical discount window loan directly to JPMorgan Chase, JPMorgan Chase would have been required to pay back the principal and interest, and it (rather than the Fed) would have borne the full risk of any depreciation in value of Bear Stearns' assets.

The Fed's statutory authority for its role in both Bear Stearns transactions comes from paragraph 3 of Section 13 of the Federal Reserve Act. In his testimony, Timothy Geithner, New York Fed president at the time, stated that the Fed did not have authority to acquire an equity interest in Bear Stearns or JPMorgan Chase.[61] Yet the LLC controlled by the Fed acquired assets from Bear Stearns, and the profits or losses from that acquisition will ultimately accrue to the Fed. It is unclear why the Fed decided to create and lend to a LLC to complete the transaction, rather than engaging in the transaction directly. Although the Fed did not buy Bear Stearns' assets directly, there are certainly important policy questions raised by the Fed's creation and financing of an LLC in order to buy Bear Stearns' assets. Typically, the Fed lends money to institutions and receives collateral in return to reduce the risk of suffering a loss. When the loan is repaid, the collateral is returned to the institution. In this case, the Fed made a loan, but to a LLC they created and controlled, not to a financial institution. From the perspective of JPMorgan Chase or Bear Stearns, the transaction was a sale (to the LLC), not a loan, regardless of whether the Fed or the LLC was the principal.

Table 1. Use of Funds Raised by Liquidation of Bear Stearns Assets

Payments from the liquidation will be made in the following order:
(1) operating expenses of the limited liability corporation
(2) $29 billion principal owed to the Federal Reserve
(3) interest due to the Federal Reserve on the $29 billion loan
(4) $1 billion principal owed to JPMorgan Chase
(5) interest due to JPMorgan Chase on $1 billion subordinated note
(6) non-operating expenses of the limited liability corporation
(7) remaining funds accrue to Federal Reserve

Source: Federal Reserve Bank of New York.

Note: Each category must be fully paid before proceeding to the next category.

Assistance to American International Group (AIG)[62]

Initial Loan

On September 16, 2008, the Fed announced, after consultation with the Treasury Department, that it would lend up to $85 billion to the financial institution American International Group. AIG had experienced a significant decline in its stock price and was facing immediate demands for $14 billion to $15 billion in collateral payments due to recent downgrades by credit rating agencies, according to press reports.[63] The Fed and Treasury feared that AIG was also "too big to fail" because of the potential for widespread disruption to financial markets that would result.

The Fed announced that AIG could borrow up to $85 billion from the Fed over the next two years. On September 18, the Fed announced that it had initially lent $28 billion to AIG.[64] The interest rate on the funds drawn is 8.5 percentage points above the London Interbank Offered Rate (LIBOR), a rate that banks charge to lend to each other. A lower interest rate is charged on any funds that it is does not draw from the facility. In return, the government agreed to receive warrants that, if exercised, would give the government a 79.9% ownership stake in AIG. The Fed named three independent trustees to oversee the firm for the duration of the loan.

The lending facility is backed by the assets of AIG's non-regulated subsidiaries (but not the assets of its insurance company). In other words, the Fed can seize AIG's assets if the firm fails to honor the terms of the loan. This reduces the risk that the Fed (and ultimately, taxpayers) will suffer a loss. The risk still remains that if AIG turned out to be insolvent, its assets would be insufficient to cover the amount it had borrowed from the Fed. Since AIG has been identified as too big to fail, it is unclear how its assets could be seized in the event of non-payment without precipitating failure.

Second Loan

On October 8, 2008, the Fed announced that it was expanding its assistance to AIG and swapping cash for up to $37.8 billion of AIG's investment-grade, fixed-income securities. These securities, belonging to AIG's insurance subsidiaries, had been previously lent out and unavailable as collateral at the time of the original agreement. It has been reported that as

AIG's loans matured, AIG realized losses on investments it had made with the collateral and some counterparties stopped participating in the lending program.[65] As a result, AIG needed liquidity from the Fed to cover these losses and counterparty withdrawals.

Although this assistance resembles a typical collateralized loan (the Fed receives assets as collateral, and the borrower receives cash), the Fed characterized the agreement as a loan of securities from AIG to the Fed in exchange for cash collateral. It appears the arrangement was structured this way because New York insurance law prevents AIG from using the securities as collateral in a loan.[66]

Revision to Agreement on November 10, 2008

On November 10, 2008, the Federal Reserve and the U.S. Treasury announced a restructuring of the federal intervention to support AIG. As evidenced by the additional borrowing after the September 16 loan, AIG had continued to see cash flow out of the company, particularly to post collateral for the credit default swaps that were arguably the primary cause of the financial problems in the company. The revised agreement points to the tension between making the terms of the assistance undesirable enough to deter other firms from seeking government assistance in the future, compared to making the terms of assistance so punitive that it exacerbates the financial problems of the recipient firm. It also points to the fact that once a firm has been identified as too big to fail, government assistance to the firm can become open-ended, as the original amounts offered were quickly revised upward.

The November 10 restructuring eased the payment terms for AIG and had three primary parts: (1) a $40 billion direct capital injection, (2) restructuring of the $85 billion loan, and (3) a $52.5 billion purchase of troubled assets.

Loan Restructuring

The initial $85 billion loan facility from the Federal Reserve was reduced to $60 billion, for a time period extended to five years, and the financial terms are eased considerably. Specifically, the interest rate on the amount outstanding is reduced by 5.5 percentage points (to Libor plus 3%) and the fee on undrawn funds is reduced by 7.75 percentage points (to 0.75%).

Purchase of Troubled Assets

While P.L. 110-343 provided for the government purchase of troubled assets, the purchases related to AIG are being done by LLCs created and controlled by the Federal Reserve. This structure is similar to that created by the Federal Reserve to facilitate the purchase of Bear Stearns by JPMorgan Chase in March 2008. There are two LLCs set up for AIG—one for residential mortgage-backed securities (RMBS) and one for collateralized debt obligations (CDO).

The agreement called for the RMBS LLC (Maiden Lane II) to be lent up to $22.5 billion by the Federal Reserve and $1 billion from AIG to purchase RMBS from AIG's securities lending portfolio. The AIG loan is subordinated and AIG will bear the first $1 billion in losses should there be future losses on these securities. AIG and the Federal Reserve will "share" in any future gains, with five-sixths of future profits accruing to the Fed and one-sixth accruing to AIG. As of March 2009, the assets had lost nearly $3 billion in value, more than AIG's total loss exposure. The previous $37.8 billion loan securities lending loan facility is to be repaid and terminated with the proceeds from this LLC plus additional AIG funds if necessary. At the end of 2008, about half of the RMBS purchased were backed by subprime mortgages, and about one quarter were backed by Alt-A mortgages. Thirteen percent of the portfolio's holdings had a credit rating of AAA and 65% had a junk rating. At the end of 2009, the Maiden Lane II assets had lost $1.1 billion in value, slightly exceeding the AIG's maximum loss sharing.

The agreement called for the CDO LLC (Maiden Lane III) to be lent up to $30 billion from the Federal Reserve and $5 billion from AIG to purchase CDOs on which AIG has written credit default swaps. The $5 billion loan from AIG is subordinated and AIG will bear the first $5 billion in future losses on these securities. As of March 2009, the assets had lost nearly $8.5 billion in value, more than AIG's total loss exposure. AIG and the Federal Reserve will "share" in any future gains, with five-sixths of future profits accruing to the Fed and one-sixth accruing to AIG. The Federal Reserve also indicates that the credit default swaps will be unwound at the same time that the CDOs are purchased. Many credit default swaps, however, are purchased by entities not holding the underlying CDOs; it is unclear how, or if, such credit default swaps written by AIG will be addressed. At the end of March 2009, 16% of the portfolio's holdings had a credit rating of AAA, and 72% had a junk rating. At the end of 2009, the Maiden Lane III assets had lost $0.9 billion in value, resulting in no losses to date for the Fed.

Direct Capital Injection

Through the TARP, the Treasury purchased $40 billion in preferred shares of AIG. In addition to $40 billion in preferred shares, the Treasury also receives warrants for common shares equal to 2% of the outstanding AIG shares. AIG was the first announced non-bank to receive TARP funds. The $40 billion in preferred AIG shares now held by the Treasury are slated to pay a 10% dividend per annum, accrued quarterly.[67] Participation in TARP triggers restrictions on executive pay as required by Congress, including a restriction on "golden parachutes" and a requirement for clawbacks on previously provided bonuses in the case of accounting irregularities. According to the November 10, 2008, AIG filings with the Securities and Exchange Commission, the amount of shares held in trust for the benefit of the U.S. Treasury will be reduced by the shares and warrants purchased under TARP, so the total equity interest currently held by the U.S. government equals 77.9% plus warrants to purchase another 2%. The warrants equal to 77.9% of AIG equity were exercised and transferred to the government on March 4, 2009.

Revision to Agreement on March 2, 2009

On March 2, 2009, the Treasury and Fed announced another revision of the financial assistance to AIG. On the same day, AIG announced a loss of more than $60 billion in the fourth quarter of 2008. In response to the poor results and ongoing financial turmoil, the ratings agencies were reportedly considering further downgrading AIG, which would most likely have resulted in further significant cash demands due to collateral calls.[68] According to the Treasury, AIG "continues to face significant challenges, driven by the rapid deterioration in certain financial markets in the last two months of the year and continued turbulence in the markets generally." The revised assistance is intended to "enhance the company's capital and liquidity in order to facilitate the orderly completion of the company's global divestiture program."[69]

The revised assistance includes the following:

- Exchange of the existing $40 billion in preferred shares purchased through the TARP program for preferred shares that "more closely resemble common equity," thus improving AIG's financial position. Dividends paid on these new shares will remain at 10%, but will be non-cumulative and only be paid as declared by AIG's board of directors. Should dividends not be paid for four consecutive quarters, the government has the right to appoint at least two new directors to the board.
- Commitment of up to $30 billion in additional preferred share purchases from TARP. As of October 2009, AIG had issued $3.2 billion of these shares.[70]
- Reduction of interest rate on the existing Fed loan facility by removing the current floor of 3.5% over the LIBOR portion of the rate. The rate will now simply be three month LIBOR plus 3%, which is approximately 4.25%.
- Limit on Fed revolving credit facility will be reduced from $60 billion to $25 billion.
- Up to $33.5 billion of the approximately $38 billion outstanding on the Fed credit facility will be repaid by asset transfers from AIG to the Fed. Specifically, (1) $8.5 billion in ongoing life insurance cash flows will be securitized by AIG and transferred to the Fed; and (2) $25 billion in preferred interests in two of AIG's large life insurance subsidiaries will be issued to the Fed. The transfer of the preferred interest in the life insurance subsidiaries was finalized in December 2009. This effectively transfers a majority stake in these companies to the Fed, but the companies will still be managed by AIG.

Assistance through the end of 2009 is summarized in **Table 2**. In addition to the new assistance, AIG announced that it was forming a new holding company to include its primary property/casualty insurance subsidiaries. Since the first assistance in September 2008, AIG has sought to sell subsidiaries, including those whose equity has been transferred to the Fed, to repay the loans and reduce its holdings to a core property/casualty business. Such sales have been difficult during the ongoing financial turmoil. By effectively transferring the two life insurance subsidiaries to the Fed and gathering property casualty subsidiaries in a new holding company, AIG is arguably progressing toward this goal.

CBO estimates that most of the expected government losses from assistance to AIG will accrue to TARP, in part because those claims are junior to the Fed's. In addition, CBO did not expect losses from the Maiden Lane asset purchases at the time of purchase because the Fed reported the assets were bought at current market value. It is unclear why it was necessary for the Fed to acquire the assets if they could have been sold at the same price in the private market, however.

Who Benefits from Assistance to AIG?

While billions of dollars in government assistance have gone to AIG, in many cases, it can be argued that AIG has essentially acted as an intermediary for this assistance. In short order after drawing on government assistance, substantial funds have flowed out of AIG to entities on the other side of AIG's financial transactions, such as securities lending or credit default swaps. If AIG had been allowed to fail and had entered bankruptcy, as was the case with Lehman Brothers, then these counterparties in many cases would have been treated as unsecured creditors and seen their claims reduced.

Seen from this view, the true beneficiaries of the billions in federal assistance that have flowed to AIG has not been AIG itself, but these counterparties. On March 15, 2009, AIG released information detailing the counterparties to many of its transactions.[71] The released information detailed $52.0 billion of direct support to AIG that went to AIGFP related transactions, $29.6 billion in Maiden Lane III CDS-related transactions, and $43.7 billion in payments to securities lending counterparties.

Legal Authority

All Fed assistance to AIG is authorized under Section 13(3) of the Federal Reserve Act, the same emergency authorization used for Bear Stearns. This authorization was needed because the Fed cannot normally lend to a financial firm that is neither primarily a depository institution (although it owns a small thrift) nor a primary dealer.

Guarantee of Citigroup's Assets

Similar to Bear Stearns and AIG, Citigroup faced a sudden drop in its stock price in late 2008. Its stock price fell from $23 per share on October 1, 2008, to $3.77 on November 21, 2008, amidst investor concern about its losses. Stepping in before a potential run began, the Federal Reserve and federal government announced on November 23 that they would purchase an additional $20 billion of Citigroup preferred shares through TARP and guarantee a pool of up to $306 billion of Citigroup's assets. (The assets were valued at $301 billion when the agreement was finalized on January 16, 2009.) Citigroup announced that the assets guaranteed include mortgages, consumer loans, corporate loans, asset backed securities, and unfunded lending commitments.[72] The guarantee was to be in place for 10 years for residential assets and five years for non-residential assets. Citigroup would exclusively bear up to the first $29 billion of losses on the pool. Any additional losses would be split between Citigroup and the government, with Citigroup bearing 10% of the losses and the government bearing 90%. The first $5 billion of any government losses would be borne by the Treasury using TARP funds; the next $10 billion would be borne by the FDIC; any further losses would be borne by the Fed through a non-recourse loan. Citigroup will pay the federal government a fee for the guarantee in the form of $7 billion in preferred stock with an 8% dividend rate and warrants to purchase common stock that were worth $2.7 billion at the time of the agreement. The assets will remain on Citigroup's balance sheet, and Citigroup will receive the income stream generated by the assets and any future capital gains.

In December 2009, Citigroup and the Treasury reached an agreement to repay the outstanding $20 billion in preferred securities and to cancel the asset guarantee. As part of this agreement, Citigroup paid a termination fee of $50 million and Treasury agreed to cancel $1.8 billion worth of the trust preferred securities originally paid as a fee for the guarantee. While the asset guarantee was in place, no losses were claimed and no federal funds paid out.

Table 2. Summary of Outstanding Assistance to AIG

	Federal Government				Terms and Conditions			
Program	**Outstanding Amount End of CY2009**	**Outstanding Amount at Peak**	**Total Income CY2009**	**Expected Gain(+) /Loss(-)**	**Dividend/ Interest Rate**	**Warrants/ Equity Interests**	**Subsequent Conversion**	**Expiration Date**
Federal Reserve Loan to AIG	$22.2 billion loan	$87.3 billion loan (Oct. 29, 2008)	$4.0 billion	-$2 billion (CBO)	3 month LIBOR+3%[a]	warrants for 79.9% (later reduced to 77.9%) of common shares	Reduced balance by $25 billion in exchange for equity in life insurance subsi-diaries; $989 million provision for loan restructuring	September 2013
TARP Preferred Share Purchase	$45.3 billion preferred shares	$45.3 billion preferred shares	$0	-$36 billion (CBO); -$45.2 billion (Treasury)	10% (dividends paid at AIG's discretion)	warrants for 2% of common shares	$1.6 billion balance outstanding[b]	Preferred Shares outstanding until repaid. No new contracts/modifica-tions to program after Oct. 3, 2010.
Fed Loan for Troubled Asset Purchases	$34.5 billion in loans to purchase assets	$43.9 billion loans to pur-chase assets (Dec. 31, 2008)	$769 million	$0	LIBOR+1%[a]	none	n/a	Securities held long- term.
Commercial Paper Funding Facility	$0	$16.7 billion (Dec 31, 2008)	n/a	$0	Overnight index swap (OIS) rate+1%; OIS+3%	none	n/a	February 2010

Source: December 2009 TARP 105(a) Report; Federal Reserve, Monthly Report on Credit and Liquidity Programs and the Balance Sheet, January 2009; Congressional Budget Office, *The Budgetary Impact of Subsidy Costs of the Federal Reserve's Actions During the Financial Crisis*, May 2010; Congressional Budget Office, *Report on the Troubled Asset Relief Program*, March 2010; U.S. Treasury, *Summary Tables of Trouble Asset Relief Program (TARP) Investments as of March 31, 2010*.

a. LIBOR = London Inter-bank Offered Rate.

b. In return for conversion of shares paying a mandatory dividend to shares paying an optional dividend, AIG took on an obligation of $1.6 billion due to the outstanding dividend balance.

In the cases of Bear Stearns and AIG, management was replaced and shareholders equity was diluted to limit moral hazard problems associated with receiving government assistance.[73] Similar steps were not taken in the case of Citigroup.

Guarantee of Bank of America's Assets

On January 16, 2009, the federal government and the Federal Reserve announced that that they would purchase an additional $20 billion of Bank of America preferred shares through TARP and guarantee a pool of up to $37 billion of Bank of America's assets and derivatives with maximum potential future losses of up to $81 billion. The guarantee would remain in place for 10 years for residential mortgage-related assets and five years for all other assets. Bank of America will bear up to the first $10 billion of losses on the assets, with any subsequent losses split 90% by the government and 10% by Bank of America. The government's share of the next $10 billion of losses will be borne jointly by the FDIC and the Treasury, and any further losses will be borne by the Fed. It was announced that the assets being guaranteed were largely acquired during Bank of America's acquisition of Merrill Lynch. Bank of America will pay the federal government a fee for the guarantee in the form of $4 billion in preferred stock with an 8% dividend rate and warrants to purchase common stock worth $2.4 billion at the time of the agreement. As part of the agreement, Bank of America was prohibited from paying dividends on common stock for three years.

The assets will remain on Bank of America's balance sheet, and Bank of America will receive the income stream generated by the assets and any future capital gains. Bank of America can further limit its cost and the benefit to the government by opting out of the guarantee early at its discretion.

In the cases of Bear Stearns and AIG, management was replaced and shareholders equity was diluted to limit moral hazard problems associated with receiving government assistance.[74] Similar steps were not taken in the case of Bank of America. On the other hand, the government has tried to encourage healthy financial firms to merge with troubled firms, and it may have felt that harsh terms on an agreement to guarantee assets that were in part acquired from Bank of America's takeover of Merrill Lynch would have discouraged future mergers. It has been reported that the asset guarantees to Bank of America were motivated by a desire to prevent them from withdrawing from their uncompleted merger agreement with Merrill Lynch.[75]

The agreement to guarantee Bank of America's assets was never finalized, and on September 22, 2009, it was announced that Bank of America would pay $425 million to exit the agreement. Although Bank of America never formally received government protection of its assets, an exit fee could be justified on the grounds that Bank of America benefited from the implicit support that the negotiations provided.

POLICY ISSUES

Cost to the Treasury

Unlike all other institutions, currency (Federal Reserve notes) is the Fed's primary liability. Along with its holdings of Treasury securities, its assets are the loans it makes (through the discount window and the new programs detailed above) and the private assets it buys directly or holds through LLCs (e.g., for AIG and the Bear Stearns takeover). It earns profits on its assets that are largely remitted to the Treasury. Its loans and asset purchases are financed by increasing its liabilities (Federal Reserve notes), and the financing does not necessarily result in any inherent cost for the Treasury. Indeed, if the loans are repaid, they would increase the profits of the Fed, which in turn would increase the Fed's remittances to the Treasury.[76] Even if the loans are not repaid, most are fully collateralized (usually over-collateralized), so the Fed would not suffer losses unless the collateral had lost value. In addition, most of its loans are made with recourse, which means that borrowers are still liable if the collateral loses value.

The Fed had net income of $38.8 billion and remitted $34.9 billion to the Treasury in 2008. Net income increased to $52.1 billion and remittances to the Treasury rose to $46.1 billion in 2009. In the past, most of the Fed's net income has derived from the interest on its Treasury securities holdings, not its loans. By the end of 2008, its loans and private assets holdings were much larger than its Treasury holdings (see **Table 4**). The earnings and any losses the Fed took on its loans would increase or reduce its net income, respectively. If loan losses caused an overall net loss, the Fed's capital (the excess of its assets compared with its liabilities) would be reduced. The Fed had capital equal to about $52 billion at end of 2009, half of which was paid-in capital of member banks and the other half of which was surplus. The Fed has not had an annual net operating loss since 1915. However, the Fed's balance sheet became more risky in 2008, due to the shift in composition of its assets from U.S. Treasuries to direct loans and private securities and due to the increase in its liabilities relative to its capital. For example, at the end of 2008, the Fed's capital would be depleted if its realized net losses were equal in value to 1.9% of its holdings of financial assets (U.S. Treasuries, loans, and other private securities).

Thus, any potential losses on loans to the Fed would not involve taxpayer dollars flowing to the Fed unless the losses exceeded the sum of its other earnings and its capital and the Treasury decided it did not want the Fed to operate as technically insolvent. However, even if the losses did not result in insolvency, any losses could result in a smaller remittance of earnings to the Treasury than would have occurred had the Fed not made the loans. Therefore, the ultimate cost to the government is the same whether loans to the financial sector are made through the Fed or the Treasury. The Fed has reported to Congress that it does not expect there to be losses on any of the actions it has undertaken under its emergency authorities (including the Maiden Lane LLCs, two of which had unrealized capital losses at the end of 2009), but it has not provided details as to how it reached that conclusion. Some analysts are concerned that a future increase in interest rates could result in losses on the Fed's asset holdings, but these losses would be realized only if the Fed were forced to sell those assets.[77]

To date, all of the Fed's lending programs have earned income for the Fed, except for Maiden Lanes I and II, whose assets have accrued unrealized capital losses.[78] In 2009, the

Fed's loan programs earned $5.5 billion, the Maiden Lane assets had fallen in value by a combined $2.3 billion, and the Fed's other assets had earned $48.8 billion, as seen in **Table 3**. (The Maiden Lane losses will not be realized until the assets are sold, and the Fed has stated that it intends to hold the assets long term.) In the aggregate, the Fed earned higher profits and increased its remittances to the Treasury.

The Fed could generate positive income from its programs but still operate those programs at a subsidy to the recipients. Subsidies would occur when the interest rates charged for loans or prices paid for assets are not high enough to fully compensate for the risks borne by the Fed in undertaking those transactions. In other words, the subsidy is equal to the difference between the price or interest rate the Fed received and what could have been received if the transaction had been made privately. CBO has estimated subsidies for each of the Fed's emergency programs, presented in **Table 3**.[79] In evaluating the program, that subsidy would need to be compared with the benefits to the broader economy from the program, which CBO does not attempt to do. CBO estimated that lending programs with high collateral requirements and done on a recourse basis (Term Auction Facility, repurchase agreements, central bank currency swaps, Primary Dealer Credit Facility, Term Securities Lending Facility) generated no subsidies. CBO also concluded that all asset purchases involved no subsidy, either because the purchases were made in the open market (e.g., purchases of Treasury and GSE-related securities) or because the Fed reported that purchases were made at market value (e.g., the Maiden Lane assets). The assumption that Maiden Lane assets were bought at prevailing market prices can be questioned because the rationale for the Fed's purchase was that these assets could not be sold in private markets at the time. CBO finds subsidies for loan facilities without recourse (the two commercial paper facilities and TALF) and for special assistance to systemically significant firms (AIG, Citigroup, and Bank of America). In total, CBO estimates that the Fed's emergency actions were done at a subsidy of $21 billion. This estimate would likely be smaller if re-estimated today, based on current information. For example, CBO finds a subsidy of $13 billion for TALF because TALF was expected to make loans of $200 billion; in reality, loans peaked at $48 billion. CBO also estimates subsidies on the asset guarantees to Citigroup and Bank of America, although those programs were ended with payments to the government and no payouts by the government.

Table 3. Estimated Subsidies and Earnings by Program (billions of Dollars)

Program/Transaction	Estimated Subsidy at Inception	2009 Earnings	2009 Capital Gains or Losses
Treasury Securities	0	22.9	0
GSE Debt/MBS	0	22.5	0.9
Central Bank Liquidity Swaps	Negative subsidy	2.2	0
Discount Window	0	0.2	n/a
Term Auction Facility	0	0.8	n/a
Primary Dealer Credit Facility	0	<0.1	n/a
TALF	13	0.4	n/a
Commercial Paper	4	4.3	4.7
Loan to AIG	2	4.0	n/a
Maiden Lane I (Bear Stearns)	0	1.3	-2.2

Table 3. (Continued)

Program/Transaction	Estimated Subsidy at Inception	2009 Earnings	2009 Capital Gains or Losses
Maiden Lane II (AIG)	0	0.4	-0.1
Maiden Lane III (AIG)	0	0.3	0
Citigroup asset guarantee	2	0.3	n/a
Bank of America asset guarantee	1	0.1	n/a
Total	21	52.1[a]	n/a

Source: Estimated subsidies from Congressional Budget Office, *The Budgetary Impact and Subsidy Costs of the Federal Reserve's Actions During the Financial* Crisis, May 2010. Earnings from Federal Reserve, *Monthly Report on Credit and Liquidity Programs and the Balance Sheet*, Tables 27-29, April 2010.

Notes: Maiden Lane capital gains or losses are those attributable to Fed, not overall. For Maiden Lanes, interest on loans from Fed are added back to earnings when Federal Reserve System's balance sheet is consolidated. CBO subsidies were calculated based on economic conditions and projections of program use at the time of inception. Negative subsidy for central bank liquidity swaps means that the Fed, according to CBO, offered the swaps on less favorable terms than foreign central banks could have received in the marketplace.

a. Net income.

Although the Fed has taken steps to minimize the risk that recent activities will result in losses, Members of Congress have raised the question of whether taxpayers should be exposed to additional fiscal risks without congressional approval, particularly because some of the Fed's actions have similarities to those authorized under TARP. H.R. 4173 requires the Fed to issue policies and procedures for emergency lending that, among other things,

- ensure that "the security for emergency loans is sufficient to protect taxpayers from losses" by assigning a lendable value to collateral that is "consistent with sound risk management practices;"[80] and
- prohibit lending to borrowers that are insolvent or establishing a lending program or facility for the purpose of helping a single and specific company to avoid bankruptcy.

How Much Can the Fed's Balance Sheet Expand? Will the Fed Run Out of Money?

As a result of the Fed's new facilities and activities, its balance sheet has increased significantly, from $874 billion on August 1, 2007, a date shortly before the financial system first experienced turmoil, to $2,312 billion at its peak on December 17, 2008, an increase of 165%. **Table 4** shows the increase in the balance sheet by category over that period. Since the size of the balance sheet peaked in December 2008, the overall size of the balance sheet has remained relatively steady, but there have been large changes in the composition of the balance sheet. For example, there has been a significant increase in the Fed's holdings of mortgage backed securities and GSE debt, and a significant decrease in lending to primary dealers, holdings of commercial paper, and swaps with central banks. The Fed also began lending through the TALF in March 2009.

When the Fed makes loans or purchases assets, the asset side of its balance sheet expands; this must be matched by an increase in its liabilities. As direct loans from the Fed multiplied, some observers questioned at what point the Fed's lending power will be exhausted. The Fed cannot "run out of money" to buy assets and extend loans because it controls its liabilities, the monetary base (federal reserve notes and bank reserves), through which it expands or contracts the amount of money outstanding. There are no statutory limits on the size of the money supply or currency outstanding and, thus, how much it can loan; the ultimate constraint on the Fed's willingness to expand the monetary base in order to expand its activities comes from the part of its congressional mandate requiring stable prices (i.e., a low and stable rate of price inflation.) If the Fed allows the money supply to grow too rapidly, then price inflation will become uncomfortably high (discussed in the section below on "Stagflation?").

Sterilization of Lending before September 2008

Earlier in the financial crisis, the Fed was concerned about inflation rising. For example, in the 12 months ending in August 2008, inflation (as measured by the consumer price index) had risen to 5.4%—significantly higher than the Fed's self-identified "comfort zone." To address that concern, the Fed initially sought to keep its balance sheet from growing in order to offset the effects of its activities on the money supply. One way to keep its balance sheet from growing would be by reducing its other assets. For example, it could "sterilize" its new loans or asset purchases through contractionary open market operations, namely, the sale of Treasury securities. In practice, before September 2008, the Fed kept the monetary base relatively constant by selling enough Treasury securities to offset the additional loans it made. (When the Fed sells Treasury securities, it removes the money it receives in the sale from circulation.) Thus, as loans outstanding rose, the Fed's holdings of Treasury securities initially declined, by $340 billion through December 17, 2008. In September 2007, 88% of its assets were Treasury securities held outright and less than 1% were loans to the financial system. On December 17, 2008, 28% of its assets were Treasury securities, 32% were loans, 17% were private securities (mostly commercial paper), and 25% were currency swaps with foreign central banks.

If sterilization through the sale of Treasury securities had continued, the Fed would eventually have held too few Treasury securities to be able to conduct open market operations.[81] As seen in **Table 4**, the overall increase in the Fed's balance sheet at its peak was $1.4 trillion, more than the Treasury securities it held before the crisis started ($816 billion) or in September 2008 ($475 billion).

The Treasury announced the Supplementary Financing Program on September 17, 2008 as an alternative method for the Fed to increase its assistance to the financial sector without increasing the amount of money in circulation.[82] Under this program, the Treasury has temporarily auctioned more new securities than it needs to finance government operations and deposited the proceeds at the Fed. (The increase in the money supply does not affect inflation because the money received by the Treasury is held at the Fed and not allowed to circulate in the economy.) Ultimately, the program will not affect the Treasury's fiscal position, however, because it will increase the profits of the Fed, which are then remitted to the Treasury. By December 17, 2008, the Treasury had borrowed and increased its deposits at the Fed by $475 billion. From January to September 2009, Treasury deposits were between $200 billion and $300 billion, and were no longer large enough to offset the growth in the asset side of the

Fed's balance sheet. Congress authorized this borrowing only indirectly by raising the statutory debt limit, in P.L. 110-343 and other subsequent legislation. In late 2009, Treasury withdrew its supplementary deposits at the Fed in order to finance government spending as the debt approached the statutory limit. Once the debt limit was increased, the Treasury increased its deposits back to around $200 billion.

The fact that the Fed has been "sterilizing" the stimulative effects of its loans on the money supply (entirely until September 2008, and partially after then) limits the effects of those loans on financial conditions. In essence, the Fed has two methods for providing the financial system with liquidity—open market operations or direct loans. The Fed increased the role of direct loans to directly meet individual financial institutions' liquidity needs. But the Fed was offsetting the effects of the direct loans on the money supply to meet its goals for inflation. Thus, the loans did not provide additional overall monetary stimulus to the economy when sterilized. Since the Fed was sterilizing the loans because of its concerns with inflation, the utility of sterilization was fundamentally a question of whether the Fed had achieved the proper balance between stabilizing the financial sector and providing price stability, two topics that are discussed below.

Quantitative Easing and Balance Sheet Growth since September 2008

As commodity prices fell later in 2008, the inflation rate also fell. The Fed became less concerned about inflation rising, and more concerned about the further deterioration in financial and economic conditions. After September 2008, the Fed further increased its direct assistance to the financial system, but no longer fully sterilized those activities. As a result, the Fed's balance sheet and the monetary base have expanded rapidly, as demonstrated in **Table 4**. The monetary base doubled from August to December 2008—an unprecedented rise.[83] Because this increase went beyond what was needed to target the federal funds rate, it has been referred to as "quantitative easing." Normally, this would trigger a rapid increase in inflation. The main force preventing such an increase is the rapid increase in excess bank reserves held at the Fed during that period. Bank reserves increased from $44 billion in August 2008 to $802 billion on December 17, 2008, as banks preferred to hold the additional reserves created by the Fed's actions in order to shore up their balance sheets to avoid runs.

In normal financial conditions, banks would lend out money they received from the Fed, and through a process referred to by economists as the "money multiplier," a $1 increase in the monetary base would lead to a much larger increase in the overall money supply. But if banks hold the money received from the Fed in bank reserves instead of lending it out, the money multiplier process will not occur, so the growth in the overall money supply will be smaller. Data from the Fed show that almost all of the increase in reserves has been through excess reserves, rather than required reserves, which is consistent with banks holding most of the increase in reserves instead of lending them out. Thus, the large increase in the monetary base since September 2008 has not been matched by a corresponding increase in the overall money supply.

Table 4. Changes in the Fed's Balance Sheet from August 1, 2007, to Peak on December 17, 2008 billions of dollars

Assets		Liabilities and Capital	
Treasury Securities[a]	-$340	Federal Reserve Notes	+$64
MBS/GSE Debt	+$18[b]	Bank Reserves at Fed	+$785
Lending to Banks	+$538	Treasury Cash Deposits at Fed	+$475
Lending to Primary Dealers	+$47[b]	Other	+$103
Lending to/Assets Purchased for AIG	+$82[b]		
Lending for/Purchase of Commercial Paper	+$346[b]		
Assets Purchased from Bear Stearns	+$27[b]		
Swaps with Foreign Central Banks	+$572[b]	**Total Liabilities**	**+$1,427**
Other	+$148	**Capital**	**+$11**
Total Assets	**+$1,438**	**Total Liabilities and Capital**	**+$1,438**

Source: CRS calculations based on Federal Reserve Board of Governors, "Factors Affecting Reserve Balances," Data Release H.4.1, Tables 1 and 7, various dates.

Notes: GSE = government sponsored enterprise, MBS = mortgage-backed securities, ABS = asset backed securities, AIG = American International Group. See text for details.

a. Includes +$176 billion of Treasury securities temporarily swapped for private securities with Primary Dealers.

b. Item equaled zero in August 2007.

Initially, the balance sheet grew because of high private demand for borrowing from the Fed, and asset purchases were not needed. But between the weeks of December 17, 2008, and March 25, 2009, the Fed's direct lending to the financial sector decreased from a weekly average of $976 billion to $848 billion. The pattern of decline was steady over that period, and presumably stemmed from the fact that as financial conditions improved, there was less financial sector demand for Fed lending. With declining loan balances, the balance sheet would have shrunk, unless other assets were added to offset the fall in direct lending.

On March 18, 2009, the Fed announced a commitment to purchase $300 billion of Treasury securities, $200 billion of Agency debt (later revised to $175 billion), and $1.25 trillion of Agency mortgage-backed securities. Since then, direct lending has continued to gradually decline, while the Fed's holdings of Treasury and Agency securities have steadily increased, as seen in Table 5. The Fed's planned purchases of Treasury securities were completed by the fall of 2009 and planned Agency purchases were completed by the spring of 2010. By April 2010, direct lending outside of TALF and AIG was modest. Because other assets on the Fed's balance sheet (most notably, liquidity swaps with foreign central banks) have also declined over that period, the net result of these purchases has been to keep the overall size of the balance sheet relatively constant. Thus, the Fed's asset purchases have prevented liquidity from being removed from the financial system as Fed lending fell.[84] But since the fall in lending was spurred by less demand among financial institutions, critics question if the level of liquidity needed in the crisis is still needed today.

Table 5. Federal Reserve Balance Sheet, June 30, 2010 billions of dollars

Assets		Liabilities and Capital	
Treasury Securities[a]	777	Federal Reserve Notes	904
MBS/GSE Debt[a]	1,283	Bank Reserves at Fed	973
Lending to Banks	1	Treasury Cash Deposits at Fed	288
Lending to Primary Dealers	0	Other	113
Lending to/Assets Purchased for AIG	90		
Lending for/Purchase of Commercial Paper	0		
Lending for/Purchase of ABS (TALF)	43		
Assets Purchased from Bear Stearns	28		
Swaps with Foreign Central Banks	1	**Total Liabilities**	**2,278**
Other	111	**Capital**	**56**
Total Assets	**2,334**	**Total Liabilities and Capital**	**2,334**

Source: CRS calculations based on Federal Reserve Board of Governors, "Factors Affecting Reserve Balances," Data Release H.4.1, Tables 1 and 7, July 1, 2010.

Notes: GSE = government sponsored enterprise, MBS = mortgage-backed securities, ABS = asset backed securities, AIG = American International Group, TALF = Term Asset-Backed Securities Lending Facility. Amounts may not add due to rounding. See text for details.

a. Includes a $14 billion of securities temporarily swapped for private securities with Primary Dealers.

Purchases of Treasury securities could also stimulate the economy if private interest rates fall in response; a similar effect could occur with purchases of MBS, although those purchases should also more directly stimulate residential investment by reducing mortgage rates. Whether these purchases were more stimulative than the direct lending they replaced depends on their relative effects on financial conditions and interest rates.

Future Concerns

Once the financial outlook improves, banks may decide to use their reserve holdings to rapidly increase their lending. At that point, if the Fed found itself fighting inflationary pressures, it would have to find a way to prevent banks from lending those reserves in order to prevent a rapid increase in the money supply.[85] The most straightforward method to achieve this would be to withdraw those reserves from the banking system, which would require the Fed to reduce both its assets and liabilities through asset sales. Some of the Fed's outstanding assets can be sold relatively quickly in theory, although there could be political resistance in reality. By April 2010, the Fed's balance sheet consisted predominantly of securities that could be sold in secondary markets. But the Fed has pledged to hold these assets long term. Given the Fed's concerns about the fragility of housing markets, it is not clear how these holdings could be reduced quickly if the Fed became concerned about rising inflation. (About $100 billion to $200 billion per year could be reduced by not replacing maturing assets, according to Chairman Bernanke.[86])

Another option would be to give banks incentives not to lend out reserves by raising the interest rate that the Fed pays on reserves, although it remains to be seen how interest-sensitive bank reserves are.[87] To better prevent these reserves from being lent out if necessary, the Fed began offering "term deposits" with a one to six month maturity for bank reserves. The interest rate on these term deposits would be set through auction; banks would presumably be willing to bid for term deposits only if the interest rate exceeded the rate paid by the Fed on normal reserves.

The Fed could also attempt to reduce liquidity by lending its assets out through "reverse repos." This would change the composition of liabilities on the Fed's balance sheet, replacing Federal Reserve notes or bank reserves with reverse repos. It is unlikely that reverse repos operations could be large enough to remove most of the new liquidity, however.[88]

Cash balances held at the Fed through the Treasury Supplemental Financing Program could also be used to tie up liquidity, but the size of this program is constrained by the statutory debt limit (since Treasury needs to borrow to acquire cash), and would be insufficient to significantly reduce liquidity without a large increase in the debt limit.

With an eye to the potential long-run inflationary effects of the growth in the Fed's balance sheet, the Fed and Treasury announced in March 2009 that they would seek "legislative action to provide additional tools the Federal Reserve can use to sterilize the effects of its lending or securities purchases on the supply of bank reserves." Many analysts interpreted this statement to express the desire for the Fed to gain authority to issue its own bonds. Returning to the balance sheet in **Table 4**, the Fed must match an increase in assets with an increase in liabilities. The only liability it can currently issue are federal reserve notes that increase the monetary base. If the Fed were granted new authority to issue bonds, they could then expand their liabilities without increasing the monetary base and increasing inflationary pressures.[89] Then, there would no longer be any statutory limit or check on the Fed's ability to directly allocate credit, provided it met the broad guidelines of Section 13(3). To date, legislation to allow the Fed to do so has not been considered.

With a federal funds rate of zero, unsterilized purchases of long-term assets could help further stimulate the economy by adding needed liquidity to the financial system reducing long-term interest rates (flattening the yield curve). But once the Fed decides to start raising rates, economic theory casts some doubt on the economic usefulness of maintaining a large balance sheet, but sterilizing its effects on the economy by paying interest on reserves, reverse repos, the Treasury Supplemental Program, or issuing Fed bonds. The large balance sheet has no positive effect on liquidity if it is offset by any of these actions that drain liquidity from the economy. And if investors have rational expectations, it is not clear how a large balance sheet could flatten the yield curve in the face of sterilization since the long end of the yield curve should be determined primarily by expectations of future interest rates, and sterilized purchases of assets in the present should not change those expectations, all else equal. Previous experience suggests that sterilized attempts to flatten the yield curve have failed to stimulate the economy. For example, a study by Ben Bernanke (before he was Fed Chairman) and other economists concluded that a similar policy in the 1960s called "Operation Twist" is "widely viewed today as having been a failure."[90]

Is the Fed Monetizing the Budget Deficit?

Some commentators have interpreted the Fed's decision to make large scale purchases of Treasury securities as a signal that the Fed intends to "monetize the federal deficit," which is projected this fiscal year to reach its highest share of GDP since World War II. Monetizing the deficit occurs when the budget deficit is financed by money creation rather than by selling bonds to private investors. Hyperinflation in foreign countries has consistently resulted from governments' decisions to monetize large deficits.

According to this definition, the deficit has not been monetized. Section 14 of the Federal Reserve Act legally forbids the Fed from buying newly issued securities directly from the Treasury, and all Treasury securities purchased by the Fed to date have been purchased on the secondary market, from private investors.[91] Moreover, the size of the Fed's purchases of Treasury securities thus far is small relative to the overall deficit, which was $1.4 trillion in 2009. The Fed has announced and completed purchases of $300 billion thus far, although that amount can be altered at its discretion.

Nonetheless, the effect of the Fed's purchase of Treasury securities on the federal budget is similar regardless of whether the Fed buys the securities on the secondary market or directly from Treasury. When the Fed holds Treasury securities, Treasury must pay interest to the Fed, just as it would pay interest to a private investor. These interest payments, after expenses, become profits to the Fed. The Fed, in turn, remits about 95% of its profits to the Treasury, where they are added to general revenues.[92] In essence, the Fed has made an interest-free loan to the Treasury, because almost all of the interest paid by Treasury to the Fed is subsequently sent back to Treasury.

The Fed could increase its profits and remittances to Treasury by printing more money to purchase more Treasury bonds (or any other asset). The Fed's profits are the incidental side effect of its open market operations in pursuit of its statutory mandate (to keep prices stable and unemployment low). If the Fed chose instead to buy assets with a goal of increasing its profits and remittances, it would be unlikely to meet its statutory mandate.

Limits on the Fed's Ability to Address Problems in the Financial Sector

The Fed's actions since 2007 have been primarily focused on restoring liquidity to the financial system—lending to financial firms to convert their illiquid assets into cash or U.S. Treasury securities. But as financial conditions deteriorated in spite of increasing Fed intervention, it became apparent that the problems facing financial firms were not exclusively related to liquidity.

The crux of the firms' problem in the fall of 2008 stemmed from the large losses on some of their assets, particularly mortgage-related assets.[93] This caused a number of problems for the firms related to *capital adequacy*, which is the difference between the value of their assets and the value of their liabilities. First, losses and write-downs associated with those assets have reduced the firms' existing capital. Second, in the current environment, investors and creditors are demanding that firms hold more capital relative to assets than before so that firms can better withstand any future losses.

Third, at the peak of the crisis, firms were unable to raise enough new capital. Firms can raise new capital through retained earnings, which had been greatly reduced for many firms by the poor performance of their assets, or by issuing new capital (equity) and selling it to new investors. But during the crisis, investors were reluctant to inject new capital into struggling firms. Part of the explanation for this is that losses made the firms less profitable. But another part of the reason was that investors feared that there would be further losses in the future that would reduce the value of their investment, and perhaps even cause the firm to become insolvent. Uncertainty about future losses was partly caused by the opacity surrounding the assets that have been declining in value, which makes it hard for investors to determine which assets remain overvalued and which are undervalued. The result for companies such as Bear Stearns, Lehman Brothers, AIG, Washington Mutual, and Wachovia was a downward spiral in their stock price, which had two self-reinforcing characteristics. First, there was little demand for existing stock since its worth would either have been diluted by new capital (raised privately or through government intervention) or lost in insolvency. Second, new capital could not be attracted because the fall in stock value had left the market capitalization of the firms so low. If a firm's capital is completely depleted, there is no longer a buffer between its assets and liabilities, and it becomes insolvent. In 2009, financial firms were again able to issue capital to private investors, and many did so successfully.

Many large financial firms, including the firms that have failed, are heavily dependent on short-term borrowing to meet their current obligations. As financial conditions worsened, some of the firms that had the problems described above had problems accessing short-term borrowing markets that in normal conditions could be taken for granted. In an atmosphere where creditors cannot perceive which firms have insufficient capital, they become unwilling to lend for even short intervals. This is the essence of the *liquidity* problem—although the firms' assets may exceed their liabilities, without access to short-term borrowing, the firm cannot meet its current obligations because it cannot convert its assets into cash quickly enough (at least not if it wishes to avoid "fire sale" prices).

The Fed has always been the "lender of last resort" in order for banks to avoid liquidity problems during financial turmoil. To borrow from the Fed, a financial firm must post collateral. In essence, this allows the firm to temporarily convert its illiquid assets into cash, enabling the firm to meet its short-term obligations without sacrificing its assets. The Fed has always lent to commercial banks (depository institutions) through the discount window. As discussed above, it has extended liquidity to non-bank financial firms since 2008 through new lending facilities.

Borrowing from the Fed increases liquidity but it does not change a firm's capital buffer since it now has a liability outstanding to the Fed. So borrowing from the Fed cannot solve the problems of undercapitalization that some firms faced. Indeed, the Fed will generally not lend to firms that are not creditworthy because it wants to provide liquidity only to firms that are solvent, and thus able to repay.[94]

H.R. 1424, which was signed into law on October 3, 2008 (P.L. 110-343), created the Troubled Asset Relief Program. The Treasury initially used TARP funds to address the capital adequacy problem directly by providing $250 billion in capital to banks directly through preferred share purchases by TARP.[95]

Some have asked whether there is any way the Fed could have addressed the financial firms' capital adequacy problems. All of the Fed's standing lending facilities involve collateralized lending, and as discussed above, any program involving collateralized lending would not change a firm's capital position. According to one legal analysis, there is no express statutory authority for the Fed to purchase corporate bonds, mortgages, or equity.[96] But the Fed's assistance through the three Maiden Lane LLCs it has created has some similarities to TARP. In the case of Bear Stearns, the Fed created a limited liability corporation called Maiden Lane I, and lent Maiden Lane $28.82 billion. Maiden Lane I used the proceeds of that loan and another loan from JPMorgan Chase to purchase mortgage-related assets from Bear Stearns. (A similar arrangement with AIG led to the creation of

Maiden Lane II and Maiden Lane III.) Thus, although the Fed created and controlled the Maiden Lanes, the assets were purchased and held by the Maiden Lanes, not the Fed. The Fed plans to hold the Maiden Lane assets until markets recover, and then sell the assets to repay its loans. The Maiden Lanes were created under the Fed's Section 13(3) emergency authority.[97] H.R. 4173 forbids "a program or facility that is structured to remove assets from the balance sheet of a single and specific company."

The Fed was presumably granted broad emergency powers under Section 13(3) so that it had the flexibility to deal with unforeseen circumstances. Nonetheless, too broad of a reading of its powers could provoke displeasure in Congress or legal challenges. Creating TARP within the Treasury through legislation rather than the Fed through emergency powers avoided the argument ofwhether such a program extended beyond the Fed's intended role.

Lender of Last Resort, Systemic Risk, and Moral Hazard

Since its early days, one of the Fed's main roles has been to act as a lender of last resort to the banking system when private sources of credit become unavailable. It does so by lending through the discount window and its new lending facilities. The lender of last resort function can be seen from the perspective of an individual institution or the financial system as a whole. From the perspective of the individual institution, discount window lending is meant to provide funds to institutions that are illiquid (cannot meet current obligations out of current cash flow) but still solvent (assets exceed liabilities) when they cannot access funds from the private market. Discount window lending was unable to end bank runs, however—bank runs did not cease until the creation of federal deposit insurance. The experience of the Great Depression suggested that bank runs placed intolerably high costs on the financial system as a whole, as they led to widespread bank failures.[98] Fed lending is not meant to help insolvent institutions, with one exception explained below.

Access to Fed lending facilities and deposit insurance creates *moral hazard* for financial institutions—they can take on more risk than the market would otherwise permit because of the government safety net. To limit moral hazard, institutions with depository insurance and access to the discount window are subject to a safety and soundness regulatory regime that includes capital requirements, reserve requirements, bank examinations, and so on.

The exception to the rule that insolvent institutions cannot access Fed lending facilities is when the institution is deemed "too big to fail." Institutions that are too big to fail are ones that are deemed to be big enough that their failure could create *systemic risk*, the risk that the financial system as a whole would cease to function smoothly.[99] For example, failure could lead to systemic instability through "contagion" effects where the losses to creditors and counterparties imposed by the bankruptcy system drove those creditors and counterparties into insolvency. A systemic risk episode could impose heavy costs on the overall economy, as the bank panics of the Great Depression demonstrated. Although too big to fail institutions are not offered explicit guarantees, it can be argued that they have implicit guarantees since the government would not be willing to allow a systemic risk episode. This accentuates the moral hazard problem described above. There is no official governmental classification of which financial institutions are too big to fail, presumably since maintaining uncertainty over which institutions are too big to fail could help reduce the moral hazard problem. But the lack of official designation arguably creates a vacuum in terms of policy preparedness. (Making the problem more complex, as one report described the situation, "Officials grimly concluded that while Bear Stearns isn't too big to fail, it was too interconnected to be allowed to fail in just one day." It is unclear how to judge which institutions are too interconnected to fail.)[100]

As the cases of Bear Stearns, Fannie Mae and Freddie Mac, and AIG illustrate, some of the modern-day financial institutions that are too big to fail are not depository institutions that fall under the strict regulatory umbrella that accompanies membership in the Federal Reserve system. Nevertheless, all received direct or indirect assistance from the Fed. This highlights the shift in financial activity from a bank-dominated financial system at the time of the Fed's creation to a system whose health now depends on many types of institutions. The Fed was set up to be a lender of last resort to only the banking system. In the current crisis, it has been able to extend its lender of last resort functions to non-bank financial institutions only because of its Section 13(3) emergency powers. A policy issue going forward is whether the extension of these functions should be made permanent, and if so, what types of regulatory safeguards should accompany it. Because Section 13(3) of the Federal Reserve Act is intended for responding to unanticipated emergencies, it grants authority that is broader and more open-ended than the Fed's normal authority.

It is possible that part of the reason these institutions failed is because they took on excessive risks in the belief that they were too big to fail. Although that theory can be debated, it is clearer that the precedent of the Fed's role in the Bear Stearns acquisition may strengthen the perception of other institutions and investors that any financial firm, regardless of whether it is a depository institution, will be bailed out in the future if it is too big to fail, or merely too interconnected to fail. If so, it could be argued that the Bear Stearns episode may have increased moral hazard going forward. The government's decision not to intervene to prevent the failure of the investment bank Lehman Brothers in September 2008, but to subsequently assist AIG, Citigroup, and Bank of America may have created further market uncertainty regarding which institutions the government views as too big to fail. Lehman Brothers was larger than Bear Stearns and involved in similar business activities. Others have argued that the failure of Lehman Brothers set off a wave of unrest in money markets (see above), interbank lending markets, and the market for credit default swaps that would make the government unlikely to allow any large institution to fail in the future.[101]

The government assistance to Bear Stearns, Fannie Mae and Freddie Mac, and AIG all include clauses that significantly reduced the value of existing shareholder equity. This was partly justified in terms of reducing moral hazard—investors would be reluctant to buy equity in too big to fail companies that were taking excessive risks if the government demanded a reduction in existing shareholder value. But government assistance in all of these cases made creditors and other counterparties whole. In these cases, the moral hazard problem manifests itself in a willingness of creditors to lend to, and counterparties to transact with, a firm they know to be taking excessive risks, thereby potentially allowing the firm to take more risks. More recent government assistance to Citigroup and Bank of America was provided without similar measures to replace management or dilute shareholders. (Warrants to purchase some common stock were issued but have not yet been exercised.) Market participants may view this decision as a signal that the government is no longer placing emphasis on avoiding moral hazard.

The current situation raises three broad points about systemic risk. First, risk is at the foundation of all financial intermediation. Policymakers may wish to curb excessive risk taking when it leads to systemic risk, but too little financial risk would also be counterproductive for the economy. (Indeed, some would argue that part of the underlying problem for the financial system as a whole at present is that investors are currently too risk averse.) Second, many analysts have argued that part of the reason that so much financial intermediation has left the commercial banking system is to avoid the costs of regulation.[102] This point applies to future regulatory changes as well. An attempt to increase regulation on banks could lead more business to move to hedge funds, for example. Third, financial markets have become significantly more complex and fast-moving in recent years. Many of the financial instruments with which Bear Stearns, Lehman Brothers, and AIG were involved did not exist until recently. For regulation to be effective in this environment, it faces the challenge of trying to keep up with innovation. If used prudently, many of these innovations can reduce risk for individual investors. Yet the Bear Stearns example implies that innovation may also lead to more interconnectivity, which increases systemic risk.

Going forward, policymakers must determine whether new regulation is needed to limit moral hazard because there may be no credible way to maintain a policy that prohibits the rescue of future institutions that are too big to fail even if such a policy were desired.

The financial crisis has led to the passage of comprehensive regulatory reform in the House and Senate that address the "too big to fail" problem and the Fed's role as a regulator and lender of last resort. CRS Report R40877, *Financial Regulatory Reform: Systemic Risk and the Federal Reserve*, analyzes the effects of this legislation on the Fed and the "too big to fail" issue.

Oversight, Transparency, and Disclosure of Emergency Programs

Because profits and losses borne by the Fed ultimately get passed on to taxpayers (see "Cost to the Treasury"), some Members of Congress have argued that more information about the Fed's emergency activities should be made available to the public. The Fed has not been subject to many of the oversight and reporting requirements applied to the TARP, although the amount of direct assistance outstanding from the Fed at its peak exceeded the authorized size of TARP.

Nonetheless, the Fed has publicly released a significant amount of information on its emergency actions. The Fed's financial statements are published weekly and audited by private sector auditors, with the results published in the Fed's annual report. The Fed has provided detailed information to the public on the general terms and eligibility of its borrowers and collateral by class for each crisis-response program.[103] It has also provided a rationale for why each crisis program has been created, and an explanation of the goals the program is meant to accomplish. The Emergency Economic Stabilization Act (P.L. 110-343) requires the Fed to report to the House Financial Services Committee and the Senate Banking, Housing, and Urban Affairs Committee on its justification for exercising Section 13(3), the terms of the assistance provided, and regular updates on the status of the loan. Beginning in June 2009, the Fed began releasing a monthly report that listed the number of and concentration among borrowers by type, the value and creditworthiness of collateral held by type, and the interest income earned for each of its facilities.[104] Contracts with private vendors to purchase or manage assets are also posted on the New York Fed's website.

But the Fed has kept confidential the identity of the borrowers from its facilities, the collateral posted in specific transactions, the terms of specific transactions, and the results of specific transactions (i.e., whether they resulted in profits or losses).[105] As historical precedent, the Fed has had a longstanding policy of keeping the identity of banks that borrow from its discount window confidential. Those calling for more disclosure note that the new Fed programs place the Fed in a more expansive role and are potentially riskier than the discount window, and, unlike the discount window, were not explicitly endorsed by legislation (many were authorized under its emergency authority).

The Fed has argued that allowing the public to know which firms are accessing its facilities could undermine investor confidence in the institutions receiving aid because of a perception that recipients were weak or unsound. A loss of investor confidence could potentially lead to destabilizing runs on the institution's deposits, debt, or equity. If institutions feared that this would occur, the Fed argues, then the institutions would be wary of participating in the Fed's programs, which, in the aggregate, would retard economic recovery. A historical example supporting the Fed's argument would be the Reconstruction Finance Corporation (RFC) in the Great Depression. When the RFC publicized to which banks it had given loans, those banks typically experienced depositor runs.[106] A more recent example provides mixed evidence—disclosure of TARP fund recipients. At first, TARP funds were widely disbursed, and recipients included all the major banks. At that point, there was no perceived stigma to TARP participation. More recently, many banks have repaid TARP shares at the first opportunity, and remaining participants have expressed concern that if they did not repay soon, investors would perceive them as weak. Arguments about investor confidence are arguably less compelling when applied to publicly disclosing collateral held by the Fed.

There are several different approaches to expanding disclosure or oversight:

- Congress could remove the Government Accountability Office's (GAO's) restrictions on conducting investigations of the Fed for Congress. While GAO has had longstanding authority to audit the Fed's non-monetary policy functions,[107] the Federal Banking Agency Audit Act of 1978 (31 USC 714(b)) restricts GAO from auditing certain Fed activities: (1) transactions with foreign central banks or governments; (2) "deliberations, decisions, or actions on monetary matters, including discount window operations, reserves of member banks, securities credit, interest on deposits, and open market operations;" and (3) "transactions made under the direction of the Federal Open Market Committee."[108] While the act does not specifically mention activities taken under the Fed's emergency authority, those activities have been interpreted as falling under the restrictions. Also included in the Federal Banking Audit Act of 1978 are restrictions on GAO disclosure of confidential information about the financial firms subject to the Fed's policies. Thus, if audit restrictions were removed but these disclosure restrictions remained in place, GAO audits would not necessarily accomplish some policymakers' goal of disclosing the identities of borrowers from Fed lending facilities. S. 896, which was signed into law on May 20, 2009 (P.L. 111-22), allows GAO audits of "any action taken by the Board under ... Section 13(3) of the Federal Reserve Act with respect to a single and specific partnership or corporation." This would allow GAO audits of the Maiden Lane facilities and the asset guarantees of Citigroup and Bank of America, but would maintain audit restrictions on non-emergency activities and broadly-accessed emergency lending facilities, such as the Primary Dealer Credit Facility or the commercial paper facilities. In performing the audit under S. 896, GAO must maintain the confidentiality of the private documents it accesses, but cannot withhold any information requested by Members of Congress on the committees of jurisdiction. H.R. 4173 allows GAO to audit emergency actions, discount window lending, and open market operations for operational integrity, accounting financial reporting, internal controls, collateral policies, favoritism, and third-party contracting policies. With the exception of the Maiden Lane facilities, GAO would be prohibited from releasing confidential information to Congress or the public about the transactions until the information was released by the Fed. H.R. 4173 also requires a GAO audit, according to the criteria listed above, of all lending between December 2007 and the date of enactment. It also requires a separate GAO audit to determine whether the selection of Federal Reserve regional bank presidents meets the criteria under Section 4 of the Federal Reserve Act, whether there are actual or potential conflicts of interest created by member banks choosing Fed regional bank directors, to examine the role regional banks played in the Fed's response to the crisis, and to propose reforms to regional bank governance.

- Congress could require the Fed to disclose more information on the identities of borrowers, the collateral accepted, or the terms and results of transactions. Congress requires the Fed to make some general policy reports, but does not typically require the Fed to disclose this type of specific information. Indeed, much of the information about monetary policy that the Fed currently makes public is done so on a voluntarily basis. H.R. 4173 requires the Fed to disclose the identities of borrowers and terms of borrowing to the committees of jurisdiction within seven days of a loan and allows for the information to be kept confidential if desired. It requires that the identities of borrowers and terms of borrowing be released to the public with up to a two year delay for the discount window and a one year delay after a facility has been terminated for other lending. It requires that the identities of counterparties and terms of sale be released to the public with up to a two year delay for open market operations. It requires that the identities of borrowers and borrowing terms be released to the public by December 1, 2010, for actions taken during the financial crisis.
- Congress could create specific oversight boards or committees that focus on the Federal Reserve. Currently, regular congressional oversight of the Fed is done at a general level through semi-annual hearings with the House Financial Services Committee and the Senate Banking, Housing, and Urban Affairs Committee, as well as ad hoc hearings on more focused topics. There is no routine, specific oversight of the Fed's crisis-response actions, and no group with monetary policy expertise tasked with evaluating the Fed's actions for Congress.

Greater disclosure and outside evaluation could potentially help Congress perform its oversight duties more effectively. The main argument against increasing Fed oversight would be that it could be perceived to reduce the Fed's operational independence from Congress. Chairman Bernanke has argued that "The general repeal of (the audit) exemption would serve only to increase the perceived influence of Congress on monetary policy decisions, which would undermine the confidence the public and the markets have in the Fed."[109] Most economists believe that the Fed's independence to carry out day-to-day decisions about monetary policy without congressional input strengthens the Fed's credibility in the eyes of the private sector that it will follow policies that maximize price and economic stability. Greater credibility is perceived to strengthen the effectiveness of monetary policy on the economy. This independence is seen as consistent with the democratic process because the Fed's mandate to pursue price and economic stability has been given to it by Congress, and choosing the interest rate policies best able to achieve these goals is viewed as relatively technocratic and non-political in nature.[110] The Fed's unprecedented response to the financial crisis moves it into new policy areas involving decisions that are arguably more political in nature, such as deciding which financial actors should be eligible to access Fed credit. While few policymakers argue for total independence or total disclosure and oversight, the policy challenge is to strike the right balance between the two. In February 2010 testimony, Chairman Bernanke has also advocated striking such a balance:

> we understand that the unusual nature of (the emergency credit and liquidity) facilities creates a special obligation to assure the Congress and the public of the integrity of their operation. Accordingly, we would welcome a review by the GAO of the Federal Reserve's management of all facilities created under emergency authorities. In particular, we would support legislation authorizing the GAO to audit the operational integrity, collateral policies, use of third-party contractors, accounting, financial reporting, and internal controls of these special credit and liquidity facilities.... We are also prepared to support legislation that would require the release of the identities of the firms that participated in each special facility after an appropriate delay. It is important that the release occur after a lag that is sufficiently long that investors will not view an institution's use of one of the facilities as a possible indication of ongoing financial problems, thereby undermining market confidence in the institution or discouraging use of any future facility that might become necessary to protect the U.S. economy.[111]

Effects on the Allocation of Capital

In normal conditions, the Fed primarily influences economic conditions through the purchase and sale of U.S. Treasury securities on the secondary market. This enables the Fed to influence overall economic conditions without favoring any particular financial firm or asset, thus minimizing its effect on the market allocation of capital.

As the Fed has shifted to an increasing reliance on more direct intervention in the financial system since 2008, its actions have had growing consequences for the allocation of private capital. Its actions can affect the allocation of capital by favoring certain classes or types of assets over others or by favoring certain financial firms or types of firms over others.

As discussed above, assisting Bear Stearns and AIG after their mistakes may encourage inefficiently high risk taking by other firms that are deemed "too big to fail." Punitive conditions attached to the assistance mitigate but do not eliminate these effects.[112] Allowing primary dealers to temporarily swap their illiquid assets for Treasuries protects those who invested poorly. The Fed has attempted to push down yields on certain assets that it feels have become inefficiently high (e.g., through the Term Asset Backed Securities Lending Facility), but it may be that at the height of the boom yields on these assets had become inefficiently low because investors underestimated their riskiness. The Fed's efforts could eventually reintroduce inefficient underpricing of risk. By purchasing commercial paper, the Fed has increased the relative demand for those assets, which confers an advantage to those firms that can access that market, which are generally large and have high credit ratings. Likewise, the Fed is purchasing GSE obligations and GSE-guaranteed MBS, but not similar securities issued by private firms. This increases the GSEs' funding advantage over private competitors.[113]

In a time when liquidity is scarce, access to Fed borrowing confers an advantage on banks and primary dealers over other types of institutions. It may also arguably retard the process of weeding out bad institutions, since reputation is needed to access private liquidity, but not Fed liquidity. On the other hand, during a panic both good and bad firms can be shut out of credit markets. Liquidity has positive externalities that means it would be underprovided by the private sector if it were not provided by the government. When financial markets are not functioning, credit allocation is an incidental but unavoidable side effect of liquidity provision. But some of the Fed's efforts, such as paying interest on bank reserves or possibly seeking to issue its own bonds, could be interpreted as signaling that the Fed intends to go beyond allocating credit for the sole purpose of providing liquidity because these initiatives allow the Fed to extend more credit than is needed for liquidity purposes.

The Fed's short-term goal is to avoid the downward spiral in conditions that could lead to a panic, causing serious disruptions to the credit intermediation process for all firms, prudent or otherwise. But in the long run, once financial stability has been restored, these distortions to the market allocation of capital could result in economic inefficiencies. There is also a risk that the Fed's activities could "crowd out" private lenders and investors in specific markets, such as the markets for bank reserves, private-label MBS, and commercial paper, leading to less robust private markets. This risk seems greater since the Fed has suggested methods to keep its balance sheet large (such as paying interest on bank reserves or issuing "Fed bonds") even after the economy has returned to normal. As demand for Fed lending facilities has fallen as financial conditions have improved, the Fed has already decided to purchase more GSE debt and MBS, rather than scale back its balance sheet. Even if some of the Fed's current programs are allowed to expire, if investors believed that they would be revived during the next downturn, capital allocation and incentives would remain altered.

Is the Economy Stuck in a Liquidity Trap? The Use of Quantitative Easing at Zero Interest Rates

Although monetary policy is credited with having contributed to an unusual degree of economic stability since at least the mid-1980s, some economists argue that it has been rendered ineffective by the current outlook. The argument is that lower interest rates will not boost spending because the economy is stuck in a credit crunch in which financial institutions are unwilling to lend to creditworthy borrowers because of balance sheet concerns. Borrower demand may increase in response to lower rates, but as long as institutions are trying to rebuild their balance sheets, they will remain reluctant to extend credit. Following September 2008, banks greatly increased their holdings of excess reserves, which could potentially be a troubling sign that banks currently prefer extremely safe, liquid assets over lending. Further, the Fed has already reduced the federal funds rate to near zero, and cannot reduce it further. By some measures, the recession was deep enough that zero interest rates are not stimulative enough to move the economy back to full employment quickly.[114]

A scenario where monetary stimulus has no effect on the economy is sometimes referred to as a "liquidity trap." Liquidity traps are rare in modern times, but the decade of economic stagnation suffered by Japan in the 1990s after the bursting of its financial bubble is cited as an example. Interest rates were lowered to almost zero in Japan, and the economy still did not recover quickly.[115]

There are some problems with this line of reasoning at present. First, liquidity traps are most likely to occur when overall prices of goods and services are falling (called *deflation*). When prices are falling, real interest rates are higher than nominal interest rates, so it is more likely that a very low nominal interest rate would still be too high in real terms to stimulate economic activity. Although prices fell at the end of 2008, they have been rising modestly since.[116] Inflation would not be expected to be steady the economy were in a liquidity trap. Second, monetary policy always suffers lags between a reduction in interest rates and corresponding increases in economic activity.

Most importantly, it would be wrong to conclude that the Fed has had no further policy options available to stimulate the economy since December 2008, when the Fed reduced the federal funds rate target to a range of 0% to 0.25%. At this point, the potential for further stimulus via traditional monetary policy channels had been exhausted, since the federal funds rate cannot be reduced below zero. But in a 2004 study, Ben Bernanke (a Fed governor at the time) and coauthors laid out policy options for how the Fed could further stimulate the economy once interest rates reached zero. In that study, the authors note that "nothing prevents the central bank from adding liquidity to the system beyond what is needed to achieve a policy rate of zero, a policy that is known as quantitative easing."[117] By that definition, the Fed has engaged in "quantitative easing" since September 2008—instead of adjusting the monetary base to meet the interest rate target, the Fed has adjusted the monetary base to meet the financial sector's liquidity needs.[118] But many different levels of Fed direct lending (and of the corresponding monetary base) are compatible with a zero federal funds rate. Once the federal funds rate hits zero, there is nothing stopping the Fed from further increases in lending that would have further expansionary effects on the economy. It could also engage in quantitative easing without direct lending by purchasing securities. From March 2009 to March 2010, the Fed purchased about $300 billion of longer-term Treasury securities, $1.25 trillion in MBS, and $175 billion of GSE obligations. Fed Vice Chairman Donald Kohn, while acknowledging great uncertainties, estimated that quantitative easing could increase nominal GDP by as much as $1 trillion over the next several years relative to a baseline forecast.[119]

The large increase in excess bank reserves casts doubt on the effectiveness of quantitative easing. Since the Fed has increased its balance sheet, excess reserves have averaged between $643 billion and $1,162 billion per month, compared with less than $2 billion before August 2007. The Fed can supply banks with unlimited liquidity, but if banks hold that liquidity at the Fed, the added liquidity will not stimulate economic activity.[120]

Even so, the Fed's actions may help bring down other interest rates in the economy, but this will be stimulative only if interest-sensitive spending is responsive to lower interest rates. This would occur through a flattening of the yield curve (i.e., pushing down long interest rates relative to short rates). Some economists argue that reductions in long-term rates are more stimulative than equivalent reductions in short-term rates.[121] But past experience with the efficacy of this method is mixed. Research by the New York Fed concludes that the recent purchases were effective in lowering interest rates based on the immediate response of rates to official announcements about the purchases, although this research could be questioned on the grounds that the rate reductions must be long-lasting to be stimulative, and for some of the maturities in question, interest rates over the entire period rose, on balance. Interpreting the overall effect on interest rates during the life of the asset purchase program is clouded by the fact that other changes in economic conditions also influence interest rates. The authors also use time-series evidence to estimate that the purchase program reduced the yield on ten-year securities relative to short-term securities by 0.38 to 0.82 percentage points. This evidence may be suffer from omitted variable bias, however—namely, the change in the risk-premium associated with MBS over the period in question, given the uncertainty prior to the purchase program caused by GSE conservatorship and the financial crisis. Another study by outside economists found small effects of the Fed's MBS purchases on interest rates after adjusting for prepayment and default risk, with the effect mainly occurring at the time the program was announced—before purchases had begun.[122]

Although a liquidity trap cannot be ruled out, it is premature to conclude the economy is stuck in one at this point in time. Liquidity traps are a threat when monetary policy has been kept too tight, but the Fed has eased monetary policy aggressively since the crisis began.

Stagflation?

Other critics have argued that the Fed has created the opposite problem of a liquidity trap—rising inflation due to excessive liquidity. They argue that the economy will enter a period of stagflation, where falling or negative economic growth is accompanied by high or rising inflation.[123]

Typically, one would expect an economic slowdown to be accompanied by a decline in the inflation rate. Excess capacity in the capital stock and rising unemployment would force firms and workers to lower their prices and wage demands, respectively. But critics believe the economy is in a situation where a modest but persistent increase in inflation in recent years has led individuals to come to expect higher inflation, and factor that expectation into their price and wage demands. Further driving up inflationary expectations, critics believe that individuals will observe the large increase in the budget deficit and monetary base and conclude that the government will inflate its way out of the crisis. Couple those higher inflation expectations with rising commodity prices, and critics argue that inflation will rise even if the economy slows. They point to the experience of the 1970s, when inflationary expectations became so ingrained that inflation continued to rise despite a fairly deep recession, as a potential parallel to the current situation.[124]

Data suggest that the fear of stagflation is premature—inflation remains relatively low at present. There is a consensus among economists that in the long run inflation is primarily a monetary phenomenon, and if the Fed's recent monetary stance were maintained for too long, it would not be consistent with stable inflation. But in the near term, a large amount of unemployment and excess capacity has removed most inflationary pressure. This can be seen in the example of Japan, where the Bank of Japan allowed the monetary base to increase by more than 10% per year after 2001, without inflation ever reaching high levels because of economic sluggishness. Furthermore, commodity prices fell in the second half of 2008, leading to a brief period of falling prices. Since then, inflation has been stable.

Ironically, if the Fed's actions succeed in reviving the economy, then the probability that its actions would boost inflation would increase. Under normal conditions, the doubling of the monetary base between August and December 2008 would have led to a sharp increase in inflation, but this did not occur because of the even greater increase in bank reserves held at the Fed that led to only a moderate increase in broader measures of the money supply. If banks responded to improved economic conditions by lending out the reserves they are now holding, the money supply and inflation would rise rapidly. The key to maintaining a stable inflation rate is finding the proper balance between the disinflationary pressures of the slowdown and the inflationary pressures of quantitative easing. The large amounts of liquidity that the Fed has added to the system must be removed soon enough that inflation does not rise, but not so soon that a nascent economic recovery is stubbed out. Removing all of the liquidity is complicated by the fact that the Fed has created some of it by buying assets it has pledged to hold long term. Given the uncertainty facing policymakers at present, finding the proper balance is extremely difficult.[125]

Concluding Thoughts

While turmoil plagues financial markets periodically, the current episode is notable for its breadth, depth, and persistence. It is difficult to make the case that the Fed has not responded to the current turmoil with alacrity and creativity. The slow financial and economic recovery is not necessarily a sign that the Fed's policy decisions have been wrongheaded—the Fed has provided the financial sector with unprecedented liquidity, but it cannot force institutions to use that liquidity to expand their lending or investing.

The Fed's response has raised statutory issues that Congress may wish to consider in its oversight capacity. Namely, the Fed's role in the Bear Stearns acquisition, the assistance to AIG, Citigroup, and Bank of America, the creation of the Primary Dealer Credit Facility (a sort of discount window for a group of non-member banks), and its intervention in the commercial paper market involved emergency authorities that had not been used in more than 70 years. This authority was needed because the actions involved financial institutions that were not member banks of the Federal Reserve System (i.e., depository institutions). But because the authority is broad and open-ended, the Fed's actions under this authority are subject to few legal parameters. The authority allows lending to non-member banks, but some of the loans in the Bear Stearns and AIG agreements were to LLCs that the Fed created and controls, and have been used to purchase Bear Stearns' and AIG's assets. These actions raise an important issue—if financial institutions can receive some of the benefits of Fed protection, in some cases because they are "too big to fail," should they also be subject to the costs that member banks bear in terms of safety and soundness regulations, imposed to limit the moral hazard that results from Fed and FDIC protections? H.R. 4173 attempts to limit future emergency lending to broadly available, collateralized facilities to avoid assistance to failing firms.

Some policymakers have questioned whether an institution largely independent from the elected branches of government should be able to (indirectly) place significant taxpayer funds at risk by providing the financial sector with hundreds of billions of dollars of assistance through use of its emergency powers. This raises the policy issue of how to balance the needs for congressional transparency and oversight against the economic benefits of Fed independence. H.R. 4173 removes most GAO audit restrictions and requires disclosure of the identities of borrowers with a delay. Furthermore, without congressional input, hundreds of billions of dollars of borrowing by the Treasury (through the Treasury Supplementary Financing Program) has allowed the Fed to increase its lending capacity without detrimental effects on inflation.

But as long as there is no government program to systematically manage financial difficulties at too big to fail institutions, the Fed is the only institution that can step in quickly enough to cope with problems on a case-by-case basis. While some had believed TARP provided the type of systemic approach that would allow the Fed to return to a more traditional role, the Fed's subsequent creation of lending facilities to support the commercial paper market, mortgage market, and asset-backed securities market suggests that TARP cannot cover all unforeseen contingencies. Furthermore, TARP is scheduled to expire in October 2010 and is limited in size, although Fed and TARP money have been coupled in order for TARP to have an impact beyond the $700 billion authorized by Congress.

The Fed's actions have resulted in an unprecedented expansion in its balance sheet and the portion of the money supply it controls. Normally, this would be highly inflationary, but inflation has remained low because of the financial crisis. As the economy improves, the Fed will need to contain this monetary expansion to prevent inflation from rising, but not so fast that it causes the financial system to destabilize again. The increase in the balance sheet could have already been automatically reversed by the decline in the Fed's direct lending, but the Fed has chosen to offset it through large-scale purchases of assets to maintain a high level of liquidity in the economy. The Fed views paying interest on bank reserves (authorized by P.L. 110-343) as an effective way to prevent inflation from rising.

End Notes

[1] For more information see CRS Report RL34182, *Financial Crisis? The Liquidity Crunch of August 2007*, by Darryl E. Getter et al.

[2] Current amounts of Fed lending outstanding can be found at Federal Reserve, "Factors Affecting Reserve Balances of Depository Institutions," statistical release H.4.1, updated weekly.

[3] Many of the loans and new programs described below are operated through the Federal Reserve Bank of New York, under the authorization of the Board of Governors. This report uses the term Federal Reserve, and does not distinguish between actions taken by the Board and actions taken by the Federal Reserve Bank of New York. The Federal Reserve System is composed of the Board of Governors and twelve regional banks (one of which is the New York Fed).

[4] Federal Reserve Bank of New York, "The Discount Window," *Fedpoint*, August 2007.

[5] Proposals for GAO to audit the Fed are discussed below in the section entitled "Oversight, Transparency, and Disclosure of Emergency Programs".

[6] Some of the Fed's purchase and sale of Treasury securities are made outright, but most are made through repurchase agreements, which can be thought of as short-term transactions that are automatically reversed at the end of a predetermined period, typically lasting a few days. Since the Fed must constantly adjust the amount of bank reserves available to keep the federal funds rate near its target, repurchase agreements give the Fed more flexibility to make these adjustments.

[7] For more information, see CRS Report RL30354, *Monetary Policy and the Federal Reserve: Current Policy and Conditions*, by Marc Labonte. For information on the federal funds market during the crisis, see Gara Afonso, Anna Kovner, and Antoinette Schoar, *Stressed, Not Frozen: The Federal Funds Market in the Financial Crisis*, Federal Reserve Bank of New York, Staff Report no. 437, March 2010.

[8] For more information, see the section below, "Is the Economy Stuck in a Liquidity Trap? The Use of Quantitative Easing at Zero Interest Rates."

[9] This occurred because financial firms were meeting their liquidity needs directly from the Fed, there was no longer adequate demand to borrow reserves in the private federal funds market, and the federal funds rate fell close to zero.

[10] For these purposes, the Fed defines Fannie Mae, Freddie Mac, the Federal Home Loan Banks, and Ginnie Mae as Agencies. For more information, see the section below entitled "Mortgage-Backed Securities Purchase Program and Purchase of GSE Obligations".

[11] Joseph Gagnon et al, *Large-Scale Asset Purchases by the Federal Reserve*, Federal Reserve Bank of New York, Staff Reports 441, March 2010.

[12] For more background, see James Clouse, "Recent Developments in Discount Window Policy," *Federal Reserve Bulletin*, November 1994, p. 965.

[13] Current data on the number of borrowers, loan concentration among borrowers, types of collateral posted, credit rating of collateral posted, and size of loans as a share of posted collateral for the Term Auction Facility and discount window can be found in the Fed's *Federal Reserve System Monthly Report on Credit and Liquidity Programs and the Balance Sheet.*

[14] The Fed has centralized information on the purpose, terms, and conditions of the facilities described in this section at the following Fed website at http://www.federalreserve.gov/monetarypolicy/bst.htm.

[15] The Fed made about 7,500 loans to non-banks each year under Section 13B of the Federal Reserve Act until that section of the act was repealed in 1959.

[16] For more information, see Olivier Armantier et al, "The Federal Reserve's Term Auction Facility," Federal Reserve Bank of New York, *Current Issues in Economics and Finance*, vol. 14, no. 5, July 2008; Charles Carlstrom and Sarah Wakefield, "The Funds Rate, Liquidity, and the Term Auction Facility," Federal Reserve Bank of Cleveland, *Economic Trends*, December 14, 2007.

[17] The dates, terms, and amounts of future TAF auctions can be accessed at http://www.federalreserve.gov/monetarypolicy/tafschedule.htm.

[18] Current data on the number of borrowers, loan concentration among borrowers, types of collateral posted, credit rating of collateral posted, and size of loans as a share of posted collateral for the TAF and discount window can be found in the Fed's *Federal Reserve System Monthly Report on Credit and Liquidity Programs and the Balance Sheet.*

[19] See James McAndrews et al, *The Effect of the Term Auction Facility on the London Inter-bank Offered Rate*, Federal Reserve Bank of New York, Staff Report no. 335, July 2008; John Taylor and John Williams, *A Black Swan in the Money Market*, Federal Reserve Bank of San Francisco, Working Paper 2008-04, April 2008; Asani Sarkar and Jeffrey Shrader, *Financial Amplification Mechanisms and the Federal Reserve's Supply of Liquidity During the Financial Crisis*, Federal Reserve Bank of New York, Staff Reports 431, February 2010.

[20] As of June 2009, Treasury securities, Agency securities, and Agency-guaranteed mortgage-backed securities were no longer accepted as collateral for the TSLF because the Fed deemed these assets to no longer be illiquid. Few of these assets were posted as collateral when the Fed discontinued their use.

[21] Current data on the number of borrowers, concentration of loans among borrowers, types of collateral, and credit rating of collateral can be found in the Fed's *Federal Reserve System Monthly Report on Credit and Liquidity Programs and the Balance Sheet.*

[22] Board of Governors of the Federal Reserve System, press release, March 11, 2008.

[23] Michael Fleming, Warren Hrung, and Frank Keane, "The Term Securities Lending Facility," Federal Reserve Bank of New York, *Current Issues in Economics and Finance*, vol. 15, no. 2 (February 2009). See also Michael Fleming, Warren Hrung, and Frank Keane, *Repo Market Effects of the Term Securities Lending Facility*, Federal Reserve Bank of New York, Staff Reports 426, January 2010. The failure of Bear Stearns set off a period of market turbulence; the decline in spreads cited in these studies may have been driven by the abatement of this turbulence.

[24] For more information, see Tobias Adrian, Christopher Burke, and James McAndrews, *The Federal Reserve's Primary Dealer Credit Facility*, Federal Reserve Bank of New York, Current Issues in Economics and Finance, vol. 15, no. 4, New York, NY, August 2009.

[25] Board of Governors of the Federal Reserve System, press release, November 25, 2008.

[26] Current data on the types of loans and names of issuers whose ABS have been used for collateral can be found in the Fed's *Federal Reserve System Monthly Report on Credit and Liquidity Programs and the Balance Sheet.*

[27] Special Inspector General for TARP, *Quarterly Report to Congress*, Washington, DC, April 29, 2009, p. 227.

[28] For more information, see CRS Report RL34730, *Troubled Asset Relief Program: Legislation and Treasury Implementation*, by Baird Webel and Edward V. Murphy.

[29] Kenneth Robinson, *TALF: Jump-Starting the Securitization Markets*, Federal Reserve Bank of Dallas Economic Letter, vol. 4, no. 6, August 2009.

[30] For more information, see Richard Anderson and Charles Gascon, "The Commercial Paper Market, the Fed, and the 2007-2009 Financial Crisis," *Federal Reserve Bank of St. Louis Review*, vol. 91, no. 6 (November/December 2009), p. 589.

[31] Figure cited in Chairman Ben Bernanke, "Financial Reform to Address Systemic Risk," speech at the Council on Foreign Relations, March 10, 2009.

[32] Current data on the number of borrowers and credit rating of collateral can be found in the Fed's *Federal Reserve System Monthly Report on Credit and Liquidity Programs and the Balance Sheet.*

[33] Current data on the number of borrowers, loan concentration among borrowers, types of borrowers, and credit rating of the commercial paper can be found in the Fed's *Federal Reserve System Monthly Report on Credit and Liquidity Programs and the Balance Sheet.* See also, Tobias Adrian, Karin Kimbrough, and Dina Marchioni, "The Federal Reserve's Commercial Paper Funding Facility," Federal Reserve Bank of New York, *Economic Policy Review*, forthcoming.

[34] Andrew Tilton, "Fed Nursing the Money Markets Back to Health," Goldman Sachs U.S. Daily newsletter, January 8, 2009.

[35] The arrangement is similar to the Fed's creation of Maiden Lane limited liability corporations to purchase Bear Stearns' and AIG's assets (discussed below), but those involved one-time purchases.

[36] See David Fettig, "Lender of More Than Last Resort," Federal Reserve Bank of Minneapolis, *The Region*, December 2002.

[37] Although much of the commercial paper bought by the CPFF was issued by financial firms, most financial firms experiencing any disruption to their liquidity needs in the commercial paper market were already eligible to borrow directly from the Fed on a collateralized basis.

[38] Brian Madigan, "Bagehot's Dictum in Practice," Speech at the Federal Reserve Bank of Kansas City's Annual Economic Symposium, August 21, 2009.

[39] See CRS Report RS22950, *Fannie Mae and Freddie Mac in Conservatorship*, by Mark Jickling.

[40] In the years before the crisis, the Fed had no GSE holdings, but the Fed had purchased GSE assets in the past. According to a New York Fed report, "Agency purchases were introduced in 1971 in order to 'widen the base for System open market operations and to add breadth to the market for agency securities.' New purchases were stopped in 1981, although some maturing funds from agency holdings were reinvested in newly issued agency securities. Beginning in 1997, all holdings of agency securities were allowed to mature without replacement. The last agency holding acquired under these programs matured in December 2003." Joseph Gagnon et al, *Large-Scale Asset Purchases by the Federal Reserve*, Federal Reserve Bank of New York, Staff Reports 441, March 2010.

[41] Federal Reserve, press release, November 25, 2008.

[42] For more information on the Treasury programs, see CRS Report RS22950, *Fannie Mae and Freddie Mac in Conservatorship*, by Mark Jickling.

[43] For more information, see Linda Goldberg, Craig Kennedy, and Jason Miu, *Central Bank Dollar Swap Lines and Overseas Dollar Funding Costs*, Federal Reserve Bank of New York, Staff Reports No. 429, Feb. 2010.

[44] Current data on swaps outstanding by central bank can be found in the Fed's *Federal Reserve System Monthly Report on Credit and Liquidity Programs and the Balance Sheet.*

[45] For more information, see CRS Report R41167, *Greece's Debt Crisis: Overview, Policy Responses, and Implications*, coordinated by Rebecca M. Nelson.

[46] This authority was originally allowed beginning in 2011 in the Financial Services Regulatory Relief Act of 2006 (P.L. 109-351). The Emergency Economic Stabilization Act of 2008 granted immediate authority.

[47] See Todd Keister et al, "Divorcing Money From Monetary Policy, Federal Reserve Bank of New York, *Economic Policy Review*, September 2008.

[48] One theory as to why the interest rate paid on bank reserves did not act as an effective floor on the federal funds rate is because the GSEs participate in the federal funds market but are not paid interest on their reserves at the Fed.

[49] See the section below entitled "Future Concerns."

[50] This section discusses the special assistance that the troubled firms received from the Fed. The same firms may also have subsequently accessed Fed resources through its normal lending facilities. All lending through facilities is confidential, so knowledge of such activity is limited to self-reporting by the firms. For example, the CEO of JPMorgan Chase testified to Congress that Bear Stearns had borrowed an additional $25 billion from the Fed. (Source: Kara Scannell and Sudeep Reddy, "Officials Say They Sought to Avoid Bear Bailout," *Wall Street Journal*, April 4, 2008, p. A1.) Similarly, AIG announced that it had accessed the Commercial Paper Funding Facility. (Source: "U.S. Treasury, Federal Reserve and AIG Establish Comprehensive Solution for AIG," AIG press release, November 10, 2008.)

[51] Federal Reserve and U.S. Treasury Department, "The Role of the Federal Reserve in Preserving Financial and Monetary Stability," joint press release, March 23, 2009.

[52] For more information, see CRS Report RL34420, *Bear Stearns: Crisis and "Rescue" for a Major Provider of Mortgage-Related Products*, by Gary Shorter.

[53] Federal Reserve Bank of New York, "New York Fed Completes Financing Arrangement Related to JPMorgan Chase's Acquisition of Bear Stearns," press release, June 26, 2008. A subordinate loan is one where the principal and interest are not repaid until after the primary loan is repaid. The originally announced terms of the loans were for up to $29 billion from the New York Fed and $1 billion from JPMorgan Chase. After more thoroughly reviewing the assets the LLC would receive, the Fed changed the terms of the loan.

[54] Federal Reserve Bank of New York, "Summary of Terms and Conditions Regarding the JPMorgan Chase Facility," press release, March 24, 2008. Many of the details of the loan, including the size, were not announced on March 16.

[55] Jamie Dimon, *Testimony Before the Senate Committee on Banking, Housing, and Urban Affairs*, April 3, 2008.

[56] Federal Reserve Bank of New York, "Summary of Terms and Conditions Regarding the JPMorgan Chase Facility," press release, March 24, 2008.

[57] Timothy Geithner, "Testimony Before the Senate Committee for Banking, Housing and Urban Affairs," April 3, 2008, p. 17.

[58] Federal Reserve Bank of New York, "Statement on Financing Arrangement of JPMorgan Chase's Acquisition of Bear Stearns," press release, March 24, 2008.

[59] Federal Reserve, *Factors Affecting Reserve Balances of Depository Institutions*, press release H.4.1, September 11, 2008. Information on the portfolio will be updated quarterly and announced through this press release.

[60] Jamie Dimon, *Testimony Before the Senate Committee on Banking, Housing, and Urban Affairs*, April 3, 2008.

[61] Timothy Geithner, "Testimony Before the Senate Committee for Banking, Housing and Urban Affairs," April 3, 2008, p. 13.

[62] This section was prepared with Baird Webel, specialist in Financial Economics. For more information, see CRS Report R40438, *Ongoing Government Assistance for American International Group (AIG)*, by Baird Webel.

[63] See, for example, "U.S. to Take Over AIG in $85 Billion Bailout; Central Banks Inject Cash as Credit Dries Up," *Wall Street Journal*, September 17, 2008, pp. A1-A6.

[64] Federal Reserve, "Factors Affecting Reserve Balances," press release H.4.1, September 18, 2008.

[65] Liam Pleven et al, "AIG Bailout Hit By New Cash Woes," *Wall Street Journal*, October 9, 2008, p. A1.

[66] N.Y. Ins. Law, Sec. 1410.

[67] Full details of the preferred shares can be found on the Treasury website at http://ustreas.gov/press/ releases/ reports/ 111008aigtermsheet.pdf.

[68] See, for example, "A.I.G. Reports Loss of $61.7 Billion as U.S. Gives More Aid," New York Times, March 2, 2009, p. A1.

[69] U.S. Treasury, "U.S. Treasury and Federal Reserve Board Announce Participation in AIG Restructuring Plan," Press Release dated March 2, 2009.

[70] U.S. Department of Treasury, *Troubled Asset Relief Program Monthly 105(a) Report to Congress*, November 10, 2009.

[71] See http://www.aig.com/aigweb/internet/en/files/Counterparties_tcm385-153017.pdf/.

[72] Citigroup, "Citigroup and U.S. Government Reach Definitive Agreement on Loss Sharing Program," press release, January 16, 2009.

[73] For a full discussion, see the section below entitled "Lender of Last Resort, Systemic Risk, and Moral Hazard."

[74] For a full discussion, see the section below entitled "Lender of Last Resort, Systemic Risk, and Moral Hazard."

[75] See, for example, Deborah Solomon, "Bailout Man Turns the Screws," *Wall Street Journal*, April 7, 2009, p. A1.

[76] Assuming that the interest rate on the loans exceeded the rate of return on the Treasuries that the Fed would have purchased if the loans had not occurred.

[77] See, for example, Peter Stella, *The Federal Reserve System Balance Sheet: What Happened and Why It Matters*, International Monetary Fund, Working Paper 09/120, May 2009.

[78] Current data on the income earned and change in asset value by Fed facility can be found in the Fed's *Monthly Report on Credit and Liquidity Programs and the Balance Sheet.*

[79] Congressional Budget Office, *The Budgetary Impact and Subsidy Costs of the Federal Reserve's Actions During the Financial* Crisis, May 2010. CBO generally estimates the rate or price needed to fully compensate for risk based on what rate or price would be charged in private markets; this became difficult to estimate during the financial crisis because private markets stopped functioning smoothly. CBO estimated the subsidy of each crisis program based on market conditions at the time the programs were started. Since market conditions have improved considerably since then, ex-post profits are not a sign that there was no subsidy; rates or prices had to reflect the risk that conditions might get much worse at the time the transaction was made.

[80] Previously, Section 13(3) required that the loan be "secured to the satisfaction of the Federal Reserve bank."

[81] It should be noted that a portfolio of Treasury securities is only needed to tighten monetary policy. Expansionary monetary policy involves the purchase of Treasury securities.

[82] The program also supplies more Treasuries to investors when there is excess demand because of a "flight to quality." The Treasuries issued under the program are indistinguishable to investors from regularly-issued securities.

[83] By comparison, the monetary base rose 2% over the four previous months.

[84] Another stated rationale for these purchases is to push down interest rates throughout the economy. It is difficult to assess whether the program has succeeded in this goal since many other factors also influence interest rates. For example, interest rates on these securities have generally trended upward since the Fed's purchases began, presumably because economic conditions have improved.

[85] The Fed's views on the issues outlined in this section can be read in Ben Bernanke, "The Fed's Exit Strategy," *Wall Street Journal*, July 21, 2009, p. A15. See also Claudio Borio and Piti Disyatat, *Unconventional Monetary Policies: An Appraisal,*" Bank for International Settlements, Working Paper 292, Nov. 2009.

[86] Chairman Ben Bernanke, "The Federal Reserve's Balance Sheet: An Update," Speech at the Federal Reserve Board Conference on Key Developments in Monetary Policy, October 8, 2009.

[87] One paper looks at international experience with paying interest on bank reserves to answer this question. There is very limited experience with raising short-term interest rates while maintaining excess reserve balances, however. Japan in the 1990s is the best-known case of quantitative easing, and it removed excess balances before raising rates. The authors found that Norway had successfully raised rates while maintaining excess reserves from 2005 to 2008, although they did reduce reserves by half during that period. David Bowman, Etienne Gagnon, Mike Leahy, "Interest on Excess Reserves as a Monetary Policy Instrument: The Experience of Foreign Central Banks," Federal Reserve Board, *International Finance Discussion Paper 996*, March 2010.

[88] The size of reverse repo operations are limited to the amount of securities held by the Fed available to lend and private investors' willingness to borrow them. In recent years, reverse repos outstanding have not exceeded $108 billion. Goldman Sachs reports that Fed officials have indicated that they do not believe private investors could absorb more than $100 billion in reverse repos. Ed McKelvey, "Fed Lays Groundwork to Offset Another Increase in Excess Reserves," *U.S. Daily Newsletter*, September 24, 2009.

[89] Economically, this would have the same effect as the Treasury Supplemental Financing Program, which has been unavailable since September 2009 because the federal debt has been too close to the statutory limit.

[90] Ben Bernanke, Vincent Reinhart, and Brian Sack, "Monetary Policy Alternatives at the Zero Bound," Federal Reserve Board of Governors, *Finance and Economics Discussion Series 2004-48*, 2004, p. 28.

[91] Until 1978, the Treasury had limited authority to "draw" from the Fed to finance its deficits, and used that authority sparingly. U.S. Congress, House Committee on Banking, Finance, and Urban Affairs, Domestic Monetary Policy, *Extending the Treasury-Federal Reserve Draw Authority*, committee print, 95th Cong., 2nd sess., April 5, 1978, 26-179 (Washington: GPO, 1978).

[92] The net addition to general revenues is reduced by the extra interest the Treasury must pay on debt it issued in order to deposit cash at the Fed.

[93] For more information, see CRS Report RS22963, *Financial Market Intervention*, by Edward V. Murphy and Baird Webel.

[94] In addition, the Fed faces some statutory limitations on lending to undercapitalized banks under normal circumstances. See, for example, Section 10B of the Federal Reserve Act.

[95] For more information, see CRS Report RL34730, *Troubled Asset Relief Program: Legislation and Treasury Implementation*, by Baird Webel and Edward V. Murphy.

[96] David Small and James Clouse, *The Scope of Monetary Policy Actions Authorized under the Federal Reserve Act*, Federal Reserve, FEDS Working Paper no. 2004-40, July 2004, p. 29.

[97] The Fed also created the Term Asset Backed Liquidity Facility (TALF) to lend to private investors to purchase illiquid assets of the same types that TARP was originally intended to purchase. TALF is also aimed at improving liquidity, and does not affect the capital adequacy problem directly, however.

[98] In this context, it is interesting to note that the Bear Stearns failure has been described as a non-bank run, meaning Bear Stearns was undermined because it was shunned by its counterparties and investors, analogous to a bank being shunned by its depositors. The defining characteristic of a run is that the fear of failure becomes self-fulfilling since it deprives an institution of the resources it needs to avoid failure.

[99] For more information, see CRS Report RL34412, *Containing Financial Crisis*, by Mark Jickling.

[100] Greg Ip, "Central Bank Offers Loans to Brokers, Cuts Key Rate," *Wall Street Journal*, March 17, 2008, p. A1.

[101] Chairman Bernanke argued that the Fed did not have the authority to assist Lehman Brothers because Lehman Brothers could not offer the Fed adequate collateral for a loan of the size needed, which according to Bernanke, would have been much larger than the assistance for Bear Stearns. See Ben Bernanke, "Current Economic and Financial Conditions," speech at the National Association for Business Economic Annual Meeting, October 7, 2008.

[102] This problem in relation to investment banking has to some degree been overtaken by events, as none of the five largest investment banks still exist in their original form. Lehman Brothers has entered bankruptcy, Bear Stearns and Merrill Lynch have merged with commercial banks, and Goldman Sachs and Morgan Stanley have reorganized as bank holding companies that are regulated by the Fed.

[103] All of the information outlined in this paragraph can be accessed at the Fed's website at http://www. Federal reserve.gov/monetarypolicy/bst.htm.

[104] Federal Reserve Board of Governors, *Federal Reserve System Monthly Report on Credit and Liquidity Programs and the Balance Sheet*.

[105] A federal judge ruled on August 25, 2009, that the Fed must turn information over to Bloomberg newsgroup on its emergency lending activities. The court case is Bloomberg LP v. Board of Governors of the Federal Reserve System, U.S. District Court, Southern District of New York (Manhattan), No. 08-9595.

[106] James Butkiewicz, "The Reconstruction Finance Corporation, the Gold Standard, and the Banking Panic of 1933," *Southern Economic Journal*, vol. 66, no. 2, October 1999, p. 271.

[107] A list of current GAO audits of the Fed can be found in the Fed's Annual Report.

[108] See U.S. General Accounting Office, *Federal Reserve System Audits*, GAO/T-GGD-94-44, October 27, 1993.

[109] Chairman Ben Bernanke, "Don't Strip the Fed of Supervisory Power," *Valley News*, December 1, 2009, p. A6. See also Federal Reserve Vice Chairman Donald Kohn, "Federal Reserve Independence," Testimony before the Subcommittee on Domestic Monetary Policy and Technology, House Financial Services Committee, July 9, 2009.

[110] See CRS Report RL31056, *Economics of Federal Reserve Independence*, by Marc Labonte.

[111] Chairman Ben S. Bernanke, Semiannual Monetary Policy Report to the Congress, Before the Committee on Financial Services, U.S. House of Representatives, Washington, DC, February 24, 2010.

[112] For example, the decision to make creditors whole in the case of Bear Stearns and AIG reduces incentives for creditors to curb lending to other institutions deemed "too big to fail."

[113] Some would argue that the GSE's funding advantage primarily stems from government conservatorship, and the effect of Fed's purchases are ancillary.

[114] For example, economist Glenn Rudebusch estimates that interest rates would need to reach -5% in 2009. Glenn Rudebusch, "The Fed's Monetary Policy Response to the Current Crisis," Federal Reserve Bank of San Francisco, *FRBSF Economic Letter*, no. 2009-17, May 22, 2009. See also John Williams, "Heeding Daedalus: Optimal Inflation and the Zero Lower Bound," *Brookings Papers on Economic Activity*, September 2009.

[115] While the term liquidity trap was often applied to Japan, it is theoretically defined as a situation where household demand for money becomes so great that normal sized changes in the money supply do not affect interest rates or spending. Under this strict definition, it is not clear that Japan, or any other economy, has ever experienced a liquidity trap.

[116] Asset prices have fallen, but they are not included in standard measures of inflation, which measures the prices of goods and services.

[117] Ben Bernanke, Vincent Reinhart, and Brian Sack, "Monetary Policy Alternatives at the Zero Bound: An Empirical Analysis," Federal Reserve Board, *Finance and Economic Discussion Series 2004-48*, 2004, p. 17. Other options for stimulus at zero short-term interest rates include buying longer-term assets to push down longer-term interest rates.

[118] Chairman Bernanke referred to the Fed's policies in 2008 as credit easing, rather than quantitative easing. He identifies quantitative easing as a policy where the central bank sets a growth rate for the monetary base and provides liquidity to achieve that growth rate. Under what he calls credit easing, the Fed has allowed the growth in the monetary base to be determined by the financial sector's demand for liquidity. He notes that both policies result in the growth of the central bank's balance sheet and the monetary base. See Chairman Ben S. Bernanke, *Speech at the Stamp Lecture*, London School of Economics, London, England, January 13, 2009.

[119] Donald Kohn, "Interactions Between Monetary and Fiscal Policy in the Current Situation," speech at Princeton University, Princeton, NJ, May 23, 2009.

[120] The Fed has argued that large excess reserves should not be seen as a sign that its policies have lost their effectiveness. See, for example, Todd Keister and James McAndrews, "Why Are Banks Holding So Many Excess Reserves?" *Federal Reserve Bank of New York Staff Reports*, no. 380, July 2009.

[121] Glenn Rudebusch, *The Fed's Exit Strategy for Monetary Policy*, Federal Reserve Bank of San Francisco, Economic Letter 2010-18, June 2010.

[122] Johannes Stroebel and John Taylor, "Estimated Impact of the Fed's Mortgage-Backed Securities Purchase Program," National Bureau of Economic Research, working paper 15626, Dec. 2009.

[123] See CRS Report RL34428, *Understanding Stagflation and the Risk of Its Recurrence*, by Brian W. Cashell and Marc Labonte.

[124] Rudebusch presents evidence that the growth in the Fed's balance sheet has had no effect on inflation expectations. Glenn Rudebusch, *The Fed's Exit Strategy for Monetary Policy*, Federal Reserve Bank of San Francisco, Economic Letter 2010-18, June 2010.

[125] For more information, see CRS Report RL34562, *Slow Growth or Inflation? The Federal Reserve's Dilemma*, by Brian W. Cashell and Marc Labonte.

In: U.S. Economic Recovery and Stimulus Measures
Editor: Jessica D. Saparito
ISBN: 978-1-61209-266-9

Chapter 7

TAX CUTS ON REPATRIATION EARNINGS AS ECONOMIC STIMULUS: AN ECONOMIC ANALYSIS

Donald J. Marples and Jane G. Gravelle

SUMMARY

At the beginning of the 111th Congress, economic stimulus proposals have dominated the legislative agenda, with a broad recognition that business tax incentives are among the policy options to consider. Two prominent proposals, H.R. 1 and S. 1, both titled the American Recovery and Reinvestment Act of 2009, were the focus of this debate. Both proposals include business tax incentives which would increase the after-tax rate of return on domestic investment and were subsequently enacted in P.L. 111-5. In contrast, little attention has been given to international policy options. An exception to this is a plan to reduce the tax rate on repatriated dividends that has received some consideration. Under such a plan, the U.S. tax that U.S. firms pay when their overseas operations remit ("repatriate") their foreign earnings as dividends to their U.S. parent corporations would be reduced. This provision was considered, but not adopted, as a floor amendment to a Senate version of the American Recovery and Reinvestment Act of 2009.

A conceptually similar proposal was enacted as part of the American Jobs Creation Act (P.L. 108-357). The provision provided a temporary reduced rate for repatriated earnings, with the condition that the repatriated earnings be used for domestic investment. While empirical evidence is clear that this provision resulted in a significant increase in repatriated earnings, empirical evidence is unable to show a corresponding increase in domestic investment or employment.

Viewed in the current debate on how to most efficiently stimulate the economy, economic theory suggests that the simulative effect of a temporary tax cut for repatriations may be partially offset by exchange rate adjustments that would reduce net exports. In addition, how businesses use repatriated earnings will impact the stimulative effect of a tax cut for repatriations. For example, repatriated earnings will have a larger stimulative effect if they are used to increase current investment. A smaller stimulative effect will result, in contrast, if the repatriated earnings are used to shore up "cash-flow" issues. This report will be updated as legislative events warrant.

The legislative agenda at the start of the 111th Congress has been dominated by efforts aimed at stimulating the U.S. economy. Two prominent proposals, H.R. 1 and S. 1, both Ttitled the American Recovery and Reinvestment Act of 2009, were the focus of this debate. Both proposals include business tax incentives which would increase the after-tax rate of return on some domestic investment and were subsequently enacted in P.L. 111-5. In contrast, little attention has been given to international policy options. One international option that has received some consideration is a plan to reduce a tax cut for repatriated dividends. Under this option, the U.S. tax that a U.S. parent corporation pays when its overseas operations repatriate foreign earnings to its U.S. parent, as dividends, would be reduced. This provision was considered, but not adopted, as a floor amendment to a Senate version of the American Recovery and Reinvestment Act of 2009.

A conceptually similar proposal was enacted as part of the American Jobs Creation Act (P.L. 108-357). The provision provided a temporary reduced rate for repatriated earnings, with the condition that the repatriated earnings be used for domestic investment. While empirical evidence is clear that this provision resulted in a significant increase in repatriated earnings, empirical evidence is unable to show a corresponding increase in domestic investment or employment by firms that utilized the repatriation provisions.

In the context of the current debate on stimulus, the use of the repatriations and not the magnitude of repatriations stimulated are likely to be the key to the proposal's effect on U.S. economic growth. This follows from two points. First, even if sizeable repatriations occur, the rate of return on U.S. investment will be unaffected by the repatriations. Assuming firms are not liquidity-constrained, it is possible that the bulk of the repatriations will be used as dividends to stockholders or used to pay down corporate debt. This scenario is especially likely for large firms.[1] Second, when the repatriations occur, those that are denominated in foreign currencies will be converted to dollars. The corresponding increase in the demand for dollars may drive up the price of the dollar in world currency markets. As a result, U.S. net exports may decline from levels that would otherwise occur, and the stimulative impact of the repatriations on the U.S. economy would be lessened.

THE U.S. INTERNATIONAL TAX SYSTEM

The United States bases its jurisdiction to tax international income on residence. As a result, U.S.-chartered corporations are taxed on their worldwide income, but foreign corporations are taxed only on their U.S.-source income. Accordingly, a U.S. firm with overseas operations can indefinitely postpone its U.S. tax on its foreign income by operating through a foreign subsidiary. Using the same principle, U.S. taxes are deferred as long as its foreign earnings remain in the control of its foreign subsidiary and are reinvested abroad. The U.S. firm pays taxes on its overseas earnings only when they are paid to the U.S. parent corporation as intra-firm dividends or other income.

Another prominent feature of the U.S. tax system is the foreign tax credit. The foreign tax credit is designed to alleviate double taxation where U.S. and foreign governments' tax jurisdictions overlap that is the U.S. firm pays taxes at the higher of the U.S. or foreign tax rate. With respect to repatriated dividends, U.S. firms can claim foreign tax credits for foreign taxes paid by their subsidiaries on the earnings used to pay the repatriated dividends. The ability to defer U.S. tax, thus, poses an incentive for U.S. firms to invest abroad in countries with low tax rates. Proposals to cut taxes on repatriations are based on the premise that even this deferred tax on intra-firm dividends discourages repatriations and encourages firms to reinvest foreign earnings abroad and that a cut in the tax would stimulate repatriations.

REPATRIATED EARNINGS PROVISIONS IN THE AMERICAN JOBS CREATION ACT

The repatriated earnings provision included in the American Jobs Creation Act (P.L. 108-357) reduced the taxes due on repatriated earnings. In particular, the provision provided a deduction equal to 85% of the increase in foreign-source earnings repatriated. For a firm paying taxes at the 35% corporate tax rate, this reduced the tax rate on repatriated earnings to the equivalent of 5.25%.

The act required firms to adopt domestic investment plans for qualifying repatriations and limited the maximum deduction allowed. The maximum allowable deduction was set equal to the greater of $500 million or the amount of earnings shown to be permanently reinvested outside the United States in a firm's books of accounts certified before June 30, 2003.

The deduction was designed and intended to be available for one year. At the taxpayer's option, the year would be the first tax year beginning on or after the date of enactment of P.L. 108-357 or the last tax year beginning before that date. The conference report for the act stated the "conferees emphasize that this is a temporary economic stimulus measure, and that there is no intent to make this measure permanent, or to 'extend' or enact it again in the future."[2]

IMPACTS OF A REDUCTION IN THE TAX ON REPATRIATED EARNINGS

A number of researchers have studied the impact of the reduction in the tax on repatriated earnings that came out of the American Jobs Creation Act. The studies have generally focused on two particular responses: the level of repatriations and the impact on economic growth. In short, the studies generally conclude that the reduction in the tax rate on repatriated earnings led to a sharp increase in the level of repatriated earnings, but that the repatriations did not increase domestic investment or employment. They further conclude that much of the repatriations were returned to shareholders through stock repurchases.

Impact on Repatriated Earnings

The impact of a reduction in the tax on repatriated earnings depends on whether the reduction is permanent or temporary. As mentioned above, the provision enacted in P.L. 108-357 was envisioned as being a temporary and one-time reduction.

A permanent reduction in the tax on repatriated earnings is not likely to result in an increase in repatriations. According to the "new view" of dividends, once a firm invests equity capital in a foreign subsidiary, the payment of home-country taxes is inevitable.[3] Given this inevitability, once the capital is abroad, repatriation taxes have no impact on the firm's decision whether to repatriate foreign earnings in the present or to instead reinvest them abroad. Instead, repatriations will follow a life-cycle model, unaffected by repatriation taxes, where young foreign subsidiaries will receive capital from their U.S. parent so long as there are profitable foreign investment opportunities, followed by a period of self-financing of foreign investment by the foreign subsidiary, and ending with a period of repatriations made by mature foreign subsidiaries.

In contrast, a temporary reduction in the tax on repatriated earnings is likely to result in an increase in repatriations in the short-run. Note that the long-run result, above, depended upon the tax on repatriated earnings being the same in the present and the future. This no longer holds for a temporary reduction, and thus repatriation taxes may affect the level of repatriations. This is not to say that all firms will increase repatriations in response to the tax reduction. It is expected that a young firm's repatriation decisions would still be unaffected by repatriation taxes, as long as the reduction expires prior to the firm intending to repatriate profits. In addition, any short-term increase in repatriations may be offset by a decrease in repatriations in later years. This is especially likely to occur if corporations view a temporary rate reduction as likely to recur.

The actual pattern of repatriations observed after enactment of the American Jobs Creation Act validated the short-run economic prediction. According to the Internal Revenue Service, 843 of the roughly 9,700 eligible corporations took advantage of the deduction.[4] This sub-set of eligible corporations repatriated $312 billion in qualified earnings and created total deductions of $265 billion. Using the most recent year of data available, the data suggest that approximately one-third of all offshore earnings were repatriated in the tax year after enactment. As way of comparison, base dividends for the same corporations total approximately $34 billion and suggest a normal repatriation rate of little more than 4%. Thus, not controlling for other factors, the rate reduction resulted in a greater-than eight-fold increase in repatriations.

The IRS study of the provision, cited above, provided information on the recipients. The benefits of the repatriation provision are not evenly spread across industries. The pharmaceutical and medicine industry accounted for $99 billion in repatriations or 32% of the total. The computer and electronic equipment industry accounted for $58 billion or 18% of the total. Thus these two industries accounted for half of the repatriations. Most of the dividends were repatriated from low tax countries or tax havens.

The benefits were also highly concentrated in a few firms. According to a recent study, five firms (Pfizer, Merck, Hewlett-Packard, Johnson & Johnson, and IBM) are responsible for $88 billion, over a quarter (28%) of total repatriations.[5] The top 10 firms (adding Schering-Plough, Du Pont, Bristol-Myers Squibb, Eli Lilly, and PepsiCo) accounted for 42%. The top 15 (adding Procter and Gamble, Intel, Coca-Cola, Altria, and Motorola), accounted for over half (52%).

Using an alternative measure of repatriations also shows a large "spike" in repatriations resulting from the American Jobs Creation Act. As seen in **Figure 1**, U.S. Multinationals increased their repatriations by approximately 266% from the prior year.

The empirical evidence also suggests that corporations expect the temporary rate reduction to recur. According to several researchers, unrepatriated earnings have rapidly grown since 2005.[6] In fact, since the last repatriation rate reduction, unrepatriated earnings for all corporations have grown by 72% to $958 billion and by 81% to $639 billion for firms that repatriated under the American Jobs Creation Act.

Impact on Economic Growth

Given the empirical evidence that a temporary reduction in taxes on repatriated earnings leads to an increase in repatriated earnings, how does this affect economic growth? Two factors that will impact the answer are how the repatriated earning are used and the role of flexible exchange rates. Simply put, the more the repatriated earnings are used to shore up a corporation's balance sheet or paid to shareholders the less the simulative effect of the repatriations. On top of that, flexible exchange rates will likely further depress the simulative impact of the repatriations.

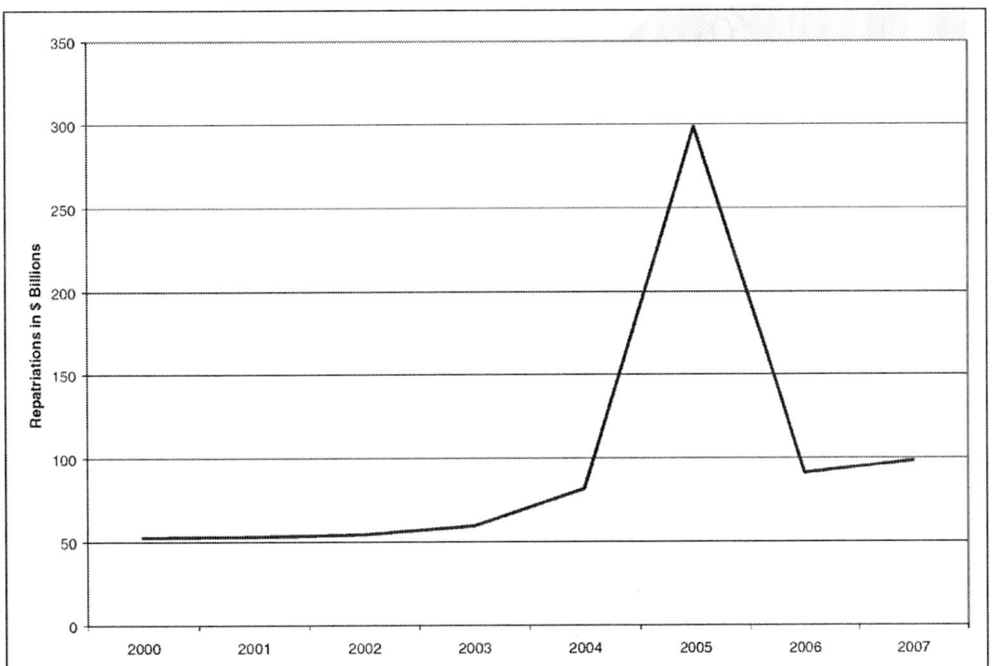

Source: Bureau of Economic Analysis, International Transactions, Table 7a.

Figure 1. Repatriations by U.S. Multinational Corporations, 2000-2007.

Use of Repatriated Earnings and Economic Stimulus

Fiscal policy, such as a reduction in the tax rate on repatriated earnings, boosts economic activity by increasing the short-run demand for goods and services. Put bluntly, the earning must be spent, in order to stimulate the economy. With this in mind, the American Jobs Creation Act required that corporations have an approved plan to reinvest the repatriated earnings prior to claiming the 85% deduction. The main criticism of the reinvestment plan provision was that it allowed an overly generous range of reinvestment options all but executive compensation and stock repurchase programs and that it was not explicitly linked to specific uses. Proponents of the reinvestment plan argue that the range of options allowed reflects a recognition of the fungibility of money.

Economic theory finds that changes in the after-tax cost of new investment are most likely to induce new investment. In contrast, incentives which increase after-tax profits (and benefit mainly cash-flow) without changing the incentive for new investment do not generally induce much new hiring or production, because these types of incentives do not alter the conditions of the pre-incentive investment equilibrium.

Two studies have attempted to quantify the impact of cash-flow incentives. According to the Sinai study, instituting repatriation provisions similar to those in the American Jobs Creation Act would improve the net cash-flow of participating companies by approximately $535 billion in 2009. The Congressional Budget Office (CBO) estimates that the stimulative impact (or multiplier) of a specific cash-flow proposal, for loss carrybacks, at between 0 and 40 cents of GDP per tax dollar not received.[7] This range of the stimulative effect for loss carrybacks should likely be viewed as an upper-bound estimate for the cash-flow effect of a repatriation rate reduction. This follows from the observation that corporations with current losses—and thus having losses to carryback are more likely to be cash constrained and able to benefit from a cash-flow provision than the relatively large multination corporations that are likely to have a better cash-flow position. (By contrast, CBO sets the multiplier for federal spending at 1 to 2.5, for transfer payments at 0.8 to 2.2, and for individual tax cuts at 0.5 to 1.7.)[8]

Which category of incentive a reduction in the tax on repatriated earnings belongs in depends upon the degree to which repatriated earnings change the incentive for new investment. This in turn depends upon the degree to which the reinvestment plan compels investment. Given a weak focus of the reinvestment plan, economic theory suggests that it is likely that a reduction in the tax on repatriated earnings falls into the less stimulative category.[9]

Empirical analyses of the stimulative effects of the repatriation provisions in the American Jobs Creation Act also suggests a limited stimulative impact from the provisions. They conclude that much of the repatriated earnings were used for cash-flow purposes and little evidence exists that new investment was spurred.

Several analysts have used public data sources, such as annual reports and press releases, to report the subsequent actions of participants in the American Jobs Creation Act, primarily firms that repatriated but also reduced employment, a sign that the scale of domestic operations was not increasing. In **Table 1** we summarize selected information from these reports for these firms. Taken together, the firms identified in **Table 1** account for nearly one-third of all repatriations under the American Jobs Creation Act. In general, two trends emerge from these analyses: (1) corporations that utilized the repatriation provisions were unable to expand domestic operations and (2) corporations in several industries appear to have increased their rate of repatriations after the expiration of the repatriation provisions. These event studies, while informative, are not able to imply any causal relationship between use of the repatriation provisions and subsequent firm responses, since they are unable to compare the response with an alternative response in the absence of utilization of the repatriation provisions. They also cannot be generalized to other firms.

Building upon the event study literature, a series of empirical econometric studies have concluded that the American Jobs Creation Act repatriation provisions did not increase domestic economic activity. Dharmapala et al. find that repatriations had a small and statistically insignificant impact both on domestic capital expenditures and employment.[10] Clemons and Kinney, similarly, are unable to find evidence that investment expenditures increased in corporations that utilized the repatriation provisions of the JOBS Act.[11] In summary, these studies both found the repatriation provisions to be an ineffective means of increasing economic growth.

There is some empirical evidence, however, that the repatriations were used to return money to shareholders though stock repurchase programs.[12] Dharmapala et al. found that a $1 increase in repatriations increased stock repurchases by $0.91, a use prohibited under the American Jobs Creation Act. (Note that because of the fungibility of money, firms that use part of the repatriation to repurchase shares may not violate the law). Clemmons and Kinney also concluded that the only significant increase in expenditures for participating corporations was on stock repurchases. Another study found similar results, estimating that 20% of the repatriation was used for stock repurchases.[13]

Table 1. Selected Information on 12 Corporations that Utilized the Repatriation Provisions in the American Jobs Creation Act

Company	JOBS Act Repatriation Amount ($ Billions)	Jobs Lost in 2005-2006	Pre-JOBS Act Accumulation of Foreign Earnings (two years, $ Billions)	Post-JOBS Act Accumulated Foreign Earnings ($ Billions)
Pfizer	37	10,000	67	101
CitiGroup	3.2	n/a	9	35.8
Merck	15.9	7,000	33	29.7
Hewlett-Packard	14.5	14,500	28.9	23.7
Proctor & Gamble	10.7	unspecified # lost	24.7	54
IBM	9.5	n/a	34.7	33
PepsiCo	7.5	200-250	16.3	25.5
Motorola	4.4	unspecified # lost	13.7	8.1
Honeywell	2.7	2,000	5.5	7
Ford	0.9	30,000-40,000	n/a	n/a
National Semiconductor	0.5	5 percent of workforce	n/a	n/a
Colgate-Palmolive	0.8	4,000	n/a	n/a

Sources: Columns 2 and 3: Lee A. Sheppard and Martin A. Sullivan, "Multinationals Accumulate to Repatriate," *Tax Notes*, January 19, 2009, pp. 295-298; and various media reports; Column 4: Sheppard and Sullivan.

In contrast to these empirical studies, the simulations conducted in the Sinai study find that a temporary reduction in the tax on repatriated earnings would increase domestic economic activity in the 2009-2013 time period.[14] According to the simulation results, the reduction in the tax on repatriated earnings would increase gross domestic product (GDP) by an average of $62 billion per year, and business capital spending and research and development by an average of $7 billion per year. The study also finds an increase in employment that peaks at 614,000 additional jobs in 2011.

Exchange Rate Adjustments and Economic Stimulus

The stimulative effect of the reduced tax rate on repatriated earnings is expected to be muted by the international system of flexible exchange rates and, subsequently, by trade. This effect will occur, because as foreign denominated earnings of foreign subsidiaries are repatriated they are also converted to U.S. dollars. This result increases the demand for dollars which leads to an appreciation, or increase, in the price of the dollar in foreign exchange markets. This stronger dollar makes U.S.-made exports more expensive and foreign imports less expensive. As a result, U.S. exports would temporarily decline, further straining the economy and at least partially offsetting any stimulative effect of the repatriated earnings.

End Notes

[1] See CRS Report RS21126, *Tax Cuts and Economic Stimulus: How Effective Are the Alternatives?*, by Jane G. Gravelle, for a more detailed discussion.

[2] U.S. Congress, Conference Committees, 2004, *American Jobs Creation Act of 2004*, conference report to accompany H.R. 4520, H.Rept. 108-755, 108th Cong., 2nd sess. (Washington: GPO, 2004), p. 314.

[3] Jane Gravelle, "Federal Corporate Income Tax," in *The Encyclopedia of Taxation and Tax Policy*, ed. Joseph J. Cordes, Robert D. Ebel, and Jane G. Gravelle (Washington, DC: The Urban Institute, 1999), p. 175.

[4] Melissa Redmiles, *The One-Time Recieved Dividends Deduction*, Internal Revenue Service, Statistics of Income Bulletin, Washington, DC, Spring 2008, http://www.irs.gov/pub/irs-soi/08codivdeductbul.pdf.

[5] Rodney P. Mock and Andreas Simon, "Permanently Reinvested Earnings: Priceless," *Tax Notes*, November 17, 2008, pp. 835-848.

[6] Allen Sinai, *Macro Economic Effects of Reducing the Effective Tax Rate on Repatriated Foreign Subsidiary Earnings in a Credit- and Liquidity-Constrained Environment,* Decisions Economics, Inc, Economic Studies Series, Dec. 11, 2008, http://www.accf.org/media/dynamic/3/media_304.pdf; and Lee A. Shepard and Martin A. Sullivan, "Multinationals Accumulate to Repatriate," *Tax Notes*, January 19, 2009, pp. 295-298.

[7] U.S. Congress, House Committee on the Budget, *The State of the Economy and Issues in Developing an Effective Policy Response*, The Economic Outlook and Budget Challenges, 111th Cong., 1st sess., January 27, 2009.

[8] The CBO multipliers are similar to those used by other forecasters. See CRS Report R40104, *Economic Stimulus: Issues and Policies*, by Jane G. Gravelle, Thomas L. Hungerford, and Marc Labonte for a complete discussion on multiplier effects.

[9] Dhammika Dharmapala, C. Fritz Foley, and Kristin J. Forbes, "The Unintended Consequences of the Homeland Investment Act: Implications for Financial Constraints, Governance, and International Tax Policy," unpublished working paper, September 2008; Roy Clemons and Michael R. Kinney," An Analysis of the Tax Holiday for Repatriations Under the Jobs Act," *Tax Notes*, August 25, 2008, pp. 759-768; and Jennifer Blouin and Linda Krull, "Bringing it Home: A Study of the Incentives Surrounding the Repatriations of Foreign Earnings Under the Jobs Creation Act of 2004," Unpublished Working Paper, Wharton School and University of Oregon, July 2008.

[10] Dhammika Dharmapala, C. Fritz Foley, and Kristin J. Forbes, "The Unintended Consequences of the Homeland Investment Act: Implications for Financial Constraints, Governance, and International Tax Policy," unpublished working paper, September 2008.

[11] Roy Clemons and Michael R. Kinney, "An Analysis of the Tax Holiday for Repatriations Under the Jobs Act," *Tax Notes*, August 25, 2008, pp. 759-768.

[12] In addition to stock repurchases, increasing dividends are a way of returning money to shareholders. Given the temporary nature of the repatriation provisions, however, stock repurchases would be the expected vehicle to return money to shareholders, since they represent less of a commitment to ongoing distributions.

[13] Jennifer Blouin and Linda Krull, "Bringing it Home: A Study of the Incentives Surrounding the Repatriations of Foreign Earnings Under the Jobs Creation Act of 2004," Unpublished Working Paper, Wharton School and University of Oregon, July 2008.

[14] Allen Sinai, *Macro Economic Effects of Reducing the Effective Tax Rate on Repatriated Foreign Subsidiary Earnings in a Credit- and Liquidity-Constrained Environment,* Decisions Economics, Inc, Economic Studies Series, Dec. 11, 2008, http://www.accf.org/media/dynamic/3/media_304.pdf.

In: U.S. Economic Recovery and Stimulus Measures
Editor: Jessica D. Saparito
ISBN: 978-1-61209-266-9

Chapter 8

THE ECONOMIC IMPACT OF THE AMERICAN RECOVERY AND REINVESTMENT ACT OF 2009: FOURTH QUARTERLY REPORT

Executive Office of the President

EXECUTIVE SUMMARY

As part of the unprecedented accountability and transparency provisions included in the American Recovery and Reinvestment Act of 2009 (ARRA), the Council of Economic Advisers (CEA) is charged with providing to Congress quarterly reports on the effects of the Recovery Act on overall economic activity, and on employment in particular. In this fourth report, we provide an assessment of the effects of the Act through the secondquarter of 2010.

Evaluating the impact of countercyclical macroeconomic policy is inherently difficult because we do not observe what would have happened to the economy in the absence of policy. Because of the challenges in the analysis, we approach the task of estimating the impact of the Recovery Act from a number of different directions, and supplement our estimates with those of numerous outside analysts.

One section of the report looks at trends in the size and composition of Recovery Act spending and tax reductions. We find that:

- The magnitude of the fiscal stimulus increased substantially in the first quarter of 2010 and has increased further in the second quarter (from \$80 billion in 2009:Q4 to \$108 billion in 2010:Q1 to \$116 billion in 2010:Q2).
- Government investment outlays in areas such as infrastructure, clean energy, and communications technology increased by roughly 50 percent between the first and second quarters of 2010.

Another section evaluates the economic impact of the Recovery Act from a number of different perspectives. The key findings are:

- Following implementation of the ARRA, the trajectory of the economy changed dramatically. Real GDP began to grow steadily starting in the third quarter of 2009 and private payroll employment has increased by nearly 600,000 since its low point in December 2009.
- The two CEA methods of estimating the impact of the fiscal stimulus suggest that the ARRA has raised the level of GDP as of the second quarter of 2010, relative to what it otherwise would have been, by between 2.7 and 3.2 percent. These estimates are very similar to those of a wide range of other analysts, including the Congressional Budget Office.
- The CEA estimates that as of the second quarter of 2010, the ARRA has raised employment relative to what it otherwise would have been by between 2.5 and 3.6 million. These estimates are broadly consistent with the direct recipient reporting data available for 2010:Q1.

A special section of the report focuses on the public investment provisions of the Recovery Act. This analysis shows that:

- The Recovery Act includes appropriations for $319 billion of public investment spending on projects ranging from roads and bridges to community health centers to a smarter electrical grid. To date, two-thirds of these appropriated funds have been obligated and more than one-quarter have been outlayed.
- CEA estimates this public investment spending has already saved or created more than 800,000 jobs as of the second quarter of 2010, an increase of 30 percent over the first quarter.
- A case study of the transportation infrastructure provisions of the Act shows that nearly 14,000 projects have been awarded in areas ranging from highway improvements to new airport runways and public transit. Recovery Act transportation expenditures by state are positively correlated with private employment growth in heavy construction.

A related special section analyzes the many direct Recovery Act programs that are designed to leverage private, non-profit, and state and local government spending:

- Some examples of Recovery Act programs that leverage other investment funds are tax credits for advanced energy manufacturing, loan guarantees for small businesses, and interest subsidies for state and local borrowing to finance essential infrastructure projects.
- CEA's analysis shows that roughly $100 billion of Recovery Act funds have leverage provisions, and these funds will ultimately support more than $380 billion of total investment spending. This implies that every $1 of Recovery Act funds invested in these programs is partnered with about$3 of outside investment spending.
- The majority of the leveraged funds come from the private sector.
- A case study of the Production Tax Credit and other incentive programs for wind energy suggests that the leverage provisions have an important impact on private sector investment spendingand hence on job creation .

I. INTRODUCTION

The American Recovery and Reinvestment Act of 2009 (ARRA) is the boldest countercyclical fiscal expansion in American history. It was enacted at a time when U.S. real gross domestic product (GDP) was contracting at an annual rate of more than 6 percent and employment was falling by more than 750,000 jobs per month. TheAct was designed to cushion the fall in demand caused by the financial crisis and the subsequent decline in consumer and business confidence, household wealth, and access to credit. Together with policies to stabilize the financial system, increase liquidity and credit, and stem the tide of foreclosures, the ARRA was part of a comprehensive policy response to the economic turmoil that gripped the United States and the world economy in the fall of 2008 and early 2009.

As part of the unprecedented accountability and transparency provisions included in the Recovery Act, the Council of Economic Advisers (CEA) was charged with providing quarterly reports to Congress on the effects of the Recovery Act on overall economic activity, and on employment in particular. In this fourth report, we provide an assessment of the effects of the Act through the secondquarter of 20 10.

As discussed in our previous reports, identifying the impact of policy actions is inherently difficult, and the estimates must be understood to be subject to large margins of error. For this reason,the CEA prepares estimates of the impact of the ARRA from two approaches, and reports estimates from a wide range of private analysts and from the Congressional Budget Office (CBO). We also regularly analyze in more detail the impact of specific programs and provisions of the Act in order to more thoroughly understand and evaluate its effects.

Our multifaceted analysis indicates that the Recovery Act has played an essential role in changing the trajectory of the economy. It has raised the level of GDP substantially relative to what it otherwise would have been and has saved or created between 2.5 and 3.6 million jobs as of the secondquarter of 2010.

The report begins in Section II with a summary of the spending and tax reductions that have occurred under the ARRA to date. As of the end of June 2010, more than 60 percent of the original $787 billion included in the Act has been outlayed or has gone to American households and businesses in the form of tax reductions. Importantly, the fiscal stimulus provided by the Act increased substantially in the first quarter of 2010 and rose even further in the second quarter. As in the first quarter of 2010, much of the higher level of stimulus in the second quarter was due to a surge in tax refunds and reduced final liabilities. However, public investment spending, which now totals $86 billion, also increased significantly. It is expected to continue risingthrough the end of the year.

Section III contains the key analysis of the overall economic impact of the Recovery Act. It shows that economic conditions have changed dramatically in the year and a half since the Recovery Act was passed. GDP began to grow in the third quarter of 2009, and has now grown for three quarters in a row. Based on the available data and a range of forecasts, GDP appears to have continued to expand solidly in the second quarter of 2010. Payroll employment grew for the first time since the recession began in November 2009, and rose modestly through the second quarter of 2010. Employment growth, excluding temporary Census workers, averaged 63,000 per month in 2010:Q1 and 123,000 per month in the second quarter. Obviously, much work remains to repair the labor market damage caused by the financial crisis and the severe recession that followed. However, the economy appears to be gradually recovering.

We estimate the role of the Recovery Act in effecting this dramatic turnaround in two ways. One uses estimates of the effects of fiscal policy from standard macroeconomic forecasting models. The second involves a comparison of the actual behavior of GDP and employment with a plausible, statistically-determined baseline. The two methods indicate that the ARRA has raised both GDP and employment substantially relative to what they otherwise would have been. A compilation of estimates from prominent private-sector and public-sector analysts shows that our estimated impacts are similar to those of economists across the ideological spectrum. We also examine the available direct job creation data provided by a fraction of ARRA fund recipients and find that the results provide further corroboration of our estimates of the overall impact of the Act.

In previous reports, the CEA has highlighted key portions of the Recovery Act, including the state fiscal relief and the tax reduction and income support components. In Section IV of this report, we focus on the public investment spending. The Recovery Act includes $319 billion of investment spending in everything from roads and bridges to schools to a smarter electrical grid and community health centers. We analyze the broad range of useful investments being made and discuss the progress in finalizing awards and getting projects underway. Our model-based analysis suggests that the investment components of the Act by themselves have already raised employment relative to what it otherwise would have been by more than 800,000 jobs as of the second quarter of 2010, 30 percent more than in the first quarter. A detailed case study of the investment in transportation infrastructure finds that higher Recovery Act transportation spending in a state is associated with higher private employment growth in heavy construction.

Much of this Recovery Act investment spending takes the form of grants that require co-investment by the recipients and tax incentives for certain types of spending. As a result, the public spending is leveraged with other funds to support even larger amounts of total investment. Section V examines these leverage provisions in more detail. The analysis shows that roughly $100 billion of Recovery Act funds have this feature and that these funds will ultimately support more than $380 billion of total investment spending. This implies that every $1 of Recovery Act funds in these programs is partnered with about $3 of other funds, the majority from the private sector. A case study of the Production Tax Credit and other incentives for wind energy suggests that the leverage provisions have an important impact on private sector investment spending and hence job creation.

II. The Progress of Spending and Tax Reductions under the Recovery Act

The first step in evaluating the effects of the Recovery Act is to analyze the data on spending and tax reductionst hat have occurred under the Act. It is certainly possible that the Act could have had effects even before any tax changes or spending had occurred. For example, its passage could have affected confidence, and expectations of a tax cut in the future could affect household spending today. But it is likely that the Act's most significant impact comes as funds are spent and tax cuts reach consumers and businesses.

A. Overall Budgetary Impact

Data on the overall budgetary impact of the Recovery Act are available on the Recovery.gov website. The data are broken down into outlays, obligations, and tax reductions. The outlays and obligations by agency are available weekly and the tax reduction data are available quarterly.[1] Outlays represent payments made by the government. Those funds represent spending that has already occurred. Obligations represent funds that have been made available but not necessarily outlayed, such as for a highway project where the builder must complete the work properly to be fully reimbursed by the Federal government. In many instances, obligations can generate economic activity because recipients may begin spending as soon as they are certain funds are available.

Table 1 shows outlays, obligations, and tax reductions as of the end of each quarter since the Act's passage (March 2009, June 2009, September 2009, December 2009, March 2010, and June 2010). As of the end of the second quarter of 2010, the sum of outlays and tax cuts was $480 billion, with an additional $147 billion obligated but not yet outlayed. This is very similar to the amount projected to have been spent by this point by the Congressional Budget Office when the Recovery Act was passed.[2] Additionally, the sum of spending, obligations in excess of spending, and tax cuts is $627 billion.

Table 1. Outlays, Obligations, and Tax Reductions

	Through the end of[a]					
	2009:Q1 (March)	**2009:Q2 (June)**	**2009:Q3 (September)**	**2009:Q4 (December)**	**2010:Q1 (March)**	**2010:Q2 (June)**
	Billions of Dollars					
Outlays	8.6	56.3	110.7	164.2	210.9	257.3
Obligations	30.5	157.8	256.3	313.9	362.1	403.8
Tax Reductions	2.4	35.3	64.7	91.4	153.1	223.0
Sum of Outlays and Tax Reductions[b]	11.0	91.7	175.4	255.6	364.0	480.3

Sources: Agency Financial and Activity Reports to the Office of Management and Budget; simulations from the Department of the Treasury (Office of Tax Analysis) based on the FY2011 Mid-Session Review.

Notes: a. Data on outlays and obligations are for the last day of each calendar quarter.

b. Items may not add to total due to rounding.

B. Components of the Recovery Act

The categorization of stimulus into outlays versus tax reductions follows accounting conventions rather than economic function. For example, the Making Work Pay tax credit, which reduced taxes for 95 percent of working families, is treated as a tax cut, while the $250 extra payment to seniors and veterans is treated as an outlay. Yet, both are thought to affect economic activity by putting more money into the hands of consumers. For this reason, it is useful to consider a more functional decomposition. The decomposition is not only interesting in its own right, but is necessary for our later model-basedanalys is of the impact of the program.

We divide the total dollars of stimulus expended to date into six categories: individual tax cuts and similar payments; the tax cut associated with the adjustment of the Alternative Minimum Tax (AMT); business tax incentives; state fiscal relief; aid to those most directly hurt by the recession; and public investment spending. The first three are tax changes of some kind and are estimated to be roughly one-third of the total package; the second two represent emergency measures and are also estimated to be roughly one-third of the total; the last encompasses a range of direct spending and covers the remainder.

We divide the outlays and tax reduction data into these functional categories as follows.

Individual tax cuts include the Making Work Pay tax credit, the child tax credit, and a number of smaller individual tax reductions. We also include direct payments that were made in lieu of a tax cut to certain groups. These include payments of $250 distributed to individuals who receive Social Security and Supplemental Security Income, Railroad Retirement benefits, or veterans' benefits. The business tax incentives and AMT relief are calculated directly by the Office of Tax Analysis(OTA) as part of itssimulation proces s.[3]

We define state fiscal relief to include just the two main programs in this category: a substantial increase in the Federal government's matching percentage for Medicaid spending (FMAP), and formula grants to state governments for education through the State Fiscal Stabilization Fund. Aid to those directly impacted by the recession includes the increase and extension of unemployment benefits, increased funds for nutritional assistance, and increases in the Temporary Assistance to Needy Families program. Similarly, the government's subsidy of continuing health insurance benefits under COBRA, which is technically a business tax cut, is treated as aid to directly impacted individuals for our functional classification.

Public investment outlays includ e everything else. The obvious components are spending on infrastructure, health information technology, research on renewable energy, and other forms of direct spending excluding transfers. Also included here are tax credits for particular types of private spending, such as weatherization, advanced energy manufacturing, or research and experimentation, since these credits are functionally similar to the direct government spending. Section IV of the report discusses in greater depth the types of public investment in the Act.

C. Trends and Developments

Table 2 shows our breakdown of aggregate outlays and tax relief into these functional categories. For the impact on the economy, what matters is less the cumulative level of expenditures under the Act, but rather the amount spent each quarter. For this reason, Table 2 also reports the change in the total budgetary impact from the end of the previous quarter.

The table shows important changes over time in the magnitude and composition of the fiscal stimulus. After being stable at $80 to $85 billion per quarter over the last three quarters of 2009, total outlays plus tax cuts rose to $108 billion in the first quarter of 2010 and $116 billion in the second quarter.

The composition of the stimulus has evolved as well. As was anticipated at the time of passage, the individual tax cuts and the state fiscal relief were the first items that could be put into effect. For this reason, they comprised a large fraction of total spending in the second quarter of 2009. Aid to those directly impacted by the recession rose substantially in the third and fourth quarters of 2009, reflecting programs like emergency unemployment compensation that provided support to people laid off during the downturn.

Public investment outlays on items such as infrastructure and clean energy are now accounting for a growing share of the stimulus. These outlays have increased from just $7 billion through the end of the second quarter of 2009 to $86 billion through the end of the second quarter of 2010. An additional $125 billion has been obligated for government investment spending, in many cases representing projects that have already begun but not yet received full federal reimbursement. As the economy continues to recover and the ARRA turns toward "reinvestment," more than half of the spending and tax credits still to come will take the form of public investment outlays.

Table 2. Fiscal Stimulus by Functional Category

	Through the end of[a]					
	2009:Q1 (March)	**2009:Q2 (June)**	**2009:Q3 (September)**	**2009:Q4 (December)**	**2010:Q1 (March)**	**2010:Q2 (June)**
	Billions of Dollars					
Individual Tax Cuts	2.3	28.4	42.1	55.0	96.7	117.0
AMT Relief	0.0	7.0	12.4	15.5	25.7	68.0
Business Tax Incentives	0.1	10.9	20.0	28.0	34.1	38.5
State Fiscal Relief	8.5	28.2	43.8	59.3	75.5	92.1
Aid to Directly Impacted Individuals	0.1	9.8	32.2	56.2	72.8	78.3
Public Investment Outlays	0.0	7.4	24.9	41.5	59.2	86.3
Total[b]	11.0	91.7	175.4	255.6	364.0	480.3
Change in Total (from End of Previous Quarter)	11.0	80.7	83.7	80.2	108.4	116.3

Sources: Agency Financial and Activity Reports to the Office of Management and Budget; simulations from the Department of the Treasury (Office of Tax Analysis) based on the FY2011 Mid-Session Review.

Notes: a. Data on outlays and obligations are for the last day of each calendar quarter.

b. Items may not add to total due to rounding.

III. Evidence of the Economic Impact of the Recovery Act

In this section, we consider a range of ways of estimating the overall impact of the Recovery Act. We begin with a straightforward examination of the behavior of GDP and employment, and then move on to more sophisticated analyses using an economic model, a statistical forecasting exercise, and the direct reporting data. Although none of these approaches is definitive, together they provide considerable evidence that the Recovery Act has played a critical role in moving the economy from accelerating decline to recovery.

A. The Change in the Economy's Trajectory

The first way that we investigate the impact of the Recovery Act is to consider the behavior of real GDP and employment. Are the changes that we have observed in these two key indicators over the past year consistent with the Act having substantial effects?

Figure 1 shows the growth rate of real GDP. The dashed line between the first and second quarters of 2009 separates the period before the Recovery Act (which was signed February 17, 2009) could have had a significant impact on the economy from the period after. GDP fell progressively more rapidly from the third quarter of 2008 to the first quarter of 2009, but then began to reverse course quickly after the passage of the Recovery Act. After declining at an annual rate of 6.4 percent in the first quarter of 2009, GDPfell at a rate of 0.7 percent in the second quarter, and then rose at a rate of 2.2 percent in the third quarter and 5.6 percent in the fourth. The improvement in growth of 12 percentage points from the first quarter to the fourth (that is, the swing from growth at a -6.4 percent rate to growth at a 5.6 percent rate) was the largest over any three quarters since 1981, and the second largest since 1958.

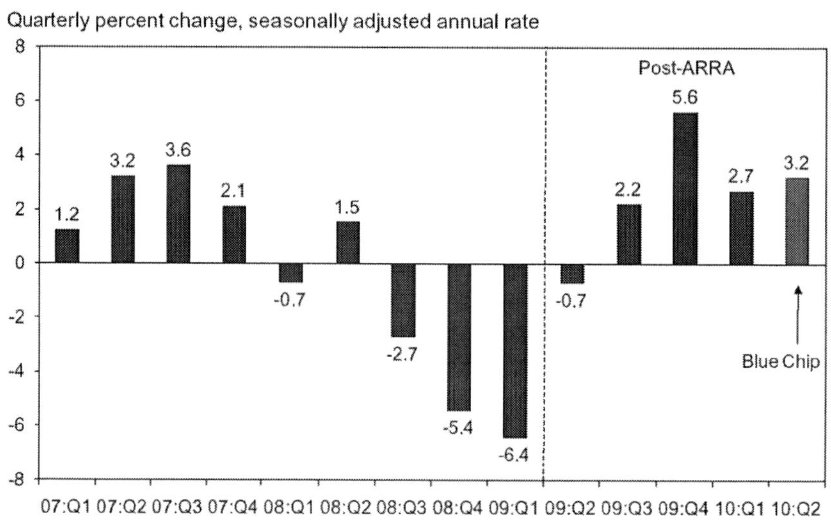

Sources: U.S. Department of Commerce (Bureau of Economic Analysis); Blue Chip consensus forecast.

Note: 2010:Q2 datapoint reflects Blue Chip consensus forecast from July 10, 2010.

Figure 1. Real GDP Growth.

After the extremely rapid growth at the end of 2009, growth moderated to 2.7 percent in the first quarter of 2010, as the influence of changes in inventory investment moderated considerably. Figure 1 also shows the July 10 Blue Chip consensus forecast for real GDP growth in the second quarter of 2010. That forecast is 3.2 percent, indicating that forecasters believe that the solid growth in the first quarter continued in the second (Blue Chip Economic Indicators, 2010). Importantly, real GDP growth is expected to remain steady in the second half of 2010 and throughout 2011. The first official GDP estimate for 2010:Q2 will be released on July30.

Figure 2 presents the behavior of the change in payroll employment. Employment shows the same pattern of an accelerating decline reversing course rapidly after the Recovery Act was passed. In the first quarter of 2009, the economy lost on average an astounding 756,000 jobs per month. Job losses fell to 476,000 per month in the second quarter, 261,000 per month in the third, and 92,000 in the fourth. The economy began adding jobs in 2010, with average gains of 63,000 per month in the first quarter and 123,000 per month in the second quarter.[4] The *change* in the average monthly change in employment over the past five quarters was among the largest on record.

The economy is obviously still far from healthy. Real GDP is substantially below its normal path, and the unemployment rate remains at 9.5 percent. While job growth has averaged 123,000 per month over the past quarter, more robust growth is needed to bring down the unemployment rate quickly. But the change in the economy over the last 18 months has been dramatic. Given what we now know about the frightening momentum of economic decline in the first quarterof 2009 , the change in the trajectory is all the more remarkable.

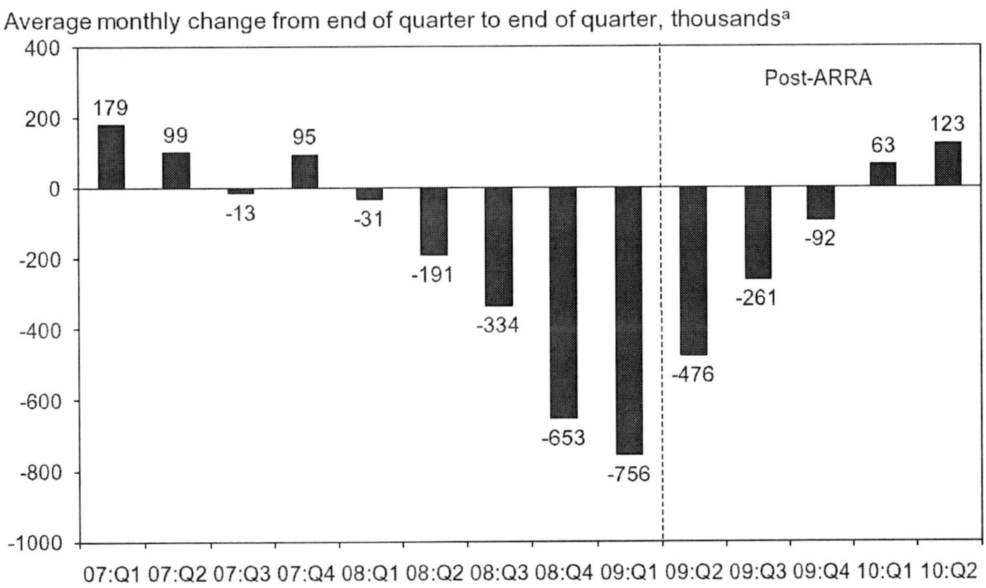

Source: U.S. Department of Labor (Bureau of Labor Statistics).

Note: a. Excludes temporary Census workers.

Figure 2. Payroll Employment Growth.

The timing of the change in trajectory is highly suggestive of an important role for the Recovery Act. At the time the Act was passed, the economy was in freefall. Real output stabilized dramatically in the quarter after the Act was passed, and began growing again in the next quarter. Similarly, job losses began to moderate rapidly in the quarter after the Act was passed, continued to slow greatly in the subsequent two quarters, and turned to modest job gains early in 2010.

B. Estimates of Effects from an Economic Model

Methodology. A key way that the CEA estimates the effects of the Recovery Act on GDP and employment is to use existing estimates of the macroeconomic effects of fiscal policy. That is, one can use mainstream estimates of economic multipliers for the effects of fiscal stimulus. The version of the approach that we use here is identical to that used in the CEA's previous quarterly reports on the Recovery Act.[5]

In its recent reports on the impact of the Recovery Act, CBO uses a similar approach. CBO reports high and low estimates for the multipliers associated with different types of spending (CBO, 2010b). Table 3 shows how the CEA multipliers compare with the CBO estimates. The CEA multipliers show the impact of a change in the fiscal component on GDP after six quarters. The comparison shows that our multiplier estimates are consistently in the middle of the CBO range, and typically toward the lower end. This reflects the fact that our multipliers were chosen to reflect as much as possible the professional consensus.

The CEA model will obviously not yield exact figures for the effects of the Recovery Act. To begin with, there is uncertainty about the size of the economic effects of a "typical" increase in public investment outlays or a "typical" tax cut. There is even more uncertainty about the precise timing of those effects, and modest changes in timing have noticeable effects on the impact at a specific point in time. In addition, the current exceptional economic environment could make the effects of stimulus somewhat larger or smaller than normal, or could cause them to occur somewhat more or less quickly. Finally, the Recovery Act—appropriately—was not just typical stimulus. For types of stimulus that are used less frequently, there is even greater uncertainty about the size and timing of the macroeconomic effects.

As in the earlier reports, we use figures on actual outlays and tax relief under the Recovery Act. Since CEA's third quarterly report, the Office of Tax Analysis of the Department of the Treasury has prepared revised estimates of the magnitude and timing of the tax provisions of the Recovery Act incorporating actual tax return data for 2009. These revised estimates have led to minor revisions in our estimates of the impact of the Recovery Act in previous quarters.

Table 3. Estimated Output Multipliers for Different Types of Stimulus

	CEA[a]	CBO Low	CBO High
Public Investment Outlays[b]	1.5	1.0	2.5
State and Local Fiscal Relief	1.1	0.7	1.8
Income Support Payments[c]	1.5	0.8	2.1
One-time Payments to Retirees	0.4	0.3	1.0
Tax Cuts to Individuals	0.8	0.6	1.5
AMT Patch	0.4	0.2	0.6
Business Tax Incentives	0.1	0.0	0.4

Source: CBO (2010b).

Notes: a. The CEA multipliers show the impact of a permanent change in the component of 1% of GDP after 6 quarters, or, equivalently, the cumulative impact of a one-time change of 1% of GDP over 6 quarters. The CBO multipliers show the cumulative impact of a one-time change of 1% of GDP over several quarters.

b. Includes transfer payments to state and local governments for infrastructure and tax incentives to businesses directly tied to certain types of spending.
c. Includes such programs as unemployment compensation, COBRA, and SNAP.

Results. The results of this analysis are shown in Table 4. They imply that the Recovery Act is having a substantial beneficial effect on production and employment. Specifically, they indicatethat the Recovery Act raised the level of real GDP in the second quarter of 2010, relative to what it otherwise would have been, by 2.7 percent. This approach also indicates that the Act increased employment relative to what it otherwise would have been by 2.5 million as of 2010:Q2.[6]

Table 4. Estimates of the Effect of the ARRA Using CEA Multiplier Model

	2009:Q2	2009:Q3	2009:Q4	2010:Q1	2010:Q2
GDP Level (Percent)	+0.8	+1.7	+2.1	+2.5	+2.7
Employment Level	+399,000	+1,120,000	+1,747,000	+2,215,000	+2,529,000

Source: CEA calculations.

C. Estimates of Effects from Comparison to a Statistical Baseline Forecast

Methodology. An entirely different approach to estimating the effects of the Recovery Act is to compare the actual paths of GDP and employment with the predictions of a sensible statistical forecast of their usual behavior. This approach has two important advantages relative to the model-based approach. The most obvious one is that because the approach is purely statistical, it does not depend on estimates of multipliersbased on past history.

The approach's other key advantage is that it can capture factors that might have caused fiscal policy to have unusual effects in the exceptional economic circumstances that prevailed when the Act was passed. For example, the Act, by stabilizing the economy and restoring confidence, may have played a role in healing the financial sector and jump-starting private demand. Because fiscal policy does not usually have such effects under normal conditions, they would not be captured by conventional multiplier estimates. But they would be reflected in a comparison of the path the economy followed after passage of the Act with the trajectory it was on.

The disadvantage of this approach is that the comparison will reflect not just the impact of fiscal policy, but all other unusual influences on the economy following passage of the Act. Most obviously, other policy actions, such as the Financial Stability Plan, monetary policy, and the Federal Reserve's program of buying agency debt and long-term U.S. government bonds, contributed to the economic turnaround. More generally, any other factors not captured by the past history of GDP and employment, such as unusual moves in foreign demand or asset prices, would also be captured in the difference.

The overall effect of the policies other than the Recovery Act and non-policy factors on GDP and employment could be either positive or negative. For example, while the various actions to improve financial conditions have surely had a positive impact, the continuing stringency in credit conditions is most likely restraining GDP and employment relative to their usual cyclical patterns. Thus, the forecast residuals could either overestimate or underestimate the impact of theRecovery Act .

Equally important, the estimates from this approach have considerable margins of error. At any time, the economy is subject to many influences that are not reflected in the past behavior of GDP and employment. These influences may be particularly large in a period as turbulent as the past eighteen months. And, the longer the time that has passed, the larger the role of those disturbances is likely to be. As a result, the estimates from this approach are likely to be less reliable as more time elapses, and should be viewed only as rough guides to the effects of the Recovery Act.

There are many ways to construct a statistical baseline forecast. The particular approach that we use is identical to that in previous CEA reports on the Recovery Act. We estimate a vector autoregression (or VAR) using the logarithms of real GDP (in billions of chained 2005 dollars) and employment (in thousands, in the final month of the quarter) over the period 1990:Q1–2007:Q4. We include four lags of each variable. Because the estimation ends in 2007:Q4, the coefficient estimates used in the prediction are not influenced by developments in the current recession. Rather, they show the usual joint short-run dynamics of the two series over an extended sample. We then forecast GDP and employment beginning in the second quarter of 2009 using actual data through the first quarter of 2009. Data through the first quarter include the monetary response to the current crisis, but not the fiscal stimulus or other actions that took effect after the first quarter. We have experimented with a variety of other ways of projecting the no-stimulus path of GDP and employment. The results of those exercises are similar to those we report below.

Results. Figure 3 shows the results of this forecasting exercise for GDP, together with the actual path of GDP. Past history would have led one to expect GDP to continue to decline in the second and third quarters of 2009 before beginning to grow moderately in the fourth quarter. The figure shows that actual GDP has risen steadily above the forecast path. It was 0.7 percent above that path in 2009:Q2, 1.4 percent above in 2009:Q3, 2.5 percent above in 2009:Q4, and 2.9 percent above in 2010:Q1. The Blue Chip forecast of 3.2 percent growth in 2010:Q2 suggests that the gap between the actual(as measured by Blue Chip) and projected levels of GDP in 2010:Q2 was about 3.2 percent.[7]

Table 5 summarizes the difference between the actual and forecasted paths of GDP using the statistical projection methodology.

Figure 4 shows the results for employment. Because employment growth normally changes relatively slowly, the usual historical patterns would have led one to expect employment losses to moderate only slowly over the course of 2009 and to continue through the middle of 2010. Actual employment losses moderated much more rapidly. As a result, employment was about 300,000 above the forecast path as of the middle of 2009:Q2, 1.1 million above as of the middle of 2009:Q3, 1.9 million above as of the middle of 2009:Q4, 2.8 million above as of the middle of 2010:Q1, and 3.6 million above as of the middle of 2010:Q2.[8] These results are also summarized in Table 5.

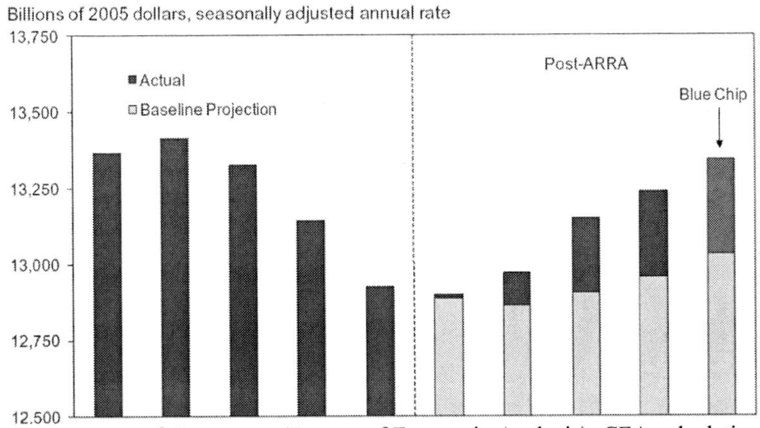

Sources: U.S. Department of Commerce (Bureau of Economic Analysis); CEA calculations; Blue Chip consensus forecast.

Note: The 2010:Q2 number for "actual" is the Blue Chip consensus forecast from July 10, 2010.

Figure 3. Real GDP: Actual and Baseline Projected Levels.

Table 5. Estimates of the Effect of the ARRA Using CEA Statistical Projection Approach

	2009:Q2	2009:Q3	2009:Q4	2010:Q1	2010:Q2
GDP Level (Percent)	+0.7	+1.4	+2.5	+2.9	+3.2
Employment Level[a]	+336,000	+1,064,000	+1,944,000	+2,840,000	+3,574,000

Source: CEA calculations.

Note: a. Estimate are for the middle month of the quarter.

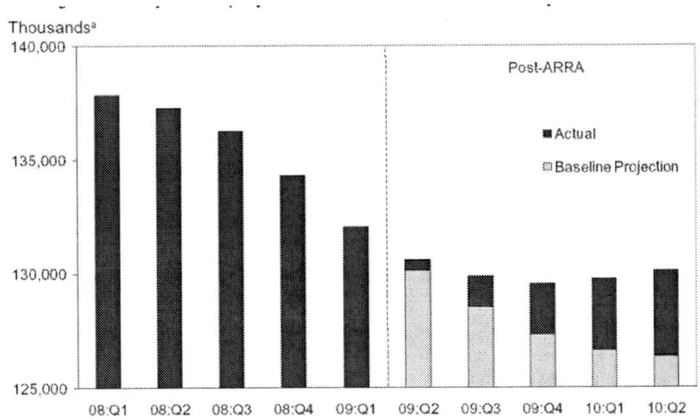

Sources: U.S. Department of Labor (Bureau of Labor Statistics); CEA calculations.

Note: a. Excludes temporary Census workers.

Figure 4. Payroll Employment: Actual and Baseline Projected Levels.

The projection methodology used here shows that using the past history of GDP and employment and actual data through 2009:Q1, one would have predicted that GDP in the second quarter of 2010 would be about 3.2 percent lower than it actually was, and that employment would be about 3.6 million lower than it actually was.

D. Evidence of Effects from Recipient Reporting

One hallmark of the Recovery Act has been an unprecedented commitment to providing timely, transparent, and accountable information about the Act's progress, allowing the public to "follow the dollar" as it is spent. In pursuit of this goal, the Act requires every prime recipient of Recovery Act funds subject to Section 1512 of the Act to file quarterly reports on the employment effects of the Act. The recipient reports are designed to reflect an estimate of individual, identifiable jobs and to provide a source of independent evidence of the effects of the Recovery Act.

Section 1512 of the Recovery Act requires prime recipients of Recovery Act funds for "projects and activities" to file quarterly reports. It is obviously not possible to identify specific jobs associated with the Recovery Act for the types of stimulus, such as individual tax cuts and extended unemployment insurance benefits, that support spending on a broad range of goods and services produced by a wide range of firms. Largely for that reason, there are no recipient reports associated with the components of the Recovery Act that consist of tax reductions, including the Making Work Pay tax credit, and with many categories of spending, including unemployment insurance benefits and aid to states under the temporary Medicaid FMAP increase. Altogether, funds subject to the recipient reporting requirement comprise about one-thirdof the total funding of the Act.

There have now been three rounds of recipient reports. The first reports were filed in October 2009 and described activity from the passage of the Act through September 30, 2009. The second reports were filed in January 2010 and covered the period between October 1 and December 31, 2009. In response to feedback from recipients and data users after the first round, the reporting requirements were changed slightly for the second round. The initial instructions asked recipients to make complex judgments about whether a job would have been filled "but for" funding under the Recovery Act. The instructions for the second reports simply asked recipients to report jobs funded by Recovery Act funds in 2009:Q4, without trying to assess whether the jobs would have existed or not in the absence of the Act. The third set of reports, covering 2010:Q1, were filed in April 2010. The fourth set of reports are being filed this month.

Table 6 shows the jobs reported by recipients for the three quarters for which there are reports. In the first quarter of 2010, recipients reported that nearly 700,000 jobs were funded by the Recovery Act.

Table 6. Recipient Reported Jobs

	2009:Q3	2009:Q4	2010:Q1
Recipient reported jobs	633,342	608,311	682,370

Source: Recipient reports downloaded from Recovery.gov on July 6, 2010.

As described in the CEA's second quarterly report, there are many reasons that the figures from the recipient reporting data do not provide a comprehensive or exact accounting of the jobs created or saved by the Recovery Act (CEA, 2010a, pp. 29-31). One key reason has already been mentioned: the reporting requirements will only apply to about one-third of the overall funding under the Act. Moreover, for the stimulus that has occurred thus far, the fraction is even smaller. The direct spending components of the Act, which are the main ones subject to the reporting requirements, are, as expected, spending out over a longer time horizon than other components and playing an important role in providing support to the economy over an extended period. As a result, spending subject to the reporting requirements has been only a relatively small fraction of the total stimulus so far.

Table 7 shows obligations, outlays, and tax reductions in each quarter for both the Recovery Act as a whole and for the subset of programs subject to recipient reporting requirements. The fraction of the stimulus—outlays and tax cuts—covered by the recipient reports has generally been around 20 percent.

Although the recipient reporting data cannot be used directly to determine the overall impact of the Recovery Act on employment, the data provide a useful check on the estimates from the aggregate approaches described in Sections III.B and III.C. One simple way to perform such a check is to note that while the funds subject to the reporting requirements have been only about 20 percent of the overall stimulus under the Act, the jobs figures from the recipient reports for each quarter are substantially more than 20 percent of the corresponding estimates from the model and projection approaches. For example, for 2010:Q1 (the most recent quarter for which there are recipient reports), only 17 percent of stimulus was subject to recipient reporting requirements. Yet the 682,000 jobs reported in the recipient reports are 31 percent of the estimated overall jobs effects from the model approach and 24 percent of the overall estimate of the projection approach. Thus, this comparison suggests that the jobs estimates from the aggregate approachesare, if anything, somewhat low.

Table 7. ARRA Spending Covered by Recipient Reporting

	For the Quarter (Not Cumulative)			
	2009:Q3	2009:Q4	2010:Q1	2010:Q2
	Billions of Dollars			
ARRA Total				
Outlays	54.4	53.5	46.7	46.4
Obligations	98.5	57.6	48.2	41.7
Tax Reductions	29.3	26.7	61.7	69.9
Outlays Plus Tax Reductions[a]	83.7	80.2	108.4	116.3
Subject to Recipient Reporting Requirement				
Outlays	14.9	17.8	18.8	25.1
Obligations	70.5	15.3	26.5	15.8
Tax Reductions	0.0	0.0	0.0	0.0
Outlays Subject to Reporting Requirement as Percent of Outlays Plus Tax Reductions	17.8%	22.1%	17.4%	21.6%

Sources: Agency Financial and Activity Reports to the Office of Management and Budget; simulations from the Department of the Treasury (Office of Tax Analysis) based on the FY2011 Mid-Session Review.

Note: a. Items may not add to total due to rounding.

In the case of the model approach, we can improve on this simple comparison by asking what the approach implies about the jobs impact not from all of the Recovery Act, but only from an amount of government spending equal to the amount subject to the recipient reporting requirement. Further, we can adjust the multipliers used in the model to omit the estimates of jobs created by the additional spending by the workers who are employed on the projects (which are obviously not included in the recipient reports); this brings the multiplier-based estimates closer to what the recipients were asked to report. This comparison again yields a considerably smaller estimate from the model approach than from the recipient reporting data for each quarter for which there are recipient reports. For 2010:Q1, for example, the model approach implies about 500,000 jobs due directly to the spending subject to reporting requirements, as opposed to the 682,000 jobs actually reported. Thus, this comparison again suggests that the model is not overstating the jobs effects.

In short, the recipient reports support the view that the ARRA has had a large, rapid impact on employment. Indeed, the recipient reports not only reinforce the reliability of the broader estimates produced by the CEA's statistical and economic models, they suggest that these models could be understating the jobs impact of the Recovery Act.

E. Comparison with Other Estimates of the Effects of the Recovery Act

Many other economists and forecasters have estimated the likely effects of the Recovery Act. Most of those estimates are based on formal macroeconomic models. These estimates serve as a check ofthe reasonableness of our own estimates.

Table 8 reports estimates of the contribution of the Recovery Act to GDP since the Act was passed from an array of public and private forecasters.[9] The first row repeats the model-based estimates from Section III.B, and the second row shows the estimates from Section III.C based on the comparison of actual outcomes with projections of the normal evolution of the economy. The next two rows show the low and high estimates prepared by the Congressional Budget Office. The estimates from both of our approaches are well below the top of the CBO range, and are generally in its lower part. The remaining lines of the table show the private sector estimates that we have been able to gather. These estimates are generally similar to ours.

Fewer estimates of the employment effects of the Recovery Act are available. Those that we have been able to gather are reported in Table 9, together with the estimates from our two approaches.[10] The CEA model-based estimates are well within the range of the other estimates, though the figures for 2010:Q1 and 2010:Q2 are toward the high end. To the degree that the estimated employment effects from our model approach are somewhat larger than those of some other forecasters, it is useful to note that our estimate is based on the most recent spending and tax reduction data, whereas some of the private sector estimates have not been updated in many months. Also, our employment effect is derived from the GDP effect using standard estimates of the usual relationship between the two series. That our GDP estimate is squarely in the middle of the range of other GDP estimates therefore adds credence to our employment estimate.

Table 8. Estimates of the Effects of the ARRA on the Level of GDP

	2009:Q2	2009:Q3	2009:Q4	2010:Q1	2010:Q2
			Percent		
CEA: Model Approach	+0.8	+1.7	+2.1	+2.5	+2.7
CEA: Projection Approach	+0.7	+1.4	+2.5	+2.9	+3.2
CBO: Low	+0.9	+1.3	+1.5	+1.7	+1.7
CBO: High	+1.5	+2.7	+3.5	+4.2	+4.6
Goldman Sachs	+0.5	+1.4	+1.9	+2.3	+2.6
IHS/Global Insight	+0.5	+1.2	+1.7	+2.0	+2.2
James Glassman, J.P.Morgan Chase	+1.2	+1.8	+2.6	+3.3	+3.7
Macroeconomic Advisers	+0.5	+1.0	+1.4	+1.7	+2.1
Mark Zandi, Moody's Economy.com	+0.8	+1.6	+2.2	+2.5	+2.7

Sources: See text for details.

Table 9. Estimates of the Effects of the ARRA on the Level of Employment

	2009:Q2	2009:Q3	2009:Q4	2010:Q1	2010:Q2
CEA: Model Approach	+399,000	+1,120,000	+1,747,000	+2,215,000	+2,529,000
CEA: Projection Approach[a]	+336,000	+1,064,000	+1,944,000	+2,840,000	+3,574,000
CBO: Low	+300,000	+700,000	+1,000,000	+1,200,000	+1,400,000
CBO: High	+500,000	+1,300,000	+2,100,000	+2,800,000	+3,400,000
IHS/Global Insight	+228,000	+689,000	+1,245,000	+1,696,000	+2,107,000
Macroeconomic Advisers	+248,000	+623,000	+1,057,000	+1,462,000	+1,847,000
Mark Zandi, Moody's Economy.com	+500,000	+1,008,000	+1,486,000	+1,893,000	+2,249,000

Sources: See text for details.
Note: a. Estimates are for the middle month of the quarter.

The CEA employment estimates based on the projection approach, in contrast, are above the range of other estimates for the past two quarters. This difference reflects two facts. First, the other estimates are largely based on economic models similar to that used in the CEA's model approach. Second, the turnaround of employment has been faster than one would have expected given the behavior of the economy before the passage of the Recovery Act and standard estimates of the effects of stimulus. Thus, an approach that takes into account the actual behavior of employment tends to yield higher estimates than ones that rely on a historical multiplier approach.

In light of the actual behavior of GDP, the estimates in Table 8 suggest that most forecasters believe that in the absence of the Act, GDP would have declined sharply in 2009:Q2 and continued to decline in 2009:Q3, and that growth would have been considerably weaker in the subsequent three quarters than it actually was. Likewise, the estimates in Table 9 imply that most forecasters believe that jobs losses would have moderated much more slowly than they actually did over the course of 2009, and that substantial job losses would have continued into 2010.

IV. THE PUBLIC INVESTMENT PROVISIONS OF THE RECOVERY ACT

The ARRA included $319 billion in public investment spending and in tax incentives linked directly to specific types of investment. We count as public investment any ARRA expenditure or tax program that directly results in activity that increases the capital stock of the Federal government, state and local governments, or private firms. We also count provisions that affect the Nation's human capital and knowledge capital, areas not measured in the national income accounts but which economists have identified as crucial to generating long-run economic growth (see e.g. CEA 2010b and sources cited therein).[11] While these programs are helping the economy to recover and put Americans back to work today, they are also making investments in areas such as clean energy, health information technology, roads, and the skills of our workers that will benefit the economy far into the future.

This section describes the types of public investment spending in the Recovery Act and the long-run benefits to the economy. It then discusses the short-run macroeconomic impact of the spending. Investment outlays increased significantly in the second quarter of 2010, corresponding to what the Vice President has called the "Summer of Recovery."[12] A final part looks in depth at one category of public investmentspending —transportation projects.

One important feature of the public investment spending programs in the Recovery Act is that many of them are leveraging outside funds. This has the potential to make government spending go even further in rescuing today's economy and rebuilding tomorrow's by partnering Recovery Act spending with investments from the private sector and other levels of government. This use of leverage is the subject of Section V of the report.

A. Categories of Public Investment Spending

The Recovery Act funded a broad variety of programs. We have classified the public investmentspending into 10 functional categories:

1. *Clean Energy.* A central piece of the ARRA is more than **$90 billion in government investment and tax incentives to lay the foundation for the clean energy economy of the future.** The CEA's second quarterly report grouped these clean energy investments into eight sub-categories: $29 billion for *Energy Efficiency*, including $5 billion to pay for energy efficiency retrofits in low-income homes; $21 billion for *Renewable Generation*, such as the installation of wind turbines and solar panels; $10 billion for *Grid Modernization* to develop the so-called "smart grid" that will involve sophisticated electric meters, high-tech electricity distribution and transmission grid censors, and energy storage; $6 billion to support domestic manufacturing of advanced batteries and other components of *Advanced Vehicles and Fuels Technologies*; $18 billion for *Traditional Transit and High-Speed Rail*; $3 billion to fund crucial research, development, and demonstration of *Carbon Capture*

and Sequestration technologies; $3 billion for *Green Innovation and Job Training* to invest in the science, technology, and workforce needed for a clean energy economy; and about $2 billion in *Clean Energy Equipment Manufacturing* tax credits that will partner with private investment to increase our capacity to manufacture wind turbines, solar panels, electric vehicles, and other clean energy components domestically.[13]

2. *Human Capital.* Investing in the knowledge and skill base of tomorrow's workers is as important as making sure they have the tools and infrastructure they need to compete in a global economy. The ARRA allocated more than **$50 billion directly to schools, students, and worker training.**[14] For example, the Act made an extra $17 billion available through Pell grants and work-study programs to help make college more affordable. It increased funding for early childhood education by $3 billion, and it sent $650 million to schools to help integrate the use of technology into 21st-century curricula. And, the Act sent $25 billion directly to elementary and secondary schools across the country that face particular educational challenges.
3. *Construction of Transportation Infrastructure.* The Recovery Act provided **$30 billion to fund much-needed infrastructure** improvements in thousands of communities across the country. Earlier this year, the Federal Highway Administration announced that it had finished obligating more than $26 billion for 12,000 road, highway, and bridge projects, and in June President Obama visited Columbus, Ohio to commemorate the breaking of ground on the 10,000th such project. Not only do these projects put Americans to work, but in many cases they will improve road safety and save hours of commuting time by easing congestion. The ARRA is also making investments in the Nation's air and sea transportation infrastructure. This includes $1.3 billion to construct new runways and improve air traffic control facilities and equipment. Finally, it is important to note that more than $18 billion in support for traditional transit and high-speed rail are classified in the clean energy category since these projects will help reduce our dependence on gas-run cars, but they can equally be thought of as improving transportation infrastructure.
4. *Health and Health IT.* The Patient Protection and Affordable Care Act signed by President Obama in March will reduce costs, improve quality and expand access to health care over the coming decade. The Recovery Act jump-started this transition with **$32 billion in investments in health care delivery and technology** that have begun to pay off already. The Act provided $2 billion to community health centers, allowing these centers to improve their facilities and hire extra staff with the potential to reach millions ofnew patients (see Box IV.1).

Box IV.1. Recovery Act Investments in Community Health Centers

The Recovery Act provided $2 billion in investments for community health centers. Community health centers offer access to primary care for medically underserved populations, including the homeless, seasonal workers, the uninsured, and others who have difficulty affording care. According to the Department of Health and Human Services (HHS), which provides grants to qualified community health centers, around 1,100 community health centers receiving federal support treated more than 16 million people in 2008, of whom nearly 40 percent were uninsured, and a third of whom were children. Treatments range from basic prenatal care, immunizations, and vaccines to cancer screenings and diagnostic laboratory and radiologic services, as well as referrals to specialists.

As the recession forced millions out of employment in 2008 and 2009—causing families to face the double burden of losing their employer-sponsored health coverage along with their job—community health centers provided an essential backstop of access to primary care. By avoiding costly emergency care through catching, diagnosing, and treating diseases before they become urgent, centers reduce uncompensated care costs passed on to state and federal budgets and privately insured individuals.

The Five ARRA Community Health Center Infrastructure Programs

The $2 billion in Recovery Act funding is divided among five programs aimed at improving the infrastructure and technology of community health centers, expanding their capacity to serve more patients due to the recession, and breaking ground on new centers. The ARRA investments in community health centers described individually below and shown in Box Table 1 have bolstered infrastructure and technology, created jobs, and resulted in the treatment of millions of uninsured patients.

1. *Capital Improvement* ($858 million). The Capital Improvement Program provides grants between $250,000 and $2.5 million to fund infrastructure investment in health centers, including construction, repair, renovation, and equipment purchase, as well as health information technology. The program was designed to help health centers meet immediate and pressing needs. Of 2,614 projects funded through this program, around 60 percent are for construction, alteration, and repair, with the rest for health information technology and electronic medical records. More than 41 percent of capital improvement grants had already been outlayed through June 2010.
2. *Facility Investment* ($521 million). Like the Capital Improvement Program, the Facility Investment Program provides infrastructure grants to support construction. The Facility Investment Program is targeted toward major investments in facility modernization and improvement and has a larger grant ceiling than the Capital Improvement Program, with awards between $750,000 to $12 million and an average award of $6 million. Because these grants were

announced in December 2009 and scheduled for later implementation than the other investments in community health centers, less than 3 percent of the grant funds had been outlayed through June 2010.

3. *New Access Points* ($157 million). Grants for New Access Points are designed to support community health centers in building new delivery sites to provide wider access to care. Nearly 60 percent of the funds for this program have been spent to date, and recipients report that these grants funded more than 1,000 jobs in the first quarter of 2010. HHS estimates that a total of more than 750,000 patients will be served by the new sites supported by this program.
4. *Health Information Technology* ($121 million). The ARRA offered grants specific to community health centers to invest in health information technology systems such as electronic medical records and networks to enhance coordination between centers. HHS had obligated nearly the entire appropriation by the end of the second quarter of 2010.
5. *Increased Demand for Services* ($343 million). In order to help health centers maintain access and quality care for an expanding uninsured population during the recession, Increased Demand for Services grants were designed to increase health center staffing, extend hours of operation, and expand existing services. More than 59 percent of these grants had been outlayed by the end of June, funding nearly 4,000 jobs in the first quarter of the year according to recipient reports. HHS estimates that more than 2 million new patients—of which more than 1 million are uninsured—will be served by the additional capacity supported through this program.

Box Table 1. ARRA Health Centers Funding

	Appropriations	Through the end of 2010:Q2	
		Obligations	Outlays
		Millions of Dollars[a]	
Health Centers Services	**500.0**	**499.1**	**298.2**
Increased Demand for Services	343.3	342.7	204.3
New Access Points	156.7	156.4	93.9
Health Centers Capital	**1,500.0**	**1,498.5**	**383.3**
Capital Improvement Program	857.7	857.0	353.8
Facilities Investment Program	520.8	520.8	13.5
Health Information Technology	121.5	120.7	16.0
Health Centers Total[b]	**2,000.0**	**1,997.6**	**681.6**

Source: Department of Health and Human Services administrative records.

Notes: a. Includes administrative costs.

b. Items may not add to total due to rounding.

Taken together, nearly the full $2 billion in community health center grants has been obligated, with just over one third of that outlayed so far. ARRA funding for community health centers has broken ground on the construction of new sites, repaired infrastructure in urgent need of renovation, and will treat more than a million uninsured patients, all while supporting thousands of jobs.

Examples of Community Health Centers Supported by ARRA Infrastructure Investment

The aggregate data make clear the effect of the community health centers funding, but it is also useful to explore the impact in individual communities.

For example, Community Health Centers of Southeast Kansas received an Increased Demand for Services grant for $336,330, and a Capital Improvement Program grant for $809,020. The network of centers—which served 16,000 patients during 59,300 visits in 2008—used the Increased Demand for Services grant to hire two new family physicians and retain a previously overburdened doctor on the staff. The centers used the Capital Improvement Program grant to add five exam rooms to an existing building, increasing the facility's capacity by 6,000 patients per year. The augmented staff and new construction will help the center respond to rising demand for care, projected to increase by 13 percent to 17,700 patients in 2010.

Halfway across the country in Washington, DC, Unity Health Care—a nonprofit operator of health centers and other social services serving 81,000 individuals and families each year—received a $12 million Facility Investment Program grant in 2009. As described by Unity Health Care, "the $12 million award will pay for a portion of the cost associated with the construction and renovation of two of Unity's busiest health care facilities; the Anacostia Health Center serving more than 7,000 patients annually and the Upper Cardozo Health Center serving more than 20,000 patients a year." The new Anacostia facility will more than quadruple the size of the previous facility, replacing a 6,000 square foot, pre-fabricated, windowless building constructed in the 1960s.

Community Health Centers and Health Insurance Reform

Just as the Recovery Act has helped families and individuals weather unemployment and uninsurance by strengthening community health centers, the comprehensive health insurance reform legislation signed into law by the President in March continues to make investments going forward. The legislation establishes a Community Health Centers and National Health Service Corps Fund that will provide $12.3 billion in support for the infrastructure and staff of community health centers between 2010 and 2019. These investments will build on the foundation established by the Recovery Actto expand access and reduce the burden and cost of disease in a reformed health care system.

The Recovery Act also included an estimated $26 billion for Health Information Technology for Economic and Clinical Health (HITECH), to make progress on the Nation's transition to health information technology (IT) by 2014. The majority of HITECH funding will be spent on Medicare and Medicaid incentive payments for physicians and hospitals who achieve "meaningful use" of health IT systems. In order to qualify for these payments, providers will have to meet IT standards that promote quality, efficiency and safety—for instance, by using electronic health records to automatically check for adverse drug interactions. Because payment is conditional on providers demonstrating performance, the HITECH incentive payment outlays will occur beginning in 2011 even though providers may have already begun to upgrade their networks. In addition, the Office of the National Coordinator for Health Information Technology is spending $2 billion on HITECH programs to facilitate expanded use of health IT.

The HITECH provisions of the Recovery Act are not just technology investments, but efforts to achieve the major goals of health reform: quality improvement and cost reduction. Diffusion of health IT will improve quality of care by reducing errors, allowing for new quality metrics, and enabling payment based on provider performance. Investments in health IT will also reduce the cost of care by eliminating redundant tests, promoting coordination across providers, and allowing for new payment models that reward coordination.

5. *Construction of Buildings*. The housing crisis set off a collapse in building construction that eliminated more than 2 million construction jobs from the pre-recession peak, one of the sharpest percentage contractions in any industry. To help stabilize employment in the sector, and to expand affordable housing options for families that may have lost their homes to foreclosure, the Recovery Act invested more than $10 billion in affordable housing in communities across America. One program provides grant funding for capital investment in low-income housing, and is anticipated to help underwrite 35,000 new affordable housing units. $2 billion is being channeled through the Neighborhood Stabilization Program in the Department of Housing and Urban Development (HUD) to purchase and redevelop foreclosed and abandoned homes in communities that have felt the foreclosure crisis hit particularly hard. Finally, the Act created a new tax credit bond program through which the Federal government pays 100 percent of the interest costs on up to $11 billion in new bond issues for school construction financing in both 2009 and 2010. To date, states and localities have issued more than 350 bonds through the program with a total face value of more than $3.5 billion. In all, the Act included **$31 billion for residential and commercial construction**.
6. *Environmental Cleanup and Preservation*. The Recovery Act made a **$23 billion investment in the Nation's environment**. The Act provides $6 billion to recapitalize states' clean water and drinking water revolving funds, providing financing for 3,000 projects that will lead to cleaner water and safer drinking water. For example, the town of Fairhaven, MA will install an anaerobic digestion and cogeneration system to convert waste into methane gas, which it can use for power generation. This will eliminate the need for the current costly practice of trucking sewer waste to an off-site location in Rhode Island and save the town an estimated $260,000 per year. The Environmental Protection Agency (EPA) is using another $600 million to help clean up Superfund sites. The Superfund program implements cleanup plans for abandoned hazardous waste sites. EPA already maintains a National Priority List of sites, which allowed the agency to obligate nearly the entire $600 million within 8 months of the Act's passage. In total, Recovery Act funding will initiate or accelerate work at 51 Superfund sites, providing jobs immediately and

accelerating the return of the sites to productive use. At the Department of the Interior, Recovery Act dollars are helping to restore landscapes and habitat, reduce the likelihood of wildfires and floods, and perform needed maintenance in our National Parks. Finally, the Army Corps of Engineers received more than $4 billion for a variety of upkeep and restoration projects.

7. *Scientific Research.* To ensure that America remains a world leader in innovation and technological discovery, President Obama announced in April 2009 the goal of boosting total national research and development (R&D) expenditures to 3 percent of GDP. As a down payment on that effort, the Recovery Act is providing **$18 billion for scientific research**—$10 billion for cutting-edge medical research through the National Institutes of Health, $3 billion to the National Science Foundation, and funding for research programs at NASA, the Department of Commerce, and the Department of Defense. These investments will help us better understand the world we live in—for example by funding the Ocean Observatories Initiative that will place hundreds of undersea sensors as far down as the ocean floor, giving scientists, students, and the public unprecedented new data on the physical systems of oceans—and better understand ourselves—with grants to build a new Genome Data Center at the Washington University School of Medicine and to fund cancer research. This category does not include scientific research related to the clean energy transformation, such as the $400 million Advanced Research Projects Agency-Energy (ARPA-E) program that funds creative research ideas aimed at accelerating the pace of innovation in advanced energy technologies, as this research is included in the category of Clean Energy.
8. *Economic Development.* The ARRA recognized that development of businesses and communities will play a vital role in our economic recovery. Thus the Act contains **$14 billion to help businesses obtain loans and communities rebuild**. The Act channels $900 million to community financial institutions, the Small Business Administration, and rural credit organizations to make loans to qualifying businesses. The Economic Development Administration in the Department of Commerce received another $147 million to give directly to projects that promote regional economic development. Importantly, and as described in the next section, many of these programs required private participation, so that the total amount of economic activity supported far surpasses the cost to the Federal government. This category also contains a number of tax programs designed to stimulate investment. For example, through the end of June local governments had issued more than 1,400 Build America Bonds that contain a 35 percent interest subsidy funded by the Federal government. Build America Bonds are being used to support individual projects that fall into almost all of the categories listed here, including school construction, environment, public safety, hospital construction, transportation, and housing.
9. *Public Safety and Defense.* The Recovery Act is spending **$7.6 billion to keep our borders secure and our communities safe**. More than $500 million will go to local airports and transportation authorities for aviation security infrastructure and technologies. The Department of Justice's Community Oriented Policing Services (COPS) received $1 billion to pay up to 3 years of full salary and benefits for newly hired law enforcement officers or to rehire officers who had been laid off due to

budget cuts. The program received more than 7,000 applications from local law enforcement agencies within two months of the Recovery Act's passage, and made 1,046 awards that will keep an additional 4,699 police officers on the streets. The Office of Justice Programs will allocate another $2 billion to support state and local law enforcement agencies in high crime areas.

10. *Broadband.* One important goal of the Recovery Act is to increase access to and drive adoption of broadband across America. An estimated 35 percent of Americans do not have a high speed internet connection, and are thus disconnected from important educational and economic opportunities. The Recovery Act aims to address this challenge, by **including $7.2 billion to upgrade the Nation's broadband infrastructure**. As part of the appropriation, $4.7 billion was provided to the Department of Commerce's National Telecommunications and Information Administration (NTIA) to deploy broadband infrastructure, support computer centers, and encourage adoption of broadband. The remaining $2.5 billion was directed to the Department of Agriculture's Rural Utilities Service (RUS) to expand broadband access in rural areas.

The RUS's Broadband Initiatives Program and NTIA's Broadband Technology Opportunities Program together received more than 3,800 applications requesting more than $52 billion in support for potential projects in all 50 states and territories. As of July 2, 2010, NTIA had invested $1.7 billion in 165 projects impacting 54 states and territories, the vast majority of which will be spent on building and improving 50,000 miles of broadband infrastructure in underserved communities. For example, the Mid-Atlantic Broadband Cooperative won funding from NTIA to connect 120 schools to fiber networks in rural Virginia with the expectation of creating potentially 200 jobs as the project progresses.[15] Moreover, over $1.4 billion had been awarded by USDA's RUS to 105 broadband projects in 37 states and one territory.

B. Classification Methodology

To describe the breakdown of the public investment spending provisions of the ARRA among these categories, we began with the nearly 300 Treasury Account Financing Symbol (TAFS) codes shown in the Agency Financial and Activity Reports available on Recovery.gov. After removing TAFS codes for the programs in the categories other than public investment spending shown in Table 2, we assigned each remaining TAFS code to one of the 10 categories above, or to an eleventh "other" category containing programs that do not fit elsewhere.

Separately, we assigned tax programs (which are not tracked in the Agency reports) that function similarly to public investment spending to one of the 10 categories. The key feature of these programs is that entities claim the tax benefits only when the associated spending occurs. For example, the Advanced Energy Manufacturing Tax Credit provides a 30 percent tax credit for investments in clean energy manufacturing. Hence, the credit is functionally equivalent to the Federal government directly spending $3 million to help cover the cost of a $10 million investment. As this example shows, public investment through tax programs almost always also involves some co-investment from a non-Federal entity. The broad range of programs in the Recovery Act with this co-investment feature isdiscussed in Section V.

The total appropriation for each category, as well as obligations and outlays through June 2010, are shown in Table 10.[16] Through the second quarter of 2010, two-thirds of the public investmentspending had been obligated and more than one-quarterh ad been outlayed.

Table 11 provides a different breakdown of the public investment spending in the Recovery Act, categorizing it by agency rather than by functional category. Appropriations to six agencies plus the tax programs account for four-fifths of the total, reflecting the prioritization of health IT (Department of Health and Human Services), infrastructure rebuilding (Department of Transportation and Department of Housing and Urban Development), support for education (Department of Education), and clean energy (mostly Department of Energy) in the Act.

The table also shows that of the money not yet obligated, more than half belongs to either HHS (almost all of which is for health IT, as described above) or to tax programs. For the tax programs, the apparent lag merely reflects how we measure "obligations" for tax provisions. In particular, the Office of Tax Analysis estimates the timing of the cost to the government of the tax provisions, which corresponds to the concept of outlays in the agency reports. Since there is no separate concept of obligations for tax programs, we also use the cost to date of tax provisions as a proxy for obligations in Tables 10 and 11. However, in many cases the tax credit beneficiary qualifies for the credit and commences the economic activity well before the government experiences the reduction in revenue or makes the tax outlay.

Table 10. Public Investment by Category

	Appropriations[a]	Through the end of 2010:Q2	
		Obligations[b]	Outlays[b]
	Billions of Dollars		
Clean Energy	94.8	51.3	19.9
Human Capital	52.8	49.7	25.3
Construction of Transportation Infrastructure	30.0	27.7	10.9
Health and Health IT	32.0	5.5	1.4
Construction of Buildings	31.2	23.6	8.3
Environmental Cleanup and Preservation	23.4	21.0	7.4
Scientific Research	18.3	14.9	4.4
Economic Development	14.4	2.1	1.7
Public Safety and Defense	7.6	6.4	2.5
Broadband	7.2	2.1	0.1
Other	6.8	6.8	4.4
Total[c]	318.6	211.2	86.3

Sources: CEA analysis of appropriations estimates from the Office of Management and Budget (OMB); agency Financial and Activity Reports to OMB through June 30, 2010; simulations from the Department of the Treasury (Office of Tax Analysis) based on the FY2011 Mid-Session Review.

Notes: a. Appropriations include estimated cost of tax provisions through 2020:Q3.

b. Include estimated costs of tax provisions through June 30, 2010.

c. Items may not add to total due to rounding.

With the Build America Bonds, for example, the cost to the government of a bond issue gets recorded as the 35 percent interest subsidy each year over the life of the bond, while the economic activity funded by the bond issue may begin immediately.

Table 11. Public Investment by Agency

	Appropriations[a]	Through the end of 2010:Q2	
		Obligations[b]	Outlays[b]
	Billions of Dollars		
Health and Human Services	49.2	19.3	7.2
Transportation	48.1	37.9	14.7
Education	44.6	42.3	21.5
Energy	42.3	29.7	5.1
Treasury[c]	21.7	10.4	6.0
Housing and Urban Development	13.6	13.4	5.0
Commerce	7.8	3.9	1.4
Agriculture	7.5	4.2	1.4
Defense	7.4	5.3	2.3
Environmental Protection Agency	7.2	7.1	2.7
Other Agencies	33.2	29.3	10.5
Tax	36.0	8.4	8.4
Total[d]	318.6	211.2	86.3

Sources: CEA analysis of appropriations estimates from the Office of Management and Budget (OMB); agency Financial and Activity Reports to OMB through June 30, 2010; simulations from the Department of the Treasury (Office of Tax Analysis) based on the FY2011 Mid-Session Review.

Notes: a. Appropriations include estimated cost of tax provisions through 2020:Q3.

b. Include estimated costs of tax provisions through June 30, 2010.

c. Includes the outlay portion of grants made under section 1602 and section 1603 of the ARRA.

d. Items may not add to total due to rounding.

C. The Short-Run Macroeconomic Effects of Public Investment Spending

The public investment spending projects in the ARRA have already begun the clean energy, health, and human capital transformations that will benefit the economy for years to come. At the same time, the $86 billion outlayed for public investment spending projects through the second quarter of 2010, and $211 billionobligated , has put Americans to work fixing roads, retrofitting homes, and restoring the environment.

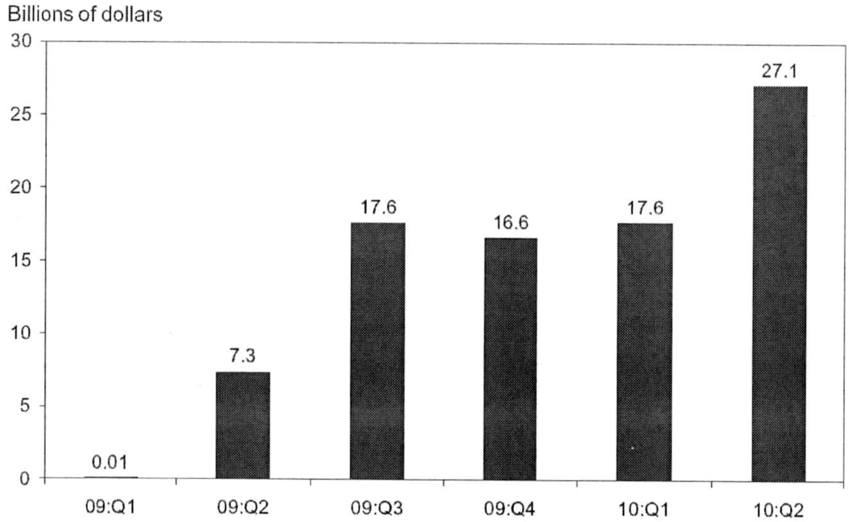

Sources: Agency Financial and Activity Reports to OMB through June 30, 2010; simulations from the Department of the Treasury (Office of Tax Analysis) based on the FY2011 Mid-Session Review.

Figure 5. Public Investment Outlays by Quarter.

To estimate the short-run jobs impact of the ARRA's public investment spending provisions, we use the CEA macroeconomic model described in Section III.B. We take the actual path of public investment spending outlays and tax reductions in each quarter and then use the model to simulate the impact of these expenditures on GDP and employment. Figure 5 shows that the pace of public investment spending has increased, with the total outlays in 2010:Q2 by far the largest to date. This pattern was expected, as it takes time for agencies to identify worthwhile projects and sign contracts, and in many cases the outlays are not actually recorded until after the project has been completed.

Table 12 provides our estimates of the jobs impact by public investment spending category. The first two columns show the estimated total impact on employment (of all types) in 2010:Q1 and 2010:Q2. We estimate that the ARRA public investment spending provisions raised aggregate employment by more than 800,000 jobs as of the second quarter of 2010. The largest impacts derive from the clean energy, human capital, and transportation infrastructure categories. Our estimates also indicate that the Recovery Act created 30 percent more jobs in the public investment spending categories in the second quarter than in the first quarter. This is consistent with the fact that the public investment component of the Act has increased substantially this summer as projects that have been in the planning stages have moved into active construction.

Spending at a point in time leads gradually to increases in GDP and employment, beginning with the direct employment effects and then, later, extending to the induced effects. Hence, to get a sense of the total near- and medium-term economic impact of the public investment spending provisions, column 3 of Table 12 shows the total job-years estimated to be saved or created by public investment spending through the end of 2012. A job-year is the equivalent of one worker employed for one year. To put these numbers in perspective, the CEA estimated that the ARRA would save or create 3.5 million jobs as of 2010:Q4, and 6.8

million job-years through the end of 2012 (CEA 2009a).[17] Column 3 shows that the public investment spending provisions will create more than 3 million of these job-years.

Of course, these figures are only estimates. The margin of error for estimates for specific programs from the CEA model is relatively large, and the number of public investment spending jobs— either in 2010:Q2 or over the life of the Act—could be somewhat smaller or larger than is indicated here. Nevertheless, it is clear that the Act is successfully putting Americans to work today to make the investments needed for tomorrow's economy.

D. A Focus on Transportation Infrastructure Spending

Infrastructure spending is one of the largest forms of public investment included in the Recovery Act. Because transportation infrastructure spending makes up a large portion of total infrastructure spending in the Act, it serves as an illustrative example of the scope and effectiveness of the infrastructure component. In this section, we examine the impact of transportation infrastructure spending. We describe the range of projects funded to give a sense of the long-term benefit of this type of spending. We use simple regression analysis and tabulations from the recipient reports to gain insight into the timeliness of expenditure and the effects on employment.

Table 12. Public Investment Jobs by Category

	CEA Model[a]		
	Jobs Saved or Created by Public Investment Outlays		Total Job-Years through 2012[b]
	(2010:Q1)	(2010:Q2)	
Clean Energy	141,400	190,700	827,000
Human Capital	174,600	222,300	573,400
Construction of Transportation Infrastructure	87,200	102,000	325,400
Health and Health IT	11,000	14,300	292,500
Construction of Buildings	60,600	80,200	292,800
Environmental Cleanup and Preservation	56,900	79,400	254,400
Scientific Research	33,200	52,400	194,000
Economic Development	14,400	18,600	73,200
Public Safety and Defense	17,400	17,900	83,000
Broadband	500	700	60,900
Other	30,200	41,100	73,400
Total[c]	627,300	819,600	3,050,000

Sources: CEA analysis of appropriations estimates from the Office of Management and Budget (OMB); agency Financial and Activity Reports to OMB through June 30, 2010; simulations from the Department of the Treasury (Office of Tax Analysis) based on the FY2011 Mid-Session Review.

Notes: a. Job numbers are rounded to the nearest 100.

b. Job-years represent all jobs supported by direct spending agency outlays and the estimated cost of tax provisions through 2012:Q4. A "job-year" is one person employed for one year.

c. Items may not add to total due to rounding.

Table 13. Transportation Infrastructure Spending by Category

	Appropriations	Through the end of 2010:Q2	
		Obligations	Outlays
		Billions of dollars	
Highway, Street, and Bridge Construction[a]	27.08	26.25	10.07
Passenger Rail	9.30	1.42	0.53
Public Transit[a]	8.82	8.75	3.29
Air and Sea Projects	1.40	1.34	0.83
TIGER Grants[b]	1.50	0.10	0.00
Total[c]	48.10	37.87	14.72

Sources: Agency Financial and Activity Reports to the Office of Management and Budget; Recovery office.

Notes: a. Through July 1, 2010, 427 million dollars have been transferred from highway, street, and bridge construction funds to public transit funds according to Flexible Funding procedures. The appropriations reported here incorporate these transfers and do not, therefore, match the legislated appropriations.

c. Items may not add to total due to rounding.

Range of Transportation Infrastructure Projects Funded by the Recovery Act. We focus on the Recovery Act spending through the Department of Transportation (DOT). We classify the Recovery Act investments of the DOT into five categories: highway, street, and bridge construction; passenger rail; public transit; air and sea projects; and TIGER grants, the DOT's competitive grant program for a wide range of transportation projects. Table 13 shows the breakdown of spending by type of transportation infrastructure.[18]

The projects within the categories of the DOT Recovery Act funding cover a variety of infrastructure spending from highway improvement to airport runway construction to high-speed rail:

1. *Highway, Street, and Bridge Construction.* The largest component of the transportation spending portion of the ARRA is highway, street, and bridge construction. **More than $26 billion has been obligated to road, highway, and bridge projects.** One of the largest highway projects is the Sepulveda Pass widening project in Los Angeles. This project will add 10 miles of high-occupancy-vehicle (HOV) lane to the San Diego Freeway (I-405), increasing capacity along one of the most clogged transportation arteries in America as well as supporting 18,000 jobs.
2. *Passenger Rail.* **The ARRA appropriated more than $9 billion for passenger rail projects.** $8 billion will be used for high-speed passenger rail infrastructure development. This funding is an important part of Congress and the Administration's plan to improve travel in the United States and will lay the groundwork for 13 high-speed rail corridors spanning 22 states. An additional $1.3 billion was awarded to Amtrak to invest in projects that will improve its railroad infrastructure and expand passenger rail capacity. These investments in passenger rail will meet the growing demand for inter-city passenger rail transportation while reducing national dependence on oil and creating clean, energy-efficient transportation solutions.

3. *Public Transit.* **About $9 billion has been appropriated to public transit projects in both urban and non-urban areas.** The ARRA has funded a wide variety of public transit projects such as: the construction of a new bus maintenance and operations facility in Raleigh, NC that is needed to accommodate a growing bus fleet; the rehabilitation of the ramps for the St. George Ferry in New York City, which provides a direct connection from Staten Island to Manhattan for 60,000 daily riders; and the purchase of five GILLIG 30' low-floor hybrid-electric buses—which use as much as 35 percent less fuel than standard diesel buses—in Montgomery, AL. $750 million of the public transit funds are reserved for modernizing existing fixed guideway systems (such as subways and trolley cars). Another $750 million is being used to improve rail and bus lines in several cities.
4. *Air and Sea Projects.* **The Recovery Act appropriated $1.4 billion to air and sea projects** that will provide immediate construction jobs as well as provide long-term benefits. Airports in nearly 300 municipalities across the Nation have been awarded grants. The money will be used to fund much-needed projects, including the refurbishment of 18 air traffic control centers that are more than 40 years old. The ARRA funds will also support capital investments and workforce training to expand the shipbuilding productivity of small shipyards by improving efficiency and by increasingcapacity to work on larger ships.
5. *TIGER Grants.* **The final component of the transportation funds comprises $1.5 billion of discretionary grants for the Transportation Investment Generating Economic Recovery (TIGER) program**, which is intended to support major capital infrastructure investments that will provide long-term economic benefits. One recipient is the National Gateway Freight Rail Corridor, where the grant will be used to double rail capacity on a major freight rail corridor serving Ohio, Pennsylvania, West Virginia, and Maryland with no increase in noise, emissions or train length.

The Rate of Obligations and Outlays. Of the total $48.1 billion that was appropriated for the Department of Transportation, $37.9 billion (or 79 percent) has been obligated. The rate is even higher in particular categories. For example, 99 percent of the funds appropriated to public transit have been obligated to almost one thousand projects.

The recipient reports provide a way of digging deeper into the timing of the construction projects. Each individual project is an observation in the recipient reported data, which include the award date and whether economic activity had yet been generated in the reporting quarter (as measured by the production of jobs). Table 14 shows how many projects have been awarded funds in each quarter. As described above, the recipient reports are only available through the first quarter of 2010.

The timing of project awards suggests the existence of "shovel-ready" projects: almost 2,000 transportation projects had been awarded more than $8 billion by the end of March 2009, just six weeks after the Recovery Act was passed.[19] As of the end of March 2010, nearly 14,000 projects had been awarded. Of these, more than 12,000 were road, highway, and bridge projects. More than 300 were airport projects for the modernization of runways and other airport infrastructure.

Transportation infrastructure tends to spread economic activity over a longer period of time than other forms of stimulus. First, not all infrastructure projects are shovel-ready. Some projects, in particular those requiring large-scale coordination among civil engineers and municipalities, take time to set up and evaluate. Of the $10 billion that has not yet been obligated, $8 billion is for high-speed rail. For these projects, environmental, engineering, and design work must be done before construction can begin.

The key reason that infrastructure spending spreads economic activity over long periods is that, unlike other forms of stimulus such as tax cuts, infrastructure spending cannot be outlayed immediately and projects take substantial time to complete even after obligations are made. Although to date 79 percent of appropriations have been obligated to specific projects, only 31 percent of appropriations have been outlayed as of June 30, 2010 (see Table 13). 58 percent of projects that were awarded in the first quarter of 2009 were still not complete in the first quarter of 2010. As outlays are spent over the next few quarters to meet obligations, job creation from transportation infrastructure is likely to rise considerably.

Employment Impact of Transportation Infrastructure Projects. An important question is how effective transportation infrastructure investment has been at increasing employment. We perform a simple analysis of the direct effect of the ARRA transportation investments on employment by looking at the relationship between DOT ARRA outlays per construction worker in each state and the change in construction employment in each state. The ARRA outlay data come from the agency financial activity reports. We use employment data from the Current Employment Statistics (the standard source of timely data on payroll employment) for heavy and civil engineering construction (NAICS code 237). The employment data we use are not available seasonally-adjusted, so we use the change from May 2009 to May 2010 to avoid seasonal issues while using the most up-to-date data available. The Bureau of Labor Statistics' strict disclosure requirements and small sample limitations mean that the Bureau reports employment for this category for only 33 states .

Figure 6 shows a strong positive relationship between the DOT funds outlayed in a state and the change in heavy and civil engineering construction employment (which includes highway, street, and bridge construction) in that state. The regression line, which is drawn in, has a positive slope coefficient that is highly statistically significant.

Table 14. Transportation Project Award Timing

	Number of projects awarded
2009:Q1	1,835
2009:Q2	4,104
2009:Q3	3,632
2009:Q4	2,109
2010:Q1	2,272
Total	13,952

Source: Recipient reports downloaded from Recovery.gov on July 6, 2010.

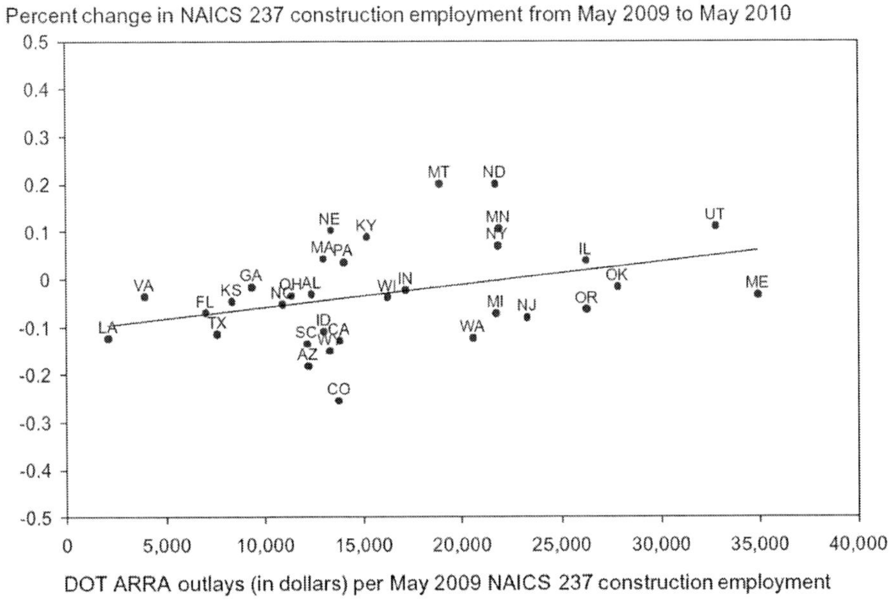

Sources: Department of Labor (Bureau of Labor Statistics); Agency Financial Activity Reports from the Office of Management and Budget; CEA calculations.

Note: Trendline comes from regression of the percent change in NAICS construction from May 2009 to May 2010 against DOT ARRA outlays through May 28, 2010 divided by NAICS 237 construction employment in May 2009. The coefficient on outlays per construction worker is 0.0000048 with a standard error of 0.0000017.

Figure 6. Change in Heavy and Civil Engineering Construction Employment Against DOT ARRA Outlays.

It is important to note that this regression only measures direct jobs produced by the construction projects within a narrow sector of the economy. More direct jobs will be produced in other sectors because some of the expenses of the projects will directly employ workers outside of the NAICS 237 category. Furthermore, this simple scatter plot does not capture any of the indirect or induced jobs produced by the infrastructure spending. Construction is particularly capital intensive, which is likely to make the ratio of indirect and induced jobs to direct jobs higher than in less capital intensive sectors.

The most recent recipient-reported data are for the first quarter of 2010. Because of a high seasonality of construction in cold states, the reported jobs from the first quarter, which includes two winter months, are a poor measure of the direct jobs created by infrastructure spending. Recipient data for the second quarter of 2010 will be released on July 30.

Overall, the relationship shown in Figure 6 is not surprising; more transportation infrastructure funds yields more direct jobs in this narrow sector of the economy. But, because the relationship is between ARRA spending and total employment in this sector, it indicates that the ARRA funds have not just crowded out investment that would have happened anyway. The Recovery Act raised employment overall in the construction sector. Furthermore, the Current Employment Statistics data for heavy construction only measures private jobs, and thus the relationship shown above suggests that the job creation from

Recovery Act infrastructure spending was not limited to the government sector. Rather, it has had a significant positive effect on private employment.

V. Provisions of the Recovery Act that Leverage other Spending

A key success of the Recovery Act has been its ability to bring in outside funds—from the private sector, non-profits, universities, and state and local governments—to complement its investments in a wide range of activities. This use of “leverage” or “co-investment” has two crucial benefits. First, it potentially increases the overall amount of support the Recovery Act is providing to the economy. This role of the Recovery Act in spurring private investment is particularly important in the current environment, when private investment is low. Second, it improves economic incentives: when the recipients of Federal funds have to put up significant funds of their own, their incentives to use the funding effectively are stronger.

The Recovery Act has literally dozens of provisions and programs that leverage outside investment. The range of the areas of co-investment is wide—from health research and clean energy manufacturing to infrastructure investment and broadband. About $100 billion of Recovery Act funds use leverage, and they will support more than $380 billion of overall investment. Thus, for every $1 the Federal government is investing in these projects, other entities are investing about another $3. And, the majority of the additional spending is coming from the private sector. As a result, the Act is playing a part in investments far beyond the Federal spending itself.

This section describes the specifics of how the Recovery Act has leveraged outside funds. It breaks down the leverage in two ways: according to the area of investment where the leveraged funds are going, and according to the designof the leverage.

Of course, as is always the case when the government encourages an activity, some of the activity would have occurred even without the government support. This section does not comprehensively address the challenging question of how much activity the use of leverage has generated that would not otherwise have taken place. Instead, it focuses on the amount of funds that are being leveraged and the amount of co-investment. However, it does look carefully at one particular area, the Production Tax Credit and other incentives for wind energy, to get a sense of the issues involved and the potential magnitude of the additional investment resulting from government support.

A. Co-investment by Area of Investment

To calculate the total amount of co-investment, we collected data from 15 different agencies with 52 programs involving outside funds, including 6 tax provisions of the Act.[20]

Importantly, the figures for total activity supported reflect only the direct amounts spent on projects supported by the Act. They do not include the activity that results from the additional demand for goods and services stemming from the higher incomes of those employed because of the programs(that is, th e multiplier effect).

We first analyze the programs using the functional categories of public investment described in Section IV. As shown in Table 15, there are programs where Federal funds are partnered with non-Federal spending in every one of the categories.

1. *Clean Energy*. The largest amount of co-investment is in clean energy, where **a Federal contribution of $46 billion will support more than $150 billion in total investments** in energy efficiency, renewable generation, research, and other areas of the transformation to a clean energy future. For example, individuals and businesses that install certain types of renewable energy generation can receive a grant equal to 30 percent of the project's cost. This program, Energy Cash Assistance, has already disbursed $4.7 billion, supporting over $13 billion in total investment activity. These investments include more than 650 solar and 17 biomass projects.
   Another example is the Department of Energy's smart grid program. The program will foster smarter, more flexible, and more efficient use of energy. Spurred by a $4.5 billion investment of Recovery Act funds, the private sector has invested an additional $6 billion in smart grid projects, bringing the total investment to over $10 billion.[21]
2. *Economic Development*. In the area of economic development, **a Recovery Act contribution of approximately $14 billion is supporting $146 billion in economic activity**. Build America Bonds, discussed in Section IV, are financing the majority of that activity.
   As of the end of June, there have been 1,446 issues of Build America Bonds in 49 states, the District of Columbia, and two territories, with a total face value of $115 billion. The bonds allow states and municipalities to originate loans with 35 percent of the interest paid by the Federal government. The bonds are attractive to a variety of investors, such as pension funds, that do not benefit from the tax-free status of traditional municipal bonds. By bringing in more sources of funding, the bonds lower interest costs for the issuers. The Department of the Treasury recently estimated that the bonds issued during the first year of the program will save state and local governments about $12 billion.[22]
   Build American Bonds currently represent 21 percent of the municipal bond market. For example, the University of Washington in Seattle has raised $150 million through two issues of the bonds. The university is using the funds to finance new and renovated housing for students who live on campus, an improved research facility, additions to buildings that house its business and medical schools, and other projects. Of course, some of the $115 billion of economic activity that is being supported by Build America Bonds surely would have occurred without the program. One reason that the cost of the program to the Federal government is low is that the bonds are only a moderately more attractive source of financing than traditional tax-free bonds. In the absence of the program, some of the activity supported by Build America Bonds would have been supported by issues of traditional tax-free bonds instead. Estimating how much additional economic activity the bond issues have created is a difficult problem, and, as noted above, one we do not attempt to resolve in this report.
   This category also contains Federal dollars that underwrite or guarantee loans to private borrowers, potentially funding a large amount of activity at little cost to the

government. For example, as a part of the Recovery Act, the Small Business Administration raised the guarantee rate and eliminated fees on loans in their small business lending programs. Loan volume increased accordingly; in the ten months following the passage of the ARRA, the average SBA monthly loan volume in their largest programs increased by more than 60 percent over the level at passage. Through June 4, 2010, $552 million of ARRA funds supported $17 billion of small business lending.

3. *Building Construction.* Another category with substantial co-investment is building construction. **All together, $6 billion of Recovery Act funds are estimated to support total investment of $29 billion.** For example, under the Low Income Housing Tax Credit Assistance Program at the Department of Housing and Urban Development, $2.25 billion in Federal funds will partner with more than $7 billion in other Federal, state, local, and private funds to build low-income housing. Due to the absence of investors, hundreds of low-income housing projects across the country have been on hold. These funds are jump-starting investment in many of these projects.
4. *Other.* **An additional $29 billion of Recovery Act funds in a wide range of programs are supporting more than $50 billion of additional economic activity.** These programs range from environmental cleanup and preservation, to transportation infrastructure, to scientific research.

Table 15. Co-Investment by Area of Investment

	Cost to Government	Co-Investment	Total Activity Supported
	Billions of Dollars		
Clean Energy	46.0	106.7	152.7
Economic Development	13.9	132.3	146.3
Environmental Cleanup and Preservation	10.9	10.5	21.5
Broadband	7.2	2.7	9.9
Construction of Buildings	6.4	23.0	29.4
Health	3.7	1.3	5.0
Scientific Research	2.9	2.8	5.7
Human Capital	2.2	0.5	2.7
Construction of Transportation Infrastructure	1.6	6.4	8.0
Public Safety and Defense	0.6	0.1	0.6
Total[a]	95.4	286.4	381.8

Source: CEA calculations based on data from Office of Management and Budget and agencies.
Notes: a. Items may not add to total due to rounding.

B. Co-investment by Design of the Program

The Recovery Act uses several different approaches to putting non-Recovery Act funds to work. In fact, the Act employs six different designs to encourage other investment spending:

1. *Private Matching Grants (Businesses, Non-profits, and Universities).* Many programs in the Recovery Act require funding matches from the private sector. As a result, Recovery Act funds are drawing in private capital to help fund economic recovery, accelerate job growth, and hasten the clean energy transformation. **In total, $32 billion of Recovery Act funds are partnering with private matching funds to support $66 billion of economic activity**.
   The largest use of private matches in the Recovery Act is at the Department of Energy: $23 billion of ARRA funds for clean energy projects are partnered with $21 billion of private funds. For example, Oregon and four other western states have been awarded $88 million from the Department of Energy Office of Electricity through the Recovery Act for a regional smart grid demonstration project. The grant has been matched by $90 million from utilities and technology companies. The project will test and evaluate new smart grid technologies, provide two-way communication between distributed generation and storage, and advance security.
2. *Tax Credits.* The Recovery Act contains numerous tax provisions to encourage energy efficiency and the production of renewable energy. **In all, $22 billion in energy tax credits will support $100 billion of investments in clean energy and energy efficiency**. For example, the Home Energy Efficiency Improvement Tax Credit and the Residential Renewable Energy Tax Credit provide credits for 30 percent of the cost of energy efficient retrofits or the installation of residential renewable energy generation capacity. Other credits function almost like government grants—the Energy Cash Assistance and 48C Advanced Energy Manufacturing Credit pay for 30 percent of the cost of clean energy investments by firms. The 48C credit was awarded on a competitive basis, with the Departments of Treasury and Energy jointly reviewing applications for more than $8 billion to award the $2.3 billion in the program.
   One project supported by the 48C tax credit is an investment by General Electric in their Appliance Park facility in Louisville, Kentucky, where $25 million of support from the 48C program is supporting an investment of over $600 million. Because of this investment, GE will be moving the production of energy efficient water heaters back to the United States from China.
3. *Loan Guarantees.* The Federal government guarantees certain types of loans made by banks to firms and individuals that otherwise might have difficulty getting access to credit. The most prominent loan guarantees in the Recovery Act are loans for small businesses and for commercialization of renewable energy technology. For example, Abengoa Solar, Inc. recently received a conditional commitment for a $1.5 billion loan guarantee under the Recovery Act Title 17 Loan Guarantee Program through the Department of Energy to build one of the world's largest solar generation plants near Gila Bend, Arizona. The plant will be the first large-scale solar plant in the United States capable of storing the energy it generates. Because many of the loan

guarantees for clean energy accompany other Recovery Act programs with leverage provisions, we conservatively exclude all of the loan guarantees through the Department of Energy in our totals. **There are roughly $1 billion of non-energy loan guarantees that support $32 billion of total investment activity associated with small businesses, rural families, and Indian-owned businesses**.

4. *Direct Loans.* The government also lends directly to borrowers. **$4 billion in public expenditures under the Recovery Act will support a total of $15.6 billion in activity**. For example, the Broadband Initiatives Program at the Department of Agriculture is providing a combination of loans and grants for installing broadband in rural communities. Over 68 projects are already underway. In total, $90 million in government funds is expected to underwrite more than $1 billion in loans, with recipients contributing another $200 million in equity capital. The Broadband Initiatives Program will also award more than $2.3 billion in grants to partner with the loans. To give another example, the Bonneville and Western Area Power Administrations, which have excellent repayment records, each received $3.25 billion in additional borrowing authority under the Recovery Act.
5. *Public Matching Grants (Federal, State, and Local Governments, and Airports).* Many Federal agencies have Recovery Act programs that require funding matches from other parts of government. **In total, $23 billion in Recovery funds will partner with $22billion in spending from other areas and levels of government to support $45 billion of total activity**. For example, the Community Development Block Grant program at the Department of Housing and Urban Development has provided an additional $980 million to local governments for improving housing and services. These funds are matched by $1.9 billion from other public sources and about $600 million in private funds.
6. *Interest subsidies.* To help cash-strapped states and localities maintain crucial infrastructure investments during the downturn, the Recovery Act introduced new financing tools for the Federal government to help pay the interest cost of local borrowing. **In total, these programs are estimated to cost the Federal government $13 billion, and to date $123 billion qualifying bonds have been issued**. The Build America Bonds are the largest program of this type. Under another program, the Qualified School Construction Bonds, the Federal government pays 100 percent of the interest cost of bonds used to finance school construction.[23]

Some of the types of leverage design—the private matching grants, tax credits, and loan guarantees—are aimed at bringing in private capital. Others—the public matching grants and interest subsidies—are designed to bring in co-investment by state and local governments. The direct loans bring in a mix a private and public co-investment. Table 16 shows the overall breakdown of co-investment in the Recovery Act according to whether the co-investment funds are private or public and according to the design of the leverage.[24] The majority of the co-investment comes from the private sector: roughly $153 billion of the total co-investment of $286 billion, or 54 percent,come from private and non -profit entities.

Table 16 also shows that while all of these designs support co-investment, the degree of leverage varies substantially. On average, $1 of Recovery Act spending in these programs is partnered with about $3 of other spending. The loan guarantees have some of the highest degrees of co-investment, while the private and public matcheshave some of the lowest.

Table 16. Co-Investment by Leverage Design Type

	Cost to Government	Co-Investment	Total Activity Supported
	Billions of Dollars[a]		
Private Co-Investment (businesses, non-profits, and universities)	**56.6**	**153.2**	**209.8**
Matching Grants	32.2	33.5	65.7
Tax Credits	22.0	78.9	100.9
Loan Guarantees	0.9	30.7	31.6
Direct Loans	1.5	10.1	11.6
Public Co-Investment (Federal, state, and local governments)	**38.7**	**133.2**	**171.9**
Matching Grants	23.4	22.0	45.4
Direct Loans	2.5	1.5	4.0
Interest Subsidies	12.8	109.7	122.5
Total[b]	95.4	286.4	381.8

Source: See Table 15.

Notes: a. Programs are categorized according to the primary type of leverage.

b. Items may not add to total due to rounding.

C. Assessing Leverage

The previous sections sketch a broad outline of the role outside funds have played in the Recovery Act, but they do not address how much outside activity was *caused* by the Act. Here, using the extensions of the Production Tax Credit and Investment Tax Credit for wind energy and the enactment of the Section 1603 Energy Cash Assistance program in the Recovery Act, we analyze one example of Federal support pulling private capital off the sidelines to sustain the Nation's transition to clean energy.

In the Energy Policy Act of 1992, Congress passed a Production Tax Credit of 1.5 cents per kilowatt-hour for energy generated by wind power for any facilities placed in service before July 1999. Firms could claim the credit for any wind energy generated for up to ten years after the place-in-service date. Since then, Congress has renewed the credit several times and the credit amount has increased (the credit is currently 2.1 cents per kilowatt-hour and indexed to inflation). Three times, however, in June 1999, December 2001, and December 2003, the credit expired, and each time, it took a number of months for it to be renewed. These short-term credit expirations have two important effects: they increase uncertainty about long-run profitability, and they delay planned investments as producers wait for the credit to be renewed.

We can look at what happened to installed wind capacity in the episodes where the credit expired to build a counterfactual for what would have happened if the credit had not been extended. The difference between the counterfactual and the actual installed capacity then represents the activity caused by the credit. As shown in Figure 7, one difficulty in using historical analysis is that the amount of annual installed capacity has grown substantially since the credit expiration episodes. Hence large changes relative to the level of installed capacity in earlier years may be small relative to the much higher level of investment in 2008 and 2009. To account for this, we analyze the effect of credit expirations on the growth rate rather than the level of investment. Using data from the American Wind Energy Association on installed wind capacity, Figure 7 shows that the one year growth rate in installed capacity in years when expiration occurs is 6.3 percent, but the medium-run growth rate in capacity including the years before and after the expiration is 33.3 percent (at an annual rate). The difference between these growth rates—which is the amount of growth temporarily delayed each time the tax credit expired in the early 2000s—is 27.0 percentage points.

Metcalf (2009) performs a related analysis of investment in wind capacity at the state level. His estimate of the elasticity of investment with respect to the user cost of capital implies that removing the production credit would typically reduce investment by 40 to 50 percent.[25] While not directly comparable to the calculation above, this estimate also suggests a substantial impact of the credit on private investment.

The Energy Improvement and Extension Act of 2008 extended the Production Tax Credit for wind, which was scheduled to expire at the end of 2008, through 2009. The Recovery Act further extended the credit through 2012. The Act also introduced the 1603 Energy Cash Assistance grants, which allow businesses to apply for a grant equal to 30 percent of the cost of the investment instead of claiming the production tax credit.[26] In the tight credit conditions that prevailed during much of 2009, the 1603 grants allowed firms to receive up-front financing for projects. To date, firms have received more than $4 billion through the 1603 grant program, about 90 percent of which has gone to wind producers.

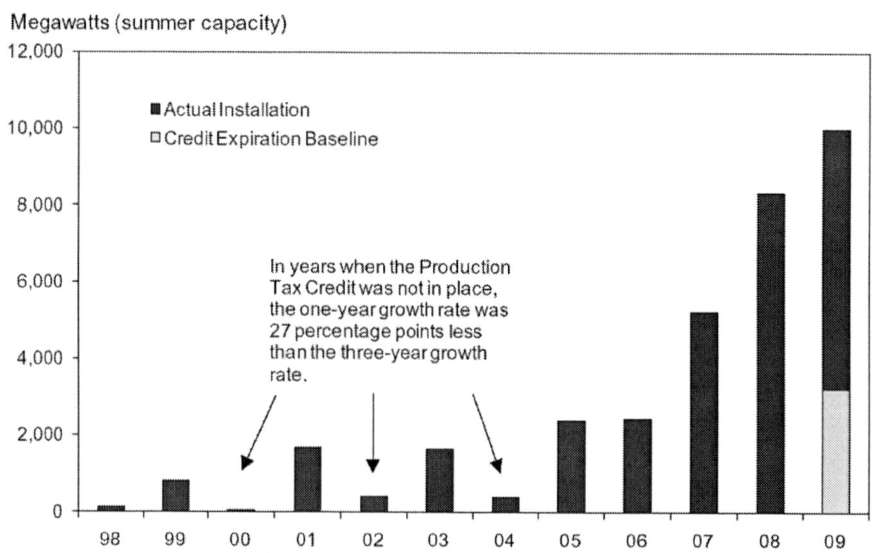

Source: American Wind Energy Association (2010).

Notes: Legislation extending the Production Tax Credit for wind passed in 2008 and again in the Recovery Act.

Figure 7. Annual Wind Energy Capacity Additions.

With these programs in place, more than 10,000 megawatts of summer wind capacity were installed in 2009, for an annual growth rate of 40 percent. Assuming that a January 2009 production tax credit expiration would have had the same 27 percentage point growth impact as in the early 2000's, the growth rate would have been 13 percent, and the level of wind energy capacity in 2009 would have been nearly 20 percent lower.[27] Thus, it appears that government support was responsible for about 6,000 megawatts of wind capacity installation that might not otherwise have occurred. Moreover, the challenging credit conditions during 2009 and the introduction of the 1603 grant program in the Recovery Act suggest that the overall effect on wind capacity installation may have been even larger.

The Lawrence Berkeley National Laboratory (LBNL) conducted an independent analysis of the 1603 grant program.[28] This study found that the program caused an increase in wind installation in 2009 of between 2,000 and 2,400 megawatts. The LBNL analysis was based on the difference between actual and forecasted installations and on estimates of whether each project would have been built given the owner and time of construction. Importantly, more than one-third of firms installing wind capacity in 2009 claimed the production tax credit instead of applying for a 1603 grant, so the LBNL study provides a lower bound for the impact of the incentive programs on wind energy installation. Even so, the LBNL study suggests a substantial impact of tax incentives on private investment.

Every program is different, and determining how much of the spending associated with the co-investment provisions of the Recovery Act would not have occurred without the Act is beyond the scope of this report. But the evidence from the analysis of the Production Tax Credit and related incentives for wind energy suggests that the additional private sector investment that is generated by these provisions may be substantial.

This fact has potentially important implications for measuring the employment effects of the Recovery Act. In our model-based analysis, we only estimate the jobs created by the direct public investment spending in the Act; we make no attempt to include any of the employment impact of the leveraged spending beyond the cost to the Federal government. As a result, the model-based estimates almost surely miss some of the employment generated by the Recovery Act. Our projection-based estimates, which simply compare actual employment to a sensible, statistically-determined baseline forecast, inherently do include any impact of the leveraged spending. This is potentially one reason why the projection-based estimates of the employment impact of the Recovery Act are larger than the model-based estimates.

VI. Conclusion

This report continues the Council of Economic Advisers' assessment of the economic impact of the American Recovery and Reinvestment Act of 2009. It reflects our attempt to monitor the progress of the Act and the response of the economy as of the second quarter of 2010.

Our analysis indicates that the Recovery Act has played a key role in the turnaround of the economy that has been occurring over the past year. Real GDP reached its low point in the second quarter of 2009 and has been growing solidly since then, in large part because of the tax cuts and spending increases included in the Act. Employment, after falling dramatically, has begun to grow again. Indeed, payroll employment (neglecting temporary Census workers) has risen for six consecutive months. As of the second quarter of 2010, we estimate that the Recovery Act has raised employment by 2.5 to 3.6 million relative to what it otherwise would have been.

We also find that the public investment programs in the Recovery Act are funding critical investments in a wide range of areas. The employment effects of these programs increased substantially in the second quarter of 2010 as many projects moved from planning to implementation; we estimate that the programs now account for almost one-third of the employment effects of the Act. This pattern fits the Vice-President's description of the summer of 2010 as the "Summer of Recovery."

One innovative feature of the Recovery Act is its leveraging of outside funds to make Federal dollars go further and to strengthen incentives for the effective use of those funds. The Act uses about $100 billion of matching grants, tax credits, and various types of lending assistance to partner with almost three times that amount of non-Federal funds, and to thereby support over $380 billion of economic activity. The leverage involves activities from advanced energy manufacturing, where 48C tax credits are partnering public and private funds, to essential infrastructure investments, where Build America Bonds are making new sources of funding available to state and local governments.

As we have emphasized, measuring what a policy action has contributed to growth and employment is inherently difficult because we do not observe what would have occurred without the policy. Therefore, it must be understood that our estimates are subject to substantial margins of error. The results, however, are strong enough and clear enough that we are confident that the basic conclusions are solid. That a wide range of private and government analysts concur with our estimates adds a reassuring check on our analysis.

APPENDIX. ESTIMATED EMPLOYMENT EFFECTS BY STATE

This report finds that the Recovery Act raised employment as of the second quarter of 2010 by between 2.5 million and 3.6 million jobs over what it would otherwise have been. There is obviously much interest in how these employment effects have been distributed across states. In this appendix, we attempt to provide a rough state-by-state breakdown for the effects of the entire ARRA. However, it is important to emphasize that these disaggregate estimates are inherently more speculative and uncertain.

The state estimates are calibrated to add up to 3.05 million jobs. This is the midpoint between the estimated employment impact of the ARRA in 2010:Q2 according to the CEA model approach and the CEA statistical projection approach (see Table 9).

Because there is no perfect way to measure state-level effects, we pursue three approaches to decomposing employment impacts across states. Our first method allocates jobs according to states' shares of national non-farm employment as of March 2009.[29] Georgia, for example, had 3.0 percent of all employment in the country in March 2009, so is allocated 3.0 percent of total job creation.

Our second method allocates jobs according to the distribution of Recovery Act outlays through June 30, 2010. Georgia has received 2.9 percent of total outlays, so is estimated to receive 2.9 percent of total job creation. This method provides a more direct measure of where ARRA impacts are likely to be felt than does the first approach, but it has an important drawback. Only a portion of the overall Recovery Act stimulus is included in the outlays data. The most important stimulus not included in this approach is tax relief, which comprises almost one-half of total spending plus tax cuts to date. Tax cuts are likely more evenly distributed across states than are outlays, so our use of outlays likely overstates the unevenness of employment effects. Similarly, this method assumes that all of the employment effects of spending in a state are felt within the state. In fact, however, there are important spillovers across states. Thus again, this approach is likely to exaggerate the differences among states.

Our third method relies on the sectoral composition of employment in each state. We estimate the number of jobs created or saved in different industries using a methodology developed in our first quarterly report.[30] Specifically, we decompose the response of employment in each sector into two components. First, a rising overall level of employment tends to increase employment in each industry in proportion to its share of the overall economy. We refer to this as the "rising tide" effect. Second, some sectors are more sensitive to the state of the business cycle than are others. The additional employment due to the Recovery Act has therefore almost certainly produced relative expansion of such procyclical sectors, while countercyclical sectors, such as utilities, health care, and government, have seen their shares of total employment shrink relative to what would have been seen in the absence of stimulus. We refer to the resulting changes in sectoral employment as the "cyclicality effect."

We then assume that any jobs saved or created in a particular industrial sector (for example, mining and logging) are distributed across states in the same way as are existing jobs in that sector.[31] Georgia has only 1.4 percent of national employment in mining and logging, so is assumed to receive only 1.4 percent of employment effects in that industry. By contrast, Georgia has nearly one-quarter of national textile product mill employment, so any employment impacts in that industry are assigned disproportionately to Georgia. Summing across 42 industries, we obtain the total impact on Georgia employment.[32] The procedure is repeated for each state to obtain the distribution across states.

None of these three approaches does a perfect job of measuring the geographic distribution of employment effects, and each has advantages and disadvantages relative to the others. Thus, to obtain a reasonable estimate of state-level job impacts, we average the three approaches. This average indicates that the ARRA has saved or created roughly 91,000 jobs in Georgia, 3.0 percent of the national total. Estimates for all fifty states, plus the District of Columbia, are reported in Appendix Table 1.

Of course, simply because their populations are larger, we estimate that larger states have seen larger jobs impacts. Similarly, because their employment is more cyclically sensitive, industrial states are estimated to have had larger employment effects relative to their populations. Finally, both because of their industrial composition and because state fiscal relief and aid to individuals directly impacted have been larger in states hit harder by the recession, we estimate that states with higher unemployment rates at the time of passage have seen larger employment effects of the ARRA relative to their populations.

Appendix Table 1. Estimated Impact of the ARRA on Employment by State

State	Jobs Impact in 2010:Q2	State	Jobs Impact in 2010:Q2
	Thousands		Thousands
Alabama	42	Montana	10
Alaska	7	Nebraska	17
Arizona	64	Nevada	29
Arkansas	26	New Hampshire	13
California	357	New Jersey	94
Colorado	50	New Mexico	19
Connecticut	38	New York	206
Delaware	9	North Carolina	90
District of Columbia	16	North Dakota	8
Florida	167	Ohio	117
Georgia	91	Oklahoma	35
Hawaii	13	Oregon	41
Idaho	15	Pennsylvania	130
Illinois	140	Rhode Island	11
Indiana	68	South Carolina	41
Iowa	34	South Dakota	8
Kansas	28	Tennessee	60
Kentucky	41	Texas	225
Louisiana	39	Utah	27
Maine	14	Vermont	7
Maryland	53	Virginia	73
Massachusetts	79	Washington	67
Michigan	102	West Virginia	16
Minnesota	60	Wisconsin	63
Mississippi	26	Wyoming	6
Missouri	59		

Sources: CEA estimates based on data from the Current Employment Statistics and the Quarterly Census of Employment and Wages.

Note: Entries sum to the midpoint of the estimated cumulative impact of policy on employment level of CEA's model approach and projection approach (3,050,000 jobs impacted).

REFERENCES

Blue Chip Economic Indicators. (2010). Aspen Publishers. Vol. *35*, No. 7, July10.

Bolinger, Mark, Ryan Wiser & Naïm Darghouth. (2010). "Preliminary Evaluation of the Impact of the Section 1603 Treasury Grant Program on Renewable Energy Deployment in 2009." Lawrence Berkeley National Laboratory. April.

Congressional Budget Office. (2009). *Letter to the Honorable Nancy Pelosi*. February 13.

Congressional Budget Office. (2010a). "*The Budget and Economic Outlook: Fiscal Years 2010 to 2020.*" January.

Congressional Budget Office. (2010b). "*Estimated Impact of the American Recovery and Reinvestment Act on Employment and Economic Output from January 2010 Through March 2010.*" May.

Council of Economic Advisers. (2009a). "*Estimates of Job Creation from the American Recovery and Reinvestment Act of 2009.*" May.

Council of Economic Advisers. (2009b). "*The Economic Impact of the American Recovery and Reinvestment Act of 2009*, First Quarterly Report." September.

Council of Economic Advisers. (2010a). "*The Economic Impact of the American Recovery and Reinvestment Act of 2009, Second Quarterly Report.*" January.

Council of Economic Advisers. (2010b). *Economic Report of the President.* February.

Council of Economic Advisers. (2010c). "*The Economic Impact of the American Recovery and Reinvestment Act of 2009, Third Quarterly Report.*" April.

Engebretson, Joan. (2010). "*Stimulus Slow to Break Ground but Generating Jobs.*" *Connected Planet*, June 2.

Glassman, James. (2010). "*Markets & the Economy / Quarterly Update.*" J.P.Morgan Chase & Co., January 4.

Goldman Sachs Group, Inc. (2009). "*Fiscal Stimulus: A Little Less in Q2, A Little More Later.*" August 4.

Macroeconomic Advisers. (2009a). "*The US Economic Outlook: Is the Upturn Imminent? How Strong?*" June 11.

Macroeconomic Advisers. (2009b). "*Outlook Commentary.*" September 3.

Metcalf, Gilbert E. (2009). "*Investment in Energy Infrastructure and the Tax Code.*" National Bureau of Economic Research Working Paper No. 15429. October.

Office of the Vice President. (2010). "*Summer of Recovery: Project Activity Increase in Summer 2010.*" June.

U.S. Department of Commerce. Bureau of Economic Analysis. (2010). "*National Economic Accounts.*" Accessed July.

U.S. Department of Labor. Bureau of Labor Statistics. (2009). "*Quarterly Census of Employment and Wages.*" Accessed September.

U.S. Department of Labor. *Bureau of Labor Statistics. (2010a). "Current Employment Statistics Survey: National.*" Accessed July.

U.S. Department of Labor. Bureau of Labor Statistics. (2010b). "*Current Employment Statistics Survey: State Employment and Unemployment.*" Accessed July.

U.S. Recovery Accountability and Transparency Board. (2010). Data from Recovery.gov website. http://www.recovery.gov/. Accessed July.

Zandi, Mark. (2010). "*The Causes and Current State of the Financial Crisis.*" Testimony to the Financial Crisis Inquiry Commission, January 13.

End Notes

[1] The outlays and obligations data are based on weekly reports by the relevant agencies. To ensure that our report is as up-to-date as possible, we use the agency Financial and Activity Reports provided directly by the Office of Management and Budget. These reports are posted on Recovery.gov with a short lag. The tax reduction

estimates are based on the Department of the Treasury Office of Tax Analysis (OTA) tax simulation model for the effect of the ARRA tax provisions. The OTA prepares new estimates semi-annually as part of the annual budget cycle and the mid-session review. The most recent data come from the FY2011 Mid-session Review. However, the data shown on Recovery.gov do not reflect many of the revisions made by OTA for the Mid-session Review. To provide the most accurate quarterly estimates of the impact of the ARRA, we report and use the revised tax estimates for all quarters. Because of these revisions, the figures in Table 1 for 2009 differ slightly from those reported in our previous reports (CEA, 2009b, 2010a, and 2010c).

[2] CBO (2009) projected that $184.9 billion would have been spent in fiscal year 2009 (that is, through the third quarter), and $399.4 billion in fiscal 2010. Assuming that the fiscal 2010 budget impact was spread evenly across the four quarters yields total projected spending of $484 billion by the end of June 2010. CBO has since published a revised estimate of the direct effect on the deficit of the ARRA of $862 billion (CBO 2010a Appendix A). This number is not comparable to the estimated cost at passage of $787 billion because it does not include adjustments for the effect of the ARRA on spending from regular appropriations or other authorizations, which CBO estimates reduced the effect on the deficit in 2009 and 2010. Most of the increase in CBO's estimate of the direct effect on the deficit comes from greater outlays on income-security programs.

[3] The quarterly estimates of AMT relief are from unpublished analysis by the OTA. The direct payment data are from the agency Financial and Activity Reports, available on Recovery.gov.

[4] These figures exclude temporary workers hired for the decennial Census.

[5] See Council of Economic Advisers (2009b, p. 23) for more details.

[6] The appendix of this report provides a breakdown of the estimated employment effects by state.

[7] These differences in the actual and projected levels of GDP imply substantial differences in the growth rates of GDP. Specifically, they imply that GDP growth in 2009:Q2 was 2.8 percentage points higher than the baseline projected growth; in 2009:Q3 it was 2.9 percentage points higher; in 2009:Q4 it was 4.4 percentage points higher; in 2010:Q1 it was 1.4 percentage points higher; and in 2010:Q2 it was 1.4 percentage points higher.

[8] Again, these figures exclude temporary Census workers.

[9] The sources are as follows. CBO: CBO (2010b). Goldman Sachs: described in Goldman Sachs (2009); updated figures from Alec Phillips, email communication, April 7, 2010. IHS/Global Insight: figures from Gregory Dago, email communication, July 1, 2010. James Glassman, J.P.Morgan Chase: Glassman (2010). Macroeconomic Advisers: Macroeconomic Advisers (2009a, 2009b); exact figures from email communication, August 10, 2009. Moody's economy.com: described in Zandi (2010); exact figures from Mark Zandi, email communication, June 24, 2010. Before using estimates from sources used in our earlier reports, we checked with each forecaster to ensure that their estimates of the effects of the Act had not changed.

[10] The sources are the same as for Table 8.

[11] These provisions also share the feature that the cost to the government corresponds directly to the occurrence of economic activity. For that reason, they all receive the same economic multiplier in the CEA model. The category does not include other business tax incentives such as bonus depreciation.

[12] Office of the Vice President (2010).

[13] These numbers differ slightly from those in CEA (2009b) because of updated cost estimates from OTA.

[14] This total excludes the $53 billion State Fiscal Stabilization Fund that went through state governments.

[15] Engebretson (2010).

[16] For spending programs, the appropriation corresponds to the 10-year cost as estimated in CBO (2009) at the Act's passage. For revenue appropriations, we use the Office of Tax Analysis's estimated cost through 2020 as calculated for the FY2011 Mid-Session Review.

[17] CEA (2010a) estimated total job-years through 2012 resulting from spending in the clean energy sector as 719,600. The new estimate reflects the increase in total clean energy tax provisions and updated assumptions on the timing of agency outlays and tax costs.

[18] This table includes all transportation infrastructure funded through the Department of Transportation. In the classification in Table 10, some transportation infrastructure funding is included in the clean energy category.

[19] Although the recipient reports allow us to observe in what month projects were awarded funds, we cannot similarly observe exactly when the outlays began to start; the recipient reported data only allow such calculations starting in 2009:Q3 when the first recipient reports were due. Through 2009:Q3, roughly $1.6 billion of ARRA funds were expended in the 1,835 transportation projects that had been awarded funds in 2009:Q1.

[20] We omit two tax programs, the Plug-in Electric Drive Vehicle Credit and the Renewable Energy Production Tax Credit, because we lack sufficient information on the dollar value of activity supported. To estimate the total amount of supported activity from projects that are still underway, we generally assume that a program's current co- investment percentage (the ratio of non-ARRA funds to ARRA funds) will be maintained for the life of the program. In a few cases where recent data are unavailable (the Community Development Block Grant, Community Development Financial Institutions, and the Tax Credit Assistance Program), we use a historical co-investment percentage. For the tax programs that provide interest subsidies on bond issues, we use the total value of issues to date as the estimate of the amount of supported activity.

[21] In these calculations of total leverage in the clean energy area of the Recovery Act, we use conservative assumptions so as not to double-count the leverage of investments that may qualify for multiple Recovery Act incentives. This suggests that our totals may understate the true level of clean energy investments supported by the Act.

[22] See http://www.ustreas.gov/press/releases/tg692.htm.

[23] Issuance of Qualified School Construction Bonds has accelerated recently, with more issued so far in 2010 than were issued in all of 2009. Accordingly, the expected 10-year cost of the program exceeds the value of issues to date, as volume is expected to rise through the rest of the year. To account for this, we conservatively set both the cost to the government and total activity supported equal to the value of issues to date.

[24] Some programs involve more than one type of leverage design. We categorize these according to the most prevalent type of leverage. For example, the Department of Agriculture Broadband Initiatives Program described above is put into the direct loan category because most of the leverage occurs through the loan portion. However, many of the loan agreements also include a government grant.

[25] This figure depends on the assumption that the elasticity of investment with respect to the user cost is constant over time. Metcalf emphasizes specifications where the level of investment is a linear function of the user cost (subject to a non-negativity constraint). The results from the linear-level specifications imply that the impact of removing the credit would be large relative to average investment over his sample period, but small relative to the very high level of investment in 2009.

[26] The Act also extended the Investment Tax Credit, which provides a tax credit equal to 30 percent of the cost of the investment. Historically wind producers have opted for the production credit over the investment credit.

[27] The assumption of proportional growth could overstate the impact of the ARRA on wind energy installation.

[28] Bolinger, Wiser, and Darghouth (2010).

[29] U.S. Department of Labor (2010b). We use seasonally adjusted estimates of total nonfarm employment.

[30] See CEA (2009b) for details.

[31] Employment by state and industry is drawn from data published by the U.S. Department of Labor (2009, 2010b). We use data from the March 2009 Current Employment Statistics to determine state employment shares and data from the 2008 Quarterly Census of Employment and Wages to determine state-by-industry employment. Because of limitations in the available data, some of the analysis here uses data beginning in 1990:Q2.

[32] For this analysis, we use a relatively detailed industry breakdown. Manufacturing is divided into 21 sectors (for example, fabricated metal products). Trade, transportation, and utilities are divided into four sectors (wholesale trade, retail trade, utilities, and transportation/warehousing); financial activities into two (finance/insurance, and real estate/rental/leasing); professional and business services into five (professional/technical services, management of companies, employment services, other administrative/support services, and waste management/remediation); education and health into two (educational services and health care/social assistance); leisure and hospitality into two (arts/entertainment/recreation and accommodation/food services). For data sources and methods used in the sectoral decomposition, see CEA (2009b).

CHAPTER SOURCES

The following chapters have been previously published:

Chapter 1 – This is an edited, excerpted and augmented edition of a United States Congressional Research Service publication, Report Order Code R41332, dated July 22, 2010.

Chapter 2 – This is an edited, excerpted and augmented edition of a United States Congressional Research Service publication, Report Order Code R41034, dated September 16, 2010.

Chapter 3 – This is an edited, excerpted and augmented edition of a United States Congressional Research Service publication, Report Order Code R40925, dated August 20, 2010.

Chapter 4 – This is an edited, excerpted and augmented edition of a United States Congressional Research Service publication, Report Order Code R41434, dated September 30, 2010.

Chapter 5 – This is an edited, excerpted and augmented edition of a United States Congressional Research Service publication, Report Order Code R40080, dated July 19, 2010.

Chapter 6 – This is an edited, excerpted and augmented edition of a United States Congressional Research Service publication, Report Order Code Rl34427, dated July 15, 2010.

Chapter 7 – This is an edited, excerpted and augmented edition of a United States Congressional Research Service publication, Report Order Code R40178, dated March 4, 2010.

Chapter 8 – This is an edited, excerpted and augmented edition of an Executive Office of the President of the United States Council of Economic Advisers Fourth Quarterly Report, dated July 14, 2010.

INDEX

F

J

K

L

S

T

U

V

W

Y